Waiting at the Mountain Pass

CONTEMPORARY ETHNOGRAPHY

Alma Gottlieb, Series Editor

A complete list of books in the series is available from
the publisher.

WAITING AT THE MOUNTAIN PASS

Coming to Terms with Solitude, Decline, and
Death in Tibetan Exile

Harmandeep Kaur Gill

PENN

UNIVERSITY OF PENNSYLVANIA PRESS

PHILADELPHIA

Published by
University of Pennsylvania Press
Philadelphia, Pennsylvania 19104–4112
www.pennpress.org

Printed in the United States of America on acid-free paper

10   9   8   7   6   5   4   3   2   1

A Cataloging-in-Publication record is available from the
Library of Congress

Paperback ISBN 978-1-5128-2735-4
Hardcover ISBN 978-1-5128-2736-1
eBook ISBN 978-1-5128-2737-8

To all my teachers

You can find a portal or a loophole in every story—trees to untangle in a plot.

—Tsering Wangmo Dhompa (2023)

CONTENTS

FIGURES

MAIN CHARACTERS

Ani Jamyang Choedon: ninety-year-old nun from the Kyirong region in southwestern Tibet. She escaped from Kyirong to Nepal before the People's Liberation Army took control of the region.

Ani Tenzin Pema: ninety-one-year-old nun from the Sakya region in southwestern Tibet. She escaped into exile in 1959.

Gen Lobsang Choedak: ninety-five-year-old monk from the Tsang region in central Tibet. He escaped into exile in 1959.

Mo Dickyi Sangmo: eighty-six-year-old female from the Kyirong region. She is the younger sister of Mo Samdrup Drolma and Ani Jamyang Choedon. Mo Dickyi and family members escaped into exile in 1963.

Mo Samdrup Drolma: ninety-three-year-old female from the Kyirong region. She escaped from Kyirong with the rest of the family in 1963.

Mo Tsering Wangmo: eighty-year-old female from the Kham region in eastern Tibet who grew up in the Tibetan capital of Lhasa from a young age. She escaped into exile in 1990.

Po Damchoe Ngawang: eighty-four-year-old male from Medrogongkar in central Tibet. He escaped into exile in 1959.

*Ages listed are as of 2024.

NOTE ON TRANSLITERATION, NAMES, PHOTOGRAPHS, THE USE OF *TIBET*, AND TIBETANS

T ibetan words—except names—are transcribed phonetically into English using the Tibetan and Himalayan Library's Simplified Phonetic Transcription of Standard Tibetan system. I refer to Tibetan institutions (with a few exceptions) by their English names, as their Tibetan names are not central to my analysis.

A note on words that are repeated throughout the book: *Mola* (short for *momo*) means "grandmother," and *Pola* (short for *popo*) means "grandfather." *Anila* means "nun"; *Acha* means "elderly sister"; and *Genla* (short for *gegen*) means "teacher," an honorific way of referring to anyone considered a teacher. Tibetans-in-exile commonly refer to monks, among others, as Genla. In this book, I use *Genla* to refer to elderly monks. I add the suffix *la* to nouns (e.g., Mo*la*, Po*la*, Ani*la*, Gen*la*) as a respectful gesture and because that is how I referred to people in person. When I refer to a person using their name preceded by a noun (e.g., *Mo* Tsering Wangmo), I do not add the suffix *la* to the noun or the name, in an effort to make it less complicated for the reader. Instead, I refer to them as *Gen* Lobsang or *Po* Damchoe.

For a more specialized audience, the titles of Tibetan Buddhist texts and literature have been transliterated according to the Wylie system for transliteration. I only provide the English translation of Tibetan sayings, with the exception of the title of the book. See the Glossary for the original Tibetan versions of various sayings.

The names of certain persons in the book—specifically, Mo Dickyi Sangmo, Mo Tsering Wangmo, and their relatives—are pseudonyms. The story of an individual in a Tibetan context is also the story of a family. Thus, I have chosen to use pseudonyms for these individuals and to invent some fictional details, because it was not possible to obtain the consent of their close family members living in foreign countries and in other parts of India. I use real names in the case of Gen Lobsang Choedak, Po Damchoe Ngawang, and the elderly Tibetans living at the Tibetan Children's Village old-age home, with the exception of Mo Yangchen, Po Ngodrup, and Po Ugyen—their names are pseudonyms.

All photographs were taken by me. It might be possible to recognize the faces of elderly individuals for whom I use real names.

Bö ("Tibet") is a vast plateau. It is a culturally, linguistically, religiously, and geographically diverse territory. It is also a colonized country, which means that the various conceptions of Tibet are contested. Academic writers tend to use one of three dominant conceptions.[1] These are not a central discussion in the book; thus, I provide a simplified note on these competing versions here. First, there is the Tibet recognized by the People's Republic of China (PRC); it is called the Tibet Autonomous Region (TAR) and was officially created by the PRC in 1965 as an administrative division after the invasion in 1950. However, the PRC acknowledges Tibetan ethnic areas outside of the TAR, specifically in the Chinese-administered regions of Qinghai, Sichuan, Gansu, and Yunnan, where ethnic Tibetans make up a substantial part of the population. TAR is understood as equivalent to the area ruled by the Lhasa government until 1951 and is referred to by scholars as "political Tibet."[2] The Chinese government is now actively attempting to erase the word "Tibet" by using the Mandarin word "Xizang." In all official communication, TAR is now referred to as "Xizang Autonomous Region."[3] A second conception, "ethnographic Tibet," denotes a vast area with a common cultural and historical heritage throughout the Tibetan plateau; it encompasses the areas Tibetans refer to as Amdo and Kham.[4] These areas are usually referred to by scholars by their Chinese administrative names (such as Qinghai, Sichuan, Gansu and Yunnan), or as Tibetan autonomous prefectures in Qinghai, Sichuan, Gansu, or Yunnan.[5] Finally, a third conception defines *Tibet* as a single political unit with roots in a historical reality dating back to the eighth and thirteenth centuries.[6] This greater political Tibet is understood to consist of Ü-Tsang (TAR), Amdo (Qinghai, parts of Gansu and Sichuan), and Kham (parts of Sichuan and Yunnan). This is Tibet as understood by Tibetans-in-exile. Since the 1980s, Tibetans inside Tibet have also clearly articulated their identification with, and recognition of, a greater political Tibet through political protests on the Tibetan plateau, in songs, poetry, books, writing, videos, and film.[7] Tibetans refer to Ü-Tsang, Amdo, and Kham as *Bö cholka sum*, meaning the "three regions of Tibet," and they regard themselves as one ethnic group.[8] National identity among exiles is asserted on the basis of their shared ethnicity and Buddhist religion. The term *Tibetans*, as used by the Central Tibetan Administration and nongovernmental organizations, refers to one unified group (something the term also denotes for the PRC), while also being aware that regional Tibetan affiliations continue to inform the identity of exiles.[9] In this book, *Tibet* refers to *Bö cholka sum*.[10]

NAMES FOR THE 14TH DALAI LAMA, TENZIN GYATSO

Phonetic Transliteration	Wylie Transliteration	English Translation
Chenrezig	spyan ras gzigs	The one who sees in all directions/ Avalokiteśvara/the Bodhisattva of Compassion
Gyalwa Rinpoche	rgyal ba rin po che	The victorious jewel/The victorious precious one
Gyalwa Yeshe Norbu	rgyal ba yid bzhin nor bu	The victorious and wish-fulfilling jewel
Kundun	sku mdun	The enlightened in person/Presence of (Dalai Lama)
Kyabgön Rinpoche	skyabs mgon rin po che	Lord protector/The protecting jewel
Kyabgön Yeshe Rinpoche/ Norbu	skyabs mgon yid bzhin rin po che/nor bu	The wish-fulfilling jewel/ The protecting jewel who fulfills all wishes
Sangye	sangs rgyas	The enlightened one/The Buddha

Prelude

Mo Samdrup Drolma was outside on the balcony of her home, overlooking her neighborhood, known as Kyirong Village. She often sat here for several hours on sunny days. Only during the monsoon or the gray and cold winter days was she forced to stay indoors. The balcony was her contact with the outside world. From here, she watched people, dogs, cats, and monkeys moving about, briefly interrupting the stillness of her days. Inside the concrete walls of her home, however, time appeared to me to stand still. Days, months, and years fused into one another.

At ninety-three years old, Mo Samdrup ("Mola") was the oldest person in her neighborhood. Most of her contemporaries in the area, the first generation of Tibetans-in-exile, had passed away. For years, she had been repeating: "*la gor thön gi dug.*" These words can be translated as, "I am about to reach the mountain pass." According to this metaphor, the journey of life is a continuous climb up to a mountain pass, and upon reaching it, the journey concludes. Then, one has to cross over and set foot on the journey of one's new rebirth. What is important to note is the particular verb ending of *gi dug* that Mola used, an ending of the English verb *to be* in the present tense. Furthermore, *gi dug* is also applied when one bears witness to something. Therefore, when Mo Samdrup said these words, I understood that death for her was not somewhere in the distant future. The mountain pass was right in front of her; in other words, she stood face-to-face with death and felt its presence in her aging body.

"I am going to die," Mola followed up next, as she tilted her head sideways with a smile, as if in an accepting gesture to herself. Apart from the mention of death, she repeated many other things, such as descriptions of her birthplace in Kyirong in Tibet, certain events in her life there, or, again and again, that her mother gave birth to twelve children, only eight of which survived. But her repetitions of her age, followed up by her usual comment that she was going to die, were more repetitive than other thoughts. Sometimes they occurred in the midst of a long silence. While the mention of death set me aback, this acknowledgment of death was spontaneous and natural for Mo Samdrup. Whatever she thought about seemed to lead to an awareness of death. She was, after all, nearly at the time-space of the mountain pass and was ready to cross it any day.

Figure 1: Mo Samdrup Drolma. Photo by Harmandeep K. Gill.

McLeod Ganj, November 2021

The Dhauladhar range was painted in white, standing tall and majestic. The hill, leaning onto the range and stretching across McLeod Ganj, was now largely barren, giving a vivid presence to the few houses nestled here and there, some clustered together like a small village.

On the opposite side, the small, yet ever expanding hill station of McLeod Ganj bustled with life, its narrow streets filled with cars honking, tourists rushing between places, dogs looking for food, and local street vendors taking note of everything passing by. Turning my gaze away from the street and toward the Dhauladhar range, silence overtook my body. The mountains are always here, generously allowing one to catch one's breath.

I have found myself drawn and connected to these mountains since I first laid my eyes on them, a connection that to me seems to transcend lifetimes. So I was rejoiced to finally return to the place that made me feel more at home in the world, after longing for it for months.

Cold air wrapped itself around my body as the auto-rickshaw sped its way from McLeod Ganj, crossing St. John's Church, the Forsyth Ganj area, and making its way uphill to the Tibetan Children's Village (TCV) old-age home. It is a ride I have taken hundreds of times. I paid the driver and stepped into the grocery shop located outside the old-age home to buy eggs, a carton of milk, and biscuits as a gift for Gen Lobsang Choedak. It had been six months since I last saw him.

I had left in mid-May 2021, after getting a research position in the United Kingdom. At the time, the second wave of the COVID-19 pandemic raged through India, and we found ourselves in the midst of a nationwide lockdown. Outsiders were forbidden to enter the premises of the old-age home, making it nearly impossible for me to meet Gen Lobsang. Yet, I could not help but send desperate messages to Youdon-la, the daily manager of the old-age home, to let me meet with Gen Lobsang one last time before my departure. Since he was ninety-two years old, it was possible we might never meet again.

Youdon-la was well aware of my affectionate relationship with Gen Lobsang ("Genla") and that I had been a constant presence in his life since 2018. She must have considered this when she generously allowed me to see him, as I had suggested, in the backyard of the old-age home, and at an appropriate physical distance from Gen Lobsang (who, at the time, had been double-vaccinated).

When I arrived, Genla was waiting patiently, sitting in the shade of a tree. Holding a conversation was a challenge, since both of us wore face masks and had to keep sufficient distance from one another. Hence, the meeting was brief. But it did not matter. I simply wanted to see my precious Genla, and to be in his presence, perhaps for the last time.

As we said our goodbyes, Genla lovingly wrapped a *khata*, a silk white scarf, around my neck, something he has done upon each goodbye. I told him I would return in a few months and would see him soon.

At a sufficient distance, I took his photo. Genla's maroon-red monastic robe stood in beautiful contrast to the light green leaves of the tree behind him. His mask was off now. He offered me a loving and accepting smile, his presence shining with an aura of grace as he stood leaning onto his walking stick, left leg slightly bent. If this were to be my last sight of Genla, I told myself, it was a beautiful one, alive with colors and warmth from the sun. A final goodbye in this setting would be all right.

Focusing on the bright day that embraced us, where life carried on as usual, I pushed myself to walk away. After taking a few steps, I turned around and caught another glimpse of Genla, who still stood under the tree with the same smile.

This image was frozen in my mind as I knocked on his door six months later on that early afternoon in November 2021. "Genla," I said excitedly, knowing that once I opened the door, time would resume, unfreezing this image and allowing us to form new encounters and deeper connections.

Genla sat on his bed with *pecha* (Tibetan Buddhist texts) on the table in front of him, a familiar sight. When I opened the door, I immediately met his expectant gaze. He looked at me with a wide smile, eyes glistening with joy. I placed the egg tray and biscuits on top of the fridge, and the milk carton inside. Genla got up from the bed and limped a step or two toward me. Holding one another's shoulders, we touched our foreheads, a Tibetan form of greeting for hello and goodbye.

Genla looked the same. The wrinkles on his face had not deepened. He looked healthy. Even though each year added another number to his age, it felt to me as if Genla, unlike my elderly female friends, did not age, as if he had reached the prime of his old age, as if in some ways he was frozen in time, until he would set off on the new journey of rebirth.

Genla asked how I was and when I had arrived, before insisting on making chai. Not wanting to burden him, I thought it better to stick with hot water and poured myself a cup from the thermos.

Genla's room was tidy, as always. His few belongings rested neatly in their designated areas, as if unmoved over the past four years I had been visiting him. The only new item I noticed was a pair of white sneakers, probably gifted by his niece, increasing Genla's total pair of outdoor shoes to five.

We chatted about his health and exercise routines before returning to the silence that accompanied his days. Genla never had much to say. Neither had anything noteworthy happened since my last visit.

Emptying my cup of hot water, I insisted on massaging Genla's leg, something I did several days a week for him and my other elderly friends during the fieldwork I carried out from 2018 to 2019. In his case, I only massaged the right leg, since his left hip was left fractured from a fall he had suffered twenty-six years ago.

I sat down on the floor in front of him. Taking off his shoe, leg warmer, and sock, I poured Tibetan medicinal oil onto his leg and foot, the same oil I have massaged my other elderly friends with. Genla's leg and foot felt the same, firm and hard with a slight swelling, but not so much that I could not get a solid grip.

We rested in each other's silence. Any effort that words would consume, I channeled into the massage. Genla was one of the most patient people I knew, never allowing himself to complain about matters to the staff at the TCV old-age home or to take the freedom to make comments on others. He silently carried the physical and emotional sufferings of his old age with so much grace and acceptance that he made it look effortless. My heart had always expanded a little extra for Genla. He had no family living close by, and, in some ways, his solitude came the closest to my own.

Touching his feet and caring for him through the act of massaging was a sort of homecoming, bringing to life our unique bond made up of cups of chai, touch, and silence.

Introduction

Gen Lobsang Choedak lives in McLeod Ganj in northwestern India, also known as the capital of Tibetans-in-exile. Born in 1929—the Tibetan year of the Earth-Snake—he is today ninety-five years old. Gen Lobsang is one of several elderly Tibetans, laypeople, and ordained monastics of a lower rank whose lives I have followed since January 2018. He was born and raised in Penpo in central Tibet. When he was fifteen years old, his parents enrolled him as a monk at Ganden Monastery. Fifteen years later, his life would forever change.

The People's Republic of China (PRC) began its invasion of the eastern Tibetan regions of Amdo and Kham in 1949. In 1959, before the Tibetan capital city of Lhasa in central Tibet came under the full control of the PRC, the highest spiritual leader of the Tibetan people, the 14th Dalai Lama, Tenzin Gyatso, the emanation of Tibet's patron deity—Chenrezig—escaped from Lhasa into exile in India. He reached the Indian border on 31 March 1959.

Gen Lobsang, like thousands of other Tibetans from all ages and walks of life—monastics, government officials, aristocrats, laypeople—followed the Dalai Lama into exile. In 1960, one year after his escape, the Dalai Lama was offered residence in McLeod Ganj. Tibetans believed that they would return to Tibet in a few years. Exile was supposed to be a temporary solution.

As of 2024, the Dalai Lama still lives in McLeod Ganj, considering it as his home-in-exile. Like the rest of the first generation of Tibetans-in-exile, the 14th Dalai Lama, Gen Lobsang Choedak, and my other elderly friends are aging and facing death on foreign soil. Many have already passed away.

I met Gen Lobsang Choedak in October 2016, when I was doing preliminary fieldwork at the Tibetan Children's Village (TCV) old-age home as preparation for a research proposal on aging and dying in exile. When I began fieldwork in January 2018, I resumed my engagements with Gen Lobsang, this time not only in the form of conversations, but also through massages. I adopted the idea of massaging the legs and feet of elderly Tibetans through work with a Tibetan nongovernmental organization (NGO) known as Tibet

Charity, where I volunteered in early 2018. Tibet Charity's small team of nurses and health-care workers regularly check on elderly Tibetans and others, providing them with free medicine or offering them leg massages. We gave a basic massage of the feet and the lower legs, in order to warm up their muscles and increase their blood circulation. During my preliminary research period in 2016, some of the elderly women had, understandably, gotten somewhat tired of my continuous presence and questions. They wanted to devote their time to Tibetan Buddhist practices without interruptions from me; therefore, they encouraged me to benefit the elderly in a practical way. Their feedback served as an important reminder of practicing reciprocity in fieldwork situations, a cornerstone of contemporary ethnographic practice. I could not just show up and hang around; I also needed to benefit them somehow, to provide them with something they would appreciate. As a result, I chose to massage their feet and legs.

Over time, these massages, along with my other efforts at assisting my elderly friends and continuing to visit them over the years, offered us an intimate access to one another, bonding us in a relationship of mutual care. My elderly friends, especially Ani Jamyang Choedon, insisted that our lives became intertwined because we share a karmic connection. With my upbringing in a community that believes in reincarnation, I have come to share Anila's belief too. The elderly related to me as an adoptive daughter, and Ani Jamyang and Mo Dickyi also insisted that we must have been relatives (*pünkya*) in a past life. This is why I refer to the elderly as friends who were like a self-chosen family; we accompanied and supported each other through the ups and downs of everyday life. According to Buddhist beliefs, we might also have met and cared for one another in past lives. The words *interlocutors* and *informants* do not capture the intimacy we came to share and how my storytelling and analysis are influenced by our ethical relationship, its possibilities and limitations alike.

Through our close friendships, I came to know the elderly Tibetans as singular personalities whose experiences could not be reduced to a grand generalization about old age in the Tibetan exile context. Neither could their experiences be simply comprehended in relation to Tibetan cultural and religious ideals. One also needed to consider the singularities of these individuals' life histories, family relationships, individual temperaments, and physical conditions. Their individual experiences remained opaque, plural, and unresolved. Perceived meanings changed from day to day, from moment to moment. Not only did I find cultural frameworks of meaning and theoretical concepts to be limited in fully encapsulating the lived experiences of my elderly friends, I also found that my friends themselves struggled to fully comprehend how bits and pieces of their lives might make a coherent whole. Nor was it always possible for them to put into words the disorientation brought on by old age and the uncertainty caused by the prospect of death. Thus, out of respect and care for my friends, whose inner lifeworlds remain far richer than the tiny fragments I glimpsed, I humbly shy away from holistic explanations that carry the illusion of completeness. Rather, I opt for an embodied knowing that is *care*-ful, hesitant, and unresolved in its claims.

Mo Samdrup Drolma's metaphor—"about to reach the mountain pass"—offers an apt visualization of old age in a Tibetan Buddhist context in exile. It is an allusion to an old Tibetan saying in which the elderly Tibetans say they are the setting sun (which is just behind the mountain pass), to suggest that they are close to death. I have also heard the elderly Tibetan neighbors of Mo Samdrup say, "We've already reached the mountain pass," followed by the remark that they were "waiting" to die. The same metaphor—an allusion to the setting sun—is phrased in different ways but comments upon a shared experience of old age: namely, that one's thoughts circle around death. One expects to be gone any day.

To pursue this metaphor, this book is a meditation on my elderly friends' last part of the journey, where they are about to reach, or have reached, the mountain pass and are waiting for death and preparing themselves for their next rebirth. I approach the mountain pass as a "borderland," defined by the Chicana poet and queer, feminist theorist Gloria Anzaldúa as an in-between world that is "a vague and undetermined" time-space.[1] It is located between this life and the next and is a time-space where the impermanence of life is crystallized, manifesting itself not only through the descent down the mountain pass but also through a series of sufferings, such as physical decline, the physical or emotional absence of significant others, dying away from one's first home, and the uncertainty of death and rebirth. The state of being in between worlds is accurately captured by the Sufi notion of *barzakh*, meaning that which lies between edges, borders, and events. The word derives from a giant beehive-like structure called by the same name in which the dead must stay separately until the Day of Judgment.[2] The great Andalusian Sufi, Ibn al-'Arabi describes *barzakh* as "something that separates a known from an unknown, an existent from a non-existent, a negated from an affirmed, an intelligible from a non-intelligible," which gives a dreamlike and even surreal quality to the state of being in between two ontological worlds.[3] This resonates with the state of waiting to set off from the mountain pass; one's physical appearance and relationship to others can appear so distant and unrecognizable that one is left wondering whether the known and intelligible past was real, or whether the often nonintelligible present, and where it is headed, is the dream. Having reached, or being about to reach, the mountain pass, my elderly friends were left suspended between worlds, living on the hinge between the known and the unknown, at the crossroads between life and death, while belonging fully to neither.

I invite the reader to join me on this journey to the in-between as I visit my elderly friends, massage their legs and feet, and share intimate moments with them. It is a time-space where everyday life traverses between past and present, in darkness and light, and in dream and reality, each fusing into one another.

This book also strives for the articulation of a phenomenological project that writes from the bottom up, putting people and sensations before the development of concepts. At the center of this phenomenological project is the ethical relationship between my elderly friends and myself. I write of them not as a distant, objective scholar, but as someone who in the moment of writing (in July 2024), continues to be entangled in their lives. Even though two of my elderly friends passed away in 2022, traces of them rest in my body, and my care extends to them through thought and in writing. Ethnographic research and writing have, for me, been practices of care and commitment.

This book asks: How is time spent at the mountain pass? What is it like to be a temporal being belonging fully to neither life nor death, but instead hanging suspended between the two? How is the anthropological project of understanding the other transformed by taking seriously the singularities of a life and the ethical responsibilities we hold toward this life? And, are there dimensions of human experience that remain *aporic*, meaning disturbing, impenetrable, and unresolved?

Old Age Among Tibetan Buddhists

A distinguished historian of Tibet, the late Elliot Sperling, wrote in 1979 that old age among Tibetans has never been at the center of attention of any scholarly work and "in fact has only rarely and indirectly been looked at by scholars at all."[4] By exploring Tibetan notions of old age in Chinese textual sources ranging from the 5th to the 7th century, Sperling suggests that the main theme running through almost all affiliated materials is that the elderly hold on to their independence as long as they are capable of sustaining it physically.[5] However, his conclusion, that "the Tibetan will come to the end of his life with the same independent outlook that carried him through his earlier years," does not reflect the lived realities of decline and frailty in old age.[6]

Since the publication of Sperling's article, a few researchers have directed attention to the cultural and religious ideals of old age and how these are practiced. Apart from Robert B. Ekvall, who briefly mentions religious practices among elderly nomadic pastoralists, the sociocultural anthropologist Melvyn Goldstein and the biological anthropologist Cynthia M. Beall were among the earliest to bring attention to old age and intergenerational relations in Tibet, based on their long-term fieldwork.[7]

In their article, Goldstein and Beall provide an overview of aging in traditional Tibetan society, which they note had many similarities to other East Asian societies—for example, in terms of patriarchal orientation.[8] As in other East Asian societies, intergenerational relationships within a household were defined in terms of "filial piety," which made loving, respecting, and taking care of aging parents the ethical responsibility of children and in-married family members.[9] Furthermore, Goldstein and Beall report that social and political norms that supported parental authority and especially male authority further reinforced the ethics of filial piety by making parents the main decision-making body of the organization of human resources.[10] In spite of being old, frail, and dependent, "they still held dominant political, legal and economic positions."[11] Things have changed significantly in Tibetan regions since the PRC took control in 1951 and introduced major socioeconomic reforms in 1959. As Tibet was incorporated into a modern economy, and with the out-migration of young people to cities, the social context of aging has changed significantly. According to Goldstein and Beall, this has redefined and delimited the norms of filial piety.[12]

Tibetan exile communities have undergone similar changes in recent years as a result of the out-migration of young people to Europe, North America, Australia, and big Indian cities,[13] much like some other communities in the highlands of Nepal and India.[14] Literature on aging and migration from other Asian and African contexts has shown that intergenerational relationships are pressurized by unequal developments caused by globalization and how out-migration of children and family members reshapes care for the elderly.[15] Nonetheless, under these shifting circumstances, older people also actively create and negotiate their social circumstances.[16] Out-migration in the Tibetan exile communities has similarly affected the experience of aging and led to renegotiations of filial piety. But in the Tibetan exile communities in India and Nepal, out-migration is not only the result of globalization; it is also driven by the status of Tibetans as a stateless people in both India and Nepal. In addition, aging away from one's homeland of Tibet affects the experience of aging in exile in significant ways.

Another crucial aspect of old age in Tibetan Buddhist communities is that it is a life phase devoted to religious preparations for death and rebirth.[17] Traditionally, the elderly left household responsibilities to their sons and in-married family members and devoted all of their time to various Buddhist practices, such as reciting mantra (*mani*), reading Tibetan Buddhist texts (*pecha*), doing circumambulation (*kora*) and prostrations (*chagtsel*), going for pilgrimage (*nekor*), or making offerings (*chöd*). These preparations for death and rebirth begin once people are in their early fifties and intensify with increasing age.

In colloquial language, Tibetans refer to the old as *genkhog*, which can be translated as "old people," or "old person." The word *gen* means "elder," or "mature" and *khog* refers to something old, decrepit, or decayed.

The elderly Tibetans I spoke to defined old age in different ways. Some said that one is old when one's children are all grown up and can handle their own lives. Others said that old age begins around the age of sixty. An old monk said that one is old when the "head" becomes white. Gen Lobsang Choedak said that old people are not thinking of staying but of dying.

I learned that death is a lingering thought among all of my elderly friends. An awareness of one's actions and the karma (*le*) they accumulate becomes more pressing in old age, and as Goldstein and Beall note, religious practices intensify.[18]

Whereas in most "Western" societies, "successful" aging is defined as staying active and healthy, and delaying sickness and death, in a Tibetan Buddhist context, "successful" aging is defined as the opposite.[19] It involves ceasing negative attachments and embracing the sufferings of old age, including the impermanence of life—ideals which are based in Tibetan Buddhist teachings.[20] Thus, old age for the elderly Tibetans comes with its own project and is a life phase devoted to karmic and moral transformations. I learned that, even though the prospect of death was fearful and unsettling for the elderly Tibetans, they did not attempt to postpone it.

Impermanence, No-Self, Suffering

In one of the two "Sūtra on Impermanence" (*mi rtag pa nyid kyi mdo*) that are found in the Tibetan canon of the "Kangyur,"[21] the Buddha speaks to his followers on one of the main characteristics of the samsaric existence: impermanence.[22] All life follows a cyclic existence (*sipe khorlo*) in Buddhism, meaning that one's present life is part of a beginningless series of rebirths. Each life unfolds according to the karma accumulated in the previous lives and in the present life, as vocalized in this proverb shared by the elderly residents of the TCV old-age home: "To know what you did before, take a look at your body. To know where you will go [in the future], take a look at your mind."

The Buddha comments that the four most cherished things in the world—good health, youth, prosperity, and life—are impermanent. Good health ends with sickness, youth ends with old age, prosperity ends with decline, and life ends in death.[23]

The impermanence of conditioned phenomena is regarded as the most fundamental teaching of the Buddha. While impermanence (*mitagpa nyi*) is described by the Buddha as the first characteristic of existence (*kartag sum*), there are two other characteristics: suffering (*dungel*) and no-self (*dagme*).[24] The Buddhist teacher and monk Nyanaponika Thera describes the first and third characteristics as applying to both the inanimate (e.g., a stone, tree, river, or house) and the animate (living beings). The second characteristic, suffering, is experienced by the animate only, whereas all three come into play for everything that is conditioned, such as human existence.[25] The concept of conditioned existence, also known as, Dependent Arising (*tendrel*), means that everything is dependent on something else for its existence, and it is one meaning of the main truth of existence in Tibetan Buddhism, which is emptiness (*tongpa nyi*). The other meaning of this truth is that everything is devoid of an intrinsic nature.[26] Thus, because everything is devoid of an inherent nature or identity, everything is conditioned by the existence of something else.

The Buddha breaks down human existence into five aggregates: the body, feeling or sensation, perception, mental formations, and consciousness, all

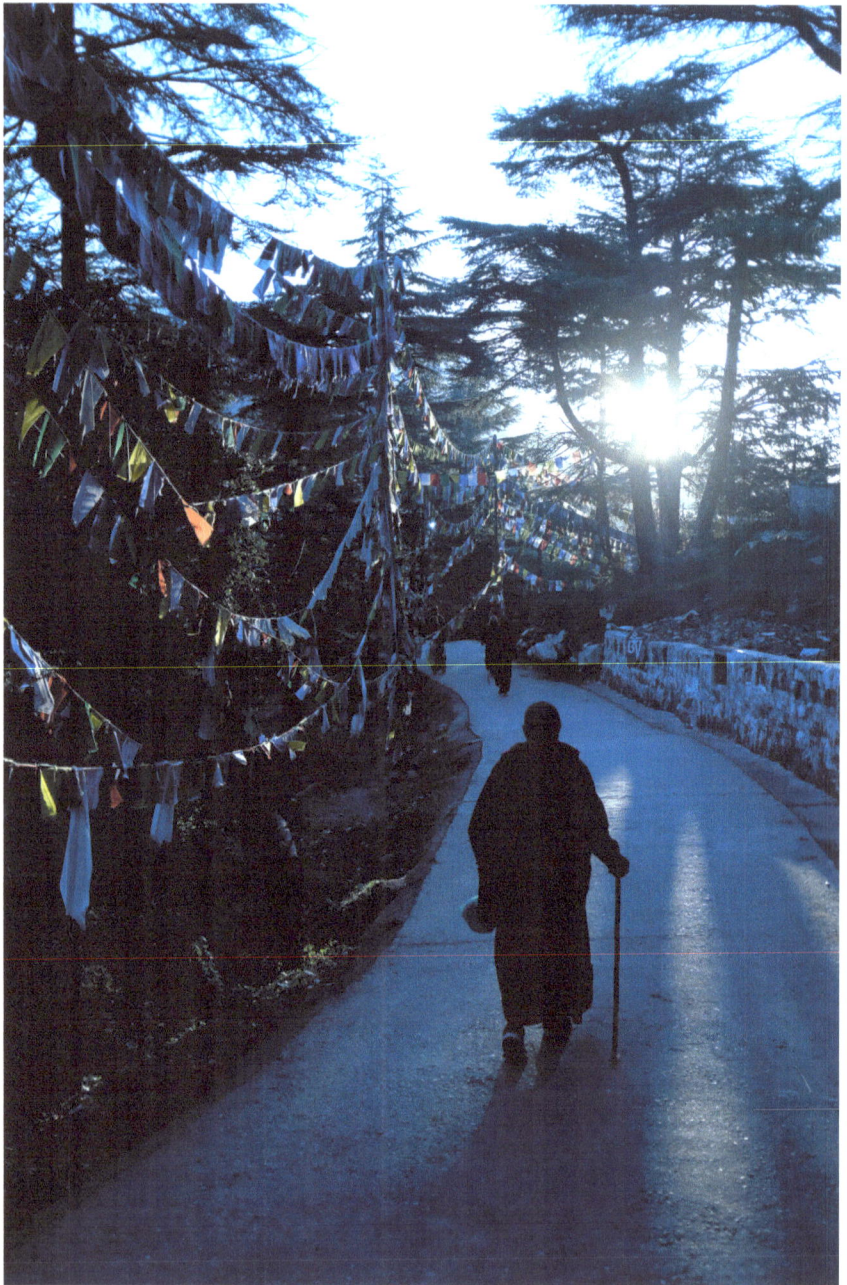

Figure 2: Tibetans doing circumambulation at *lingkor* in McLeod Ganj. Photo by Harmandeep K. Gill.

five are forever changing and thus impermanent. He explains how suffering arises from clinging to that which is impermanent.[27] It is conditioned by the ignorance of the three principal characteristics of existence, whereas "perfect wisdom" would be to recognize them and liberate oneself from the endless sufferings of samsara and rebirth.

Human beings are described as experiencing the following types of suffering: the suffering of change, suffering upon suffering (the suffering of unhappiness), and the suffering of everything composite. Furthermore, humans also suffer from four main streams of suffering: birth, old age, sickness, and death.[28] I shall briefly expand on these various types of sufferings.

Suffering of change basically entails suffering of impermanence: happiness does not last forever and gives in to suffering at some point. Suffering upon suffering means that suffering is preceded by another kind of suffering. In old age, the suffering of physical decline gives rise to mental distress or loneliness for those who become confined to their homes. In general, human life is wrapped in sufferings. The third type of suffering, the suffering of everything composite, means that because all life is conditioned, one's actions lead to the suffering of others, as, for example, our consumption of meat leads to the suffering of animals. These three kinds of sufferings come into play throughout one's lifetime. Furthermore, human life, in and of itself, is a form of suffering—the process of birth is suffering for the mother and child, and from the moment of birth one moves toward the sufferings of illness, old age, and death. Thus, suffering, as described by the Buddha, is the human condition. It cannot be overcome, and to be alive is to suffer. Buddhists perceive the suffering of old age as the worst of all sufferings. One faces physical decline, illness, disability, loneliness, and death, which can intensify the three main types of sufferings.

The only consolation for people caught in the samsaric existence lies in devoting themselves to Buddhist practice, meditating on the words of the Buddha, and attempting to reconcile with the three basic characteristics of existence, so that one learns to come to terms with the suffering (meaning one accepts it as part of the human condition), ceases attachments, accepts one's impermanence, and denounces the illusion of an independent self.

Generally, laypeople and monastics both attempt to improve their karma by devoting themselves to Buddhist practice and engaging in virtuous behavior, which increases the chances for a good rebirth and continuance on the path toward liberation.

This process can take eons of lifetimes (thousands of years) for most, but for devoted Buddhists, enlightened beings—like the historical Buddha, Siddhartha Gautama, who overcame his ignorance and achieved enlightenment step by step and over many life times—are living examples of the possibility to transcend the samsaric existence.[29]

The three truths of impermanence, suffering, and no-self, which are described as intensifying in old age, run throughout the ethnographic material presented in this book. However, most of my elderly friends did not know the depth of the Buddha's teachings as presented by such Tibetan Buddhist teachers as Patrul Rinpoche or the 14th Dalai Lama. Nonetheless, they were familiar with the main ideas of karma, impermanence, emptiness, interdependence, suffering, and no-self through their lifelong practice of Tibetan Buddhism. While waiting to cross the mountain pass, they strive to live up to Tibetan Buddhist ideals for old age. But, as highlighted by the Buddha's teachings, and as this book shows, that endeavor is not an easy process and is fraught with afflictions and fears. Simply to emphasize Buddhist models of "successful" aging—for example, by researching exemplary Buddhists or devoting attention exclusively to religious practice—would entail a romanticization and simplification of Buddhist ways of aging and dying. It would also mean an exclusion and stigmatization of those who are not perceived to age "successfully" and, as Lawrence Cohen notes, effectively an "exiling" of such individuals from the cultural order.[30] Moreover, foregrounding Buddhist ideals of old age, especially in the case of monastics, can blind us to their singular lives and to the fact that they are not untainted by worldly concerns and common human emotions.[31]

Cohen's critique—directed at "successful" and "normal" models of aging—makes clear not only the consequences of academic knowledge production on people's moral worlds but also the scholarly bias inherent in our choice of research subjects and topics. I suggest that a bias is also present in the academic tendency—with many notable exceptions[32]—to focus on privileged, wealthy, and socially supported Tibetan men and women, considered to be *a priori* "extraordinary" and, thus, typically Buddhist. This has resulted in hierarchies within academic knowledge production wherein the everyday lives and struggles of persons deemed to be *a priori* "ordinary," such as non-exemplary lay Buddhists or low-ranking monastics, are made invisible and are "exiled" not only from the cultural order but also from the academic order of Tibetan and Himalayan studies.

Despite the best intentions of my elderly friends—laypeople and monastics alike—to act as ideal Buddhists, it was not easy for them to accept impermanence, the sufferings of old age, and the emptiness of self as part of their reality, as one is supposed to at the last stage at the mountain pass. How does one then, in the philosopher Judith Butler's words, "lead a life when not all life processes that make up a life can be led, or when only certain aspects of a life can be directed or formed in a deliberate or reflective way, and others clearly not?"[33]

Whereas the Buddha's teachings describe the nature of existence, the general types of sufferings that befall all human beings in samsara, and the ways of transcending those sufferings, this book orients toward providing a phenomenological and a first-person perspective on how the sufferings of old age manifested for my elderly friends and their individual efforts at handling and enduring them.[34]

Between Worlds

The elderly at the TCV old-age home where I did parts of my fieldwork used to repeat the following Tibetan saying to explain to me that solitude is the human condition: "One is born alone. One must live alone. One must die alone." Some of them lived at the home with their spouses, but nearly all of them were aging in the absence of their children. I understood this familiar saying—influenced by Tibetan Buddhist teachings—as their way of accepting their children's absence. Yet, I also understood it was not always easy for them to come to terms with the absence of their children, especially when those children failed to provide emotional support.

Although Buddhist teachings emphasize emptiness and solitude as the human condition, there is an equal emphasis on interdependence as the human condition. The concept of interdependence is at the base of Tibetan Buddhist ethics, and it guides human coexistence with all sentient beings. Interdependence is also reflected in the concept of karma, according to which actions and intentions from the past and present life shape one's present and future. The interdependency of human existence is further reflected in Tibetan Buddhist death rituals. In these rituals, which last for forty-nine days, the dead are dependent on the living for moving on to a new rebirth, and the living are dependent on having the dead cease their attachments to the living. Even death does not cease the human and karmic interdependencies that hold together this life and countless rebirths.

Approaching life through the lens of interdependence means that every phenomenon comes into being through a relation. Our existence, including our sense of self, is codependent on others, a fact that becomes starkly visible during fragile life phases such as old age. Although we are born alone, live alone, and die alone, as articulated by the elderly Tibetans, Tibetan Buddhist ethics also emphasize that we can only come into being and seek meaning, such as our pursuit for happiness, through coexistence with others.

The mountain pass, by contrast, was a time-space where my elderly friends often found themselves disconnected from all that was familiar—significant others, their lived lives, and imagined possibilities. The main characteristics and truths of existence—impermanence and emptiness—which remain invisible to the naked eye, manifested themselves through a series of sufferings: (1) physical decline; (2) the physical or emotional absence of significant others; (3) dying far away from one's first home; and (4) the uncertainty of death and rebirth. These sufferings are addressed in four different chapters of this book.

Importantly, the sufferings of old age unsettled my friends, often bringing a strong reminder of that which was absent and could have been otherwise. Thus, waiting at the in-between time-space at the mountain pass, they found themselves on an ambiguous ground, often dominated by feelings of longing, uncertainty, and loss.[35] In facing the sufferings of old age, their connections to others and their surroundings, which had been built up through a lifetime and informed their selfhood, began to unravel, often leading to a fragmented sense of self.

However, the possibility for transformation is also inherent in the sufferings of old age.[36] Paul Stoller notes that the in-between can also be a space of creative imagination and transformation, as stressed in the Sufi notion of *barzakh*.[37] Thus, being oriented toward what was absent—the past and imagined futures—also enabled one to momentarily transcend the sufferings of old age. For my friends, these temporary escapes from the in-between-ness at the mountain pass and to different worlds made it possible for them to hold on to lived realities and imaginaries. At certain times, such escapes were vital in holding together moral worlds and reorienting their sense of self. At other times, such escapes reminded them to let go of what no longer was and come to terms with the reality of old age.

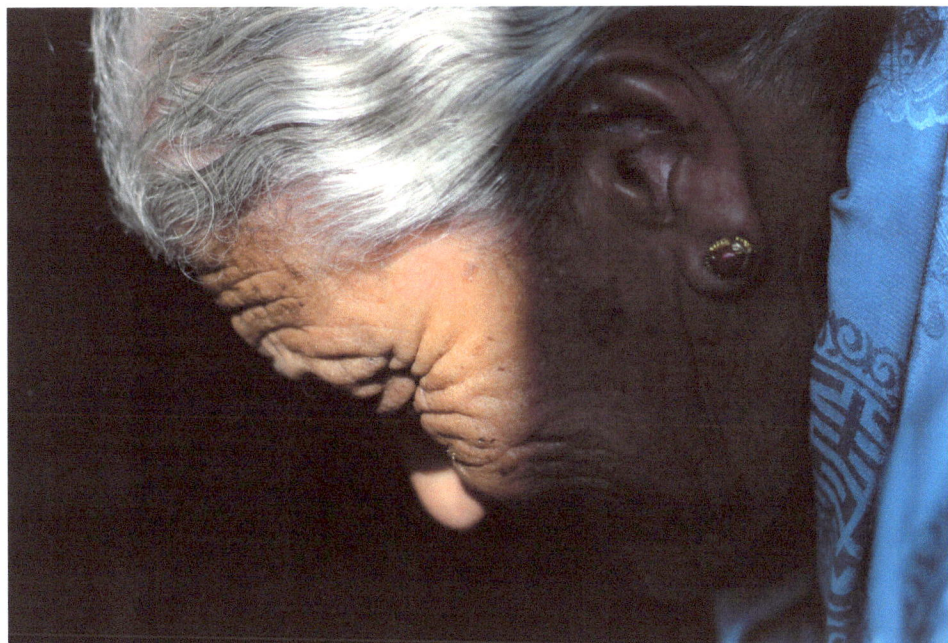

Figure 3: Mo Yangchen, an elderly resident at the Tibetan Children's Village old-age home. Photo by Harmandeep K. Gill.

In other words, in telling the stories of my elderly friends, I try to strike a balance between living with the pains and the potentiality of transformations inherent in them. As Julietta Singh powerfully reminds us, "In pain, something had been uncovered that could not be covered over again."[38] Although Singh is speaking of physical pain, I believe that this statement also holds true for emotional pain that has been endured over a long time. And tracing the "portals" or "loopholes"[39] that will allow us to uncover and be touched by the pain of others, demands, I suggest, an attention to the singular.

The Singular: Merging Ethics, Critique, and Epistemology

My elderly friends were present to me during fieldwork and continue to be present in my mind with specific bodies, faces, voices, gestures, and moods, just as I must have been for them. This might sound obvious, but features distinct to how we remember, feel, and imagine someone often tend to be glossed over while taken-for-granted notions and truths within an academic discipline are accentuated in our analysis and theory-making.

Scholars such as Cheryl Mattingly, João Biehl, Kirin Narayan, Lila Abu-Lughod, Michael Jackson, Paul Stoller, Robert Desjarlais, Ruth Behar, Unni Wikan, Veena Das, and Vincent Crapanzano, among others, have called for a more experience-near ethnography that does justice to life as actually lived.[40] They argue that human experience cannot be reduced to categories of difference, or neatly fitted into them. Several of them argue that taken-for-granted presumptions easily downgrade people's singular experiences to stand as "token of a type."[41] The exiled Tibetan poet and editor Bhuchung D. Sonam remarks how similar taken-for-granted narratives about Tibetans that favor an emphasis on spirituality have "flattened the experience of Tibetans."[42]

As a feminist scholar and a "halfie"—a person of mixed national or cultural identity—Abu-Lughod argues that academic generalizations of the other, often centered on the concept of culture, belong to the discourse of objectivity and expertise. She remarks that such generalizations, based in a historically unequal relation between the "West" and "non-Western" worlds, are thus "a language of power," a critique that has also been advanced by other postcolonial theorists.[43] Such generalizations work to produce "homogeneity, coherence and timelessness" and deny the other, who is being theorized, the complexity we give our own selves.[44] As also argued by the Jamaican-British cultural studies scholar Stuart Hall, the West's fascination with "otherness" resulted in racialized stereotypes of nonwhite subjects, which were embedded in simplified binaries between the West and the non-West.[45] In anthropology, the realities of the other have tended to be presented and interpreted as "cultural" rather than "individual," notes Ruth Behar.[46] This has resulted in a tendency to let one person's experience in so-called traditional societies stand for anyone's experience, remarks Veena Das.[47]

Abu-Lughod argues that by "breaking coherence and introducing time," we respect that the lives of others remain beyond our comprehension and cannot be claimed objectively, rationally, or holistically, not by the feminists and "halfies"—who muddle the anthropological separation between self and other and were criticized for their partiality when Abu-Lughod wrote her article—nor by everybody who engages with ethnography.[48]

Nonetheless, Abu-Lughod, Das, Jackson, and Mattingly are not suggesting that we get rid of concepts or categories (these also matter to people). Michael Jackson notes that by putting the singular before the general, a shift in analysis occurs through an attention to experience above theoretical knowledge. Instead of carrying on with the antinomies between self and other, observer and observed, writing and world, reality and imagination, and knowledge and doubt, we need to better explore the dialectics between the kinds of experiences these terms designate.[49] For Jackson, starting off with human experience before concepts and theories means putting emphasis on the relational and the transitive, and not substantives and intransitives.[50] Reading Jackson, I find strong resonance with the Buddhist notion of dependent origination, in which phenomena and meanings are always relational. Combined with impermanence, this further signifies that meanings and contexts are always in flux and changing. Thus, to pin down definitive meanings becomes an almost impossible task. They are dependent on contexts, situations, language, and, above all, the person who deduces these meanings. In the words of the 14th Dalai Lama, "There is no independent objectivity."[51]

Abu-Lughod proposes three different possibilities for writing "against" generalizations that tend to be centered on the concept of culture and, in the process, she better captures the ambiguous nature of the human condition.[52] The possibility that I am concerned with in my own work is that of *ethnographies of the particular*, which also bears resonance with Cheryl Mattingly's approach to *singularity*, and Kirin Narayan's attention to creating *fully fleshed-out* individuals.[53] Abu-Lughod argues that by attending to people's particular (or singular) lives, we can produce forms of writing that can better convey the interrelations between individual actions, words, and wider historical, cultural, or political structures. In Das's words, this would uncover how forces "from pasts known and unknown, can come together to define a life—not life in its general but life in its singularity."[54]

In conveying a type of knowing about aging and dying in Tibetan exile that gives people a singular face and is inseparable from my relationship to my elderly friends, I present two ways of attending to singularity, or particulars. On the one hand, I consider how people's experiences emerge through social, historical, political, or material forces (that shape categories of difference, such as "Tibetan Buddhists" or "old people") and through people's responses to these forces.[55] On the other hand, I attempt to surpass the distinctions between self and other, observer and observed, or writing and world,[56] and attend to my elderly friends' singularity as emerging through the relational encounters between us. It is singularity in the latter sense— embedded in mutual, caring friendships—that lies at the heart of my writings and guides my analysis and theorizing. The fundamental Buddhist truth about life and self underlies these two ways of attending to singularity— namely, that singularity emerges through a relation: between the elderly and categories of difference and through the relation between the elderly and me.[57]

Through our intimate engagements and our singular responses to one another, both during moments of connection and friction, I came to know the elderly Tibetans as individual personalities, shaped not only by historical and sociopolitical conditions but also by their upbringing, family dynamics, and critical events. Being attuned to their idiosyncrasies, I came to know them not only as Tibetan Buddhists or elderly Tibetans, but also as Po Damchoe Ngawang, Ani Jamyang Choedon, and Mo Tsering Wangmo, who carried themselves and responded to their surroundings in singular ways and continue to unsettle what I think I understand about them. Ethnographers' relationships and commitments to their interlocutors thus make ethnography not just "something to know" but also "a unique way of knowing," as remarked by Carole McGranahan.[58]

Based on such a unique way of knowing my elderly friends, my choice to write about them in their singularity has also been a conscious effort to transform perceptions of their lives from "tokens of a type" into something irreplaceable, both in the field of Tibetan and Himalayan studies and in Tibetan society at large. In doing so, I also hope to convince the reader that "extraordinariness" is not merely a trait that belongs with certain people or events; rather, it emerges from a deep care and respect for the other that refuses to trivialize anyone's life, pains, or hopes. By building on artistic and academic works from Tibet and the Himalayas that have enriched and brought nuance to our understanding of people's lives, traditions, and histories,[59] my attention to the singular is a call to see people in Tibetan and Himalayan communities as, in the words of Bhuchung D. Sonam, "human beings first and foremost."[60] Their actions and minds cannot be made transparent with the help of cultural, religious, or academic truths.

My approach to singularity, however, should not be confused with a continental philosophical view of the self as a unitary subject, or as a search for the "real," or "thisness," that, in Sara Ahmed's words, is turned "into a property of her body or her speech."[61] By drawing on the works of Latina feminist scholars Gloria Anzaldúa and Mariana Ortega, I propose a view of the self as both multiplicitous and singular.[62] For Ortega, the term *multiplicity*, in contrast to *plurality*, or plural selves, implies "a complexity associated with one self."[63] While the self, especially in the case of those whom Anzaldúa sees as constantly traveling between worlds and who tend to find themselves living at the margins (immigrants, exiles, multicultural beings), shifts its shape in accordance with people, situations, or contexts, there is, however, a oneness to the self.[64] Ortega unpacks at length the existential multiplicity of the self as it moves through different contexts, becoming its unique strength and fragility; however, she does not provide a satisfactory answer to what is meant by oneness of the self.

I interpret the self's oneness to be how people have been marked by life. It is composed of the innermost pains, desires, wounds, or hopes that make people vulnerable. These cannot be openly exposed to the world, one might not even have a language to express them as with some of my elderly friends, nonetheless, they rest in the body, sometimes silently, while also impacting how one moves about in life or relates with others. And after having known a person long enough, if one were to look, listen and receive *care*-fully, their vulnerabilities can be felt lurking behind the smile, in the tone of voice, events that make them alert, or how their body moves through a space and around others. It is the singularity of my elderly friends, with all of their vulnerabilities, hinted at through their words and silences, that I was called to respond to and made it possible for me to know them as individual personalities. And through my responses to them, by receiving or rejecting whatever they had uncovered, I inevitably lay bare my own vulnerabilities.

Throughout the chapters, I show the multiplicity of my elderly friends, as in how they appeared and reacted differently to me and others, or how they handled diverse situations. Simultaneously, they had a oneness, singular ways of carrying themselves that set them apart from other "Tibetan Buddhists" or "old Tibetans," as remarked by their friends, acquaintances, and as observed by me. Over time, I learned what brought them joy and suffering, even though my understanding of why something brought them greater joy or suffering than did something else remains ambiguous. And in this lack of clarity, and in recognizing their opacity, lies also their multiplicity; they were more than what I saw and understood.[65]

Yet, a lack of answers does not stop me from empathizing with them and challenging myself to understand them better. As the French-Caribbean poet and philosopher Édouard Glissant states, it is not necessary to "grasp" someone in order to stand in solidarity with them.[66] I suggest that people's singularity emerges through this touch of compassion; by opening up for and standing in solidarity with the desirable and undesirable in them, and in pushing oneself to better understand how these characteristics emerged or were reinforced.[67]

So even though there may be no external objective reality, and everything may be a reflection of our minds as Buddhist thinkers, such as the Indian philosopher Dharmakīrti argues, I suggest that it is still possible to connect with and be touched by other minds and bodies by appropriately receiving whatever they reveal.[68]

Seeing and Listening That Is Like Touching

How can we come closer to sensing someone as a person while also attuning ourselves to a form of seeing and listening that recognizes the opacity of other minds?

In "Eye and Mind," the French philosopher Maurice Merleau-Ponty offers a compelling analysis of painting as a form of vision. He contrasts art with the domain of science, the latter representing a form of thinking which, according to him, "looks on from above," manipulating things instead of "living in them."[69] The painter, on the other hand, explores the process of seeing through painting—in other words, how an object, person, or landscape makes itself visible *in* their eyes.[70] By doing so, the painter (unlike the scientist) opens up for what can be called a "haptic vision," in which the senses "are not independent and discrete faculties, they converge, they overlap, they assist, and they compete with one another."[71]

Importantly, as Pablo Maurette notes, a haptic vision involves a simultaneity—to see something is also to see oneself; to feel something is also to feel oneself—something that Dharmakīrti and other Buddhist philosophers recognized long before any continental philosopher did.[72] "Blue and the awareness of blue are not different, because they must always be apprehended together," says Dharmakīrti.[73] Artist Paul Cézanne, too, echoed this simultaneity when he said, "The landscape thinks itself in me . . . and I am its consciousness."[74]

In a similar vein, it might be necessary to reflect upon how we, as persons, writers, or ethnographers, not only see but also listen to others—including their silences—in person and in writing, in order to better understand how they make themselves visible *in* us. Just like the painter, who according to Merleau-Ponty "takes" the body with him in order to paint, we too "take" our bodies with us during fieldwork.

It is through our bodily sensations and acts of receiving from others and giving to them, in words and actions, and the imprints these leave on our bodies, that we, to rephrase Merleau-Ponty, transform the world into words, images, or films. Thus, vision and movement are intertwined for us, as they are for the painter and anybody else.[75] So maybe we need to slow down and trace carefully how our perspective is intertwined with our movements—in more practical terms, how our ways of seeing and listening to others affect how we relate to them, and vice versa. In the process, we may need to attune ourselves to the untold stories people's bodies and gestures hint at and not merely attend to the ones they are able to tell in words. We may need to pay attention to the hopes, desires, or fears they did not act on, or were not able to act on, instead of only devoting ourselves to the lives they ended up living.

Writing about my elderly friends in their singularity by combining intimate descriptions and images is an attempt to better understand how something makes itself visible in me. Just like the massages, writing, too, has demanded an effortful and tender touch, a *care*-ful engaging with, listening after, and responding to the experiences of the elderly and giving them shape.[76]

Writing has demanded surpassing a type of seeing (and listening) that Naisargi Davé defines as looking, possessing, or being indifferent to, a type of looking and listening the Indian poet Rabindranath Tagore and Merleau-Ponty would argue is about capturing objective facts, as it concerns the scientist and not the ambiguous, personal, or the unique that is sought by the artist.[77]

A *care*-ful form of seeing and listening, by contrast, demands an openness to letting oneself be grasped *by* someone or something, seeing *with* it, and thereby opening oneself up to its "call to imagine."[78] To let oneself be grasped by someone or something entails, I believe, an exchange of both receiving and giving. For me, it has been a process of moving out of my own skin, literally and figuratively, and allowing others to enter it. And by doing so, I have opened up for a haptic vision that demands a type of seeing and listening that, to borrow Maurette's words, is "like touching."[79] This type of touch, "at its best, is also to see; to see, at its best, is also to touch,"[80] the nonintelligible between people, that which rests in the gaps between our words, or the marks others leave in us. To see and listen in a relational and imaginative way also means that the other reflects back on the self, making the assumed separations between subject and object (i.e., the seer and the seen) blurry and unsettling.[81]

This book thus invites a creative reimagining of ethnographic practice by moving toward a (*care*-ful) form of listening and seeing that is like touching, referring, in other words, to an embodied form of knowing that rests under the skin. Being "touched" by my elderly friends occurred through the process of massaging their legs and feet; by listening to their words, moods, and silences; and by assisting them in minor tasks (e.g., washing their hair, helping them urinate, cleaning their portable toilets) or during moments of vulnerability (e.g., when Mo Dickyi was bedridden and in grave physical pain, or when Gen Lobsang, unlike many others at the old-age home, had no family members visiting him during the Tibetan New Year, except nonkin like me).

Attempting to put into words an embodied form of knowing has also meant acknowledging that the marks my elderly friends have left in me cannot be neatly explained or pinned down. Moreover, they confer on me a responsibility, meaning that I treat parts of them handed over to me, or accidently spilled over, with respect and dignity. Occasionally, I was, and often continue to be, unsettled by who my elderly friends appeared to be, and I failed to elicit a desired response to their words, silences, and actions. In striving to write about them in a sensorial and caring way, I am guided by the awareness that my insights into their lives remain fractured and uncertain, making my epistemological claims inseparable from the affective connections, interdependencies, and responsibilities within which they are embedded.

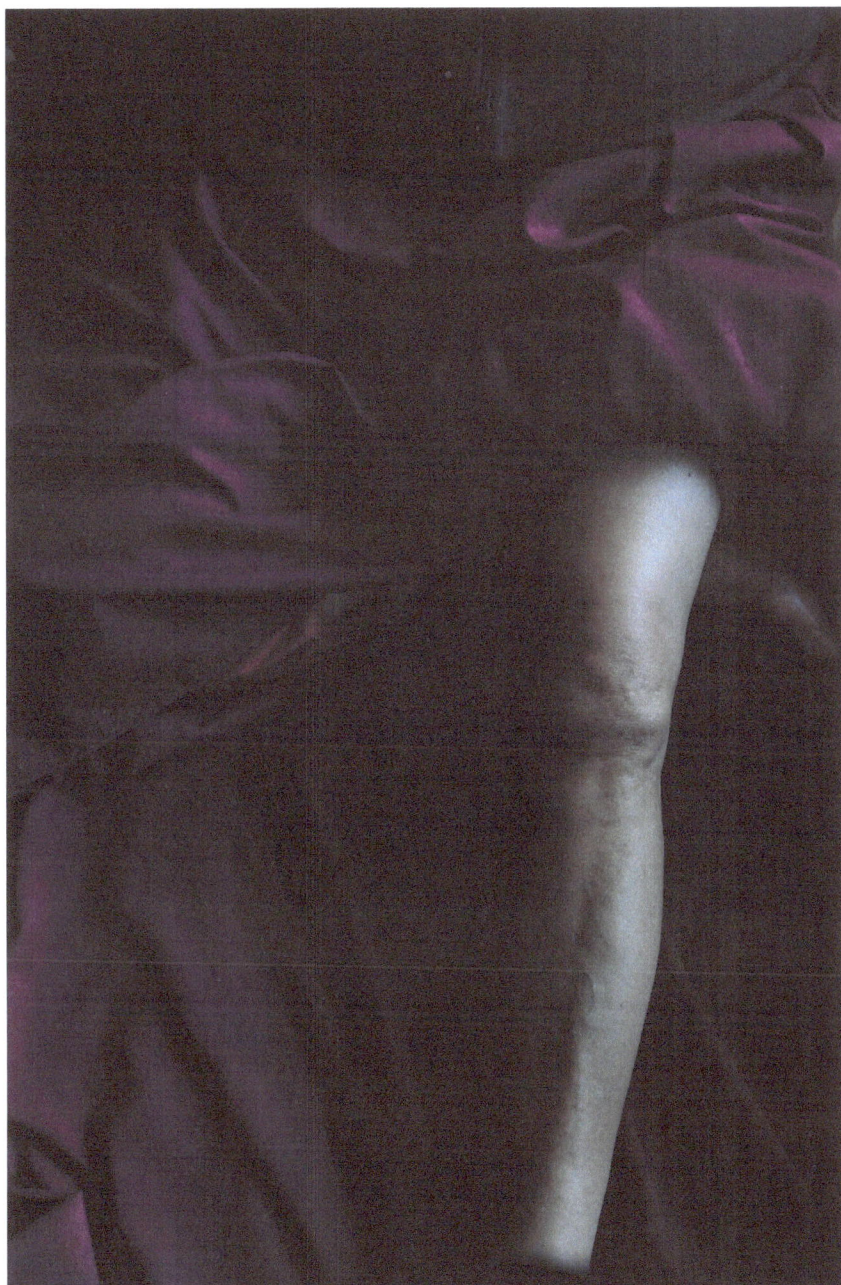

Figure 4: Red monastic robe and a leg. Photo by Harmandeep K. Gill.

Moreover, evoking an embodied form of knowing requires a sensorial and imaginative mode of expression that surpasses the barriers of a scientific language. Like a poem, painting, or image, an embodied form of knowing sends hints but remains opaque and unresolved. To this end, my understanding of the elderly in their singularity is presented not only as an empirical or theoretical argument but also through my writing style, including through the titles of chapters, interludes between chapters, and, finally, the images. These images portray bodies, objects, or spaces, carrying in them traces of the intangible that existed between my elderly friends and me, leaving them in half shadow, and thereby calling out to the imagination to uncover the gaps.[82] In some of the images, the faces of my elderly friends are concealed; in others, their faces are not exposed to bright light. This is a conscious choice on my part, not only to protect the identity of some of them but also to disclose a distance that remained between us, despite our close friendships. Yet, with the map of their bodies, such as their hands, feet, eyes, wrinkles, and posture, I also hope the reader will be touched by the stories their bodies silently tell.

Like the images, each chapter title (Chapters 2–5)—"Melancholia," "Desperation," "Nostalgia," and "Acceptance"—conveys the *feeling* of being-between-worlds at the mountain pass, evoking uncanniness and sometimes also a way out. However, in titling a chapter for a particular emotion, I do not mean to present people and phenomena as one-dimensional. My elderly friends moved between various emotional states, and their attitudes evolved over time, shifting between suffering and joy, or boundedness and movement. Nonetheless, certain ways of being and relating with others seemed to be more dominant among some individuals and in the context of aging and dying in Tibetan exile, as conveyed by the chapter titles. The interludes— unlike the prelude and postlude—are meant to be short intervals that offer an in-between space between the chapters; they detail my literal hands-on practice of leg and foot massages as phenomenological method, offering moments of physical touch.

By moving toward a sensorial and imaginative way of seeing and listening, I hope to bring my elderly friends to life as people—people whose emotional lifeworlds remain beyond my grasp but which can nonetheless be felt and connected with.

Fieldwork, Massaging, and Listening

The name Dharamsala—the other, more familiar name for McLeod Ganj—refers in Hindi to a shelter or resting place for spiritual pilgrims. For over a hundred years, it has indeed embraced people of diverse ethnicities and religions, including British officials, Tibetan refugees, and Kashmiri traders. As it was for them, McLeod Ganj has been a resting place for me: a temporary safe haven, perched below the majestic Himalayas. If I am not obliged to stay in Europe, it is in McLeod Ganj that I am always found.

I became interested in Tibet in 2011 when I visited McLeod Ganj for the first time and learned about the Tibetan people's ongoing fight for freedom and justice against the colonization of their country. My academic and political engagements with Tibetans-in-exile began shortly after, in 2012, when I began researching a topic for my bachelor's degree essay. I chose to write about Tibetan self-immolations (the act of setting oneself ablaze), and from the fall of 2013 I pursued my master's degree studies on the same topic. This brought me to McLeod Ganj for six months of fieldwork in 2014. After finishing my studies, I moved back to McLeod Ganj from September 2015 to July 2017, with only three months spent elsewhere. Upon my return in 2015, I did not anticipate that this place would become the closest I have felt to home as an adult. When I return after being away for months, the shopkeepers, my neighbors, and various acquaintances from the streets are surprised into smiles, inquiring about when I arrived, where I have been, or how long I plan to stay. I know on what corner I will find which dog, where I can expect to spot a particular face, and what kinds of Tibetan and Indian men and monks I need to steer away from. I can navigate through the more hidden paths in the forest of my mind. Every street has a unique mood, in which I move through multiple memories from times gone by. I have attended Tibetan teachings, weddings, language classes, parties, Miss and Mister Tibet pageants, *losar* (Tibetan New Year) celebrations, film festivals, protests, death rituals, and much more.

I have been with this place during days of heavy snowfall, when the cuckoo sings during the late afternoons of spring, in the merciless rains of the monsoon, and during the serene, crispy winter mornings and evenings of golden sunlight. Even at a distance, McLeod Ganj is forever close to my heart. Its people, animals, streets, and mountains are a part of me.

As someone who was born in India and, from the age of ten, raised in Norway, I relate on a personal level to Gloria Anzaldúa's notion of *los*

Figure 5: View of McLeod Ganj from Tipa Road. Photo by Harmandeep K. Gill.

atravesados—people, such as immigrants, exiles, and multicultural beings, who find themselves living between different worlds.[83] As is the case for my Tibetan exiled friends, home has been an elusive phenomenon for me since childhood. But our reasons differ. As an immigrant, one becomes disconnected and even estranged from one's homeland. Nonetheless, I can still revisit my place of birth and live there, something that is impossible for the majority of Tibetan exiles.

Having lived, worked with, and invested in the community of McLeod Ganj since 2014, including keeping a place in town in a Tibetan neighborhood known as Töpa Village since 2015, I find that McLeod Ganj is perhaps the only place that I have, to use bell hooks's words, felt "wedded to."[84] Whenever I am there, I have no desire to escape to someplace else. Thus, doing fieldwork in McLeod Ganj was like doing fieldwork "at home." Yet, despite caring for this place and its inhabitants, including people and animals, as if it were my home, I also realize that in the face of the natural and current environmental and development threats to McLeod Ganj (Chapter 1), I have much less at stake than the local Tibetans and Indians.

Apart from knowing McLeod Ganj more or less like a local, I selected it as a field site in 2017 for practical reasons—the location of the Dalai Lama's residence and temple makes it one of the holiest places in exile and an auspicious place to age in and die. My fieldwork was carried out from January 2018 to December 2018. During this period, I also did ten days of fieldwork among elderly Tibetans in Boudhanath in Kathmandu. Between March 2019 and the time of this writing, I returned to McLeod Ganj eight times, for periods ranging from approximately three to four weeks to approximately five to eight months, to live and to spend time with my elderly friends, massaging their legs and offering other types of assistance to those who lived alone.[85]

Finding My Elderly Friends

My fieldwork took an unexpected turn from the start, though I have come to see those events as a stroke of luck.

Heavy tears rolled down my face as the daily manager of the Jampaling Old People's Home, located in McLeod Ganj and the largest of the old-age homes run by the Central Tibetan Administration (CTA), informed me that I could not pursue my fieldwork there. The permission that had been granted by the Home Department, CTA—just five months ago and confirmed a week before the start of my fieldwork in January 2018—was suddenly with-drawn. I was never provided solid reasons for this decision, except that others, including Tibetan and foreigner researchers, writers, journalists, or photographers, tend to be subjected to the same access constraints. One is typically only granted the permission to be at the old-age home for a few hours to interview elderly residents who have been preselected by the daily manager of the home.

As a consolation, but in reality just to get me out of his office, the daily manager advised me to speak with the person in charge of the CTA's old-age homes. If they allowed me to pursue fieldwork at the home, he would not stand in my way. I left his office knowing that the decision would not be al-tered, but in the hopelessness of the situation, I held onto the false promise he had offered. The person in charge of the old-age homes did not change their decision and left me with the permission to do a few formal interviews with the elderly, something I pursued later on in my fieldwork.

The only option I had left was to try to gain access to private households. It would not be an easy task, as I could not simply knock on people's doors and request that they let a random stranger come around for one year. Know-ing that McLeod Ganj has a hub of NGOs, I hoped to gain access through volunteer work. And if that did not work out, I could always reach out to my Tibetan friends, who could at least help me gain access to one or two elderly Tibetans.

None of the NGOs I contacted was able to help. As my hope began to fade, an acquaintance told me about an NGO called Tibet Charity, which provides welfare services, such as leg massages, to elderly Tibetans. After submitting my project proposal to this organization and clarifying my intentions, the chairman generously allowed me to volunteer with their staff of nurses and health-care workers for a month and a half.

Starting in the middle of January 2018, I began accompanying a Tibet Charity staff member on her daily rounds to various elderly Tibetans in the McLeod Ganj area. When my volunteer period concluded at the end of February, I chose to continue visiting two of the elderly women I had be-come acquainted with, offering them leg and feet massages. During this same period (in early February), I also initiated engagements with a group of three sisters, relatives of a Tibetan friend. One of these sisters, the eldest of the three, was Mo Samdrup Drolma, whom I had known since October 2015. I also contacted the TCV old-age home, and after gaining permission from the head office of the TCV school and the daily manager of the old-age home, who was more than happy to have me there, I began massaging and visiting Gen Lobsang Choedak.

Toward the end of February 2018, I was following six elderly Tibetans on a weekly basis for massages. These were: Mo Dickyi Sangmo (female, age eighty-six), Ani Jamyang Choedon (female, age ninety), Mo Tsering Wangmo (female, age eighty), Mo Sangye (female, age sixty-five, from the Kham region in eastern Tibet), and Gen Lobsang Choedak (male, age ninety-five, TCV old-age home). Because I had known Mo Samdrup Drolma since October 2015, and had spent considerable time with her, I chose to devote more time to her younger sisters, Mo Dickyi Sangmo and Ani Jamyang Choedon, during my fieldwork. Nonetheless, I kept visiting Mo Samdrup whenever I had the time, but I did not massage her legs regularly. Spending time with these three sisters over the years and observing their family dynamics, miscommunications, and moments of togetherness has guided me in creating "fully fleshed-out" portraits of them.

By June 2018, the lack of men in the project became a serious concern, so I recruited two laymen to my fieldwork. For various reasons, however, they did not stay long. In August, through my network at the TCV school, I was able to recruit another layman, Po Damchoe Ngawang (age eighty-four), who was also a former employee of the school and a veteran of the Chushi Gangdrug, the Tibetan guerrilla army formally established in 1958.

Apart from massaging the legs and feet of my elderly friends, I also stepped in to buy groceries, purchase medicine, accompany them on hospital visits, or help them out with other practicalities, such as toilet visits. I visited my friends from Monday to Saturday. Some days I massaged three people a day, and on other days, two people. On a regular basis, my daily rounds began around 10:30 A.M. and concluded around 4:00 or 5:00 P.M.

Massaging, listening, and spending time with the elderly became a part of my life in McLeod Ganj. While, at the start of my fieldwork, I was merely a stranger to the elderly Tibetans—the "Indian girl" who offered them company and wrote about their lives—during the second half of my fieldwork in 2018, I became a personality to them and a part of their everyday lives, just as they did for me. From time to time, I reminded them of my project by writing field notes in their presence, by recording their speech, or by sharing about the "book" I was writing about the elderly Tibetans that included their individual stories.

Practicalities

From the start, I informed the elderly Tibetans that I was spending time with them and others, including the time spent massaging their legs and feet, because I was doing research (*nyamshib or shibjug*) about the lives of elderly Tibetans-in-exile. However, *research* was an alien word to most of them, especially those who were illiterate. Thus, I had to explain that it meant I was writing a "book" by spending time with and talking to them about their lives, their feelings (*tsorwa*), and their thoughts (*samlo*), including the difficulties and pains (*kangel*) of aging and dying in exile and in the absence of family, so they understood that their stories would be accessible to others to read.

My storytelling is guided by whatever the elderly chose to share with me and whatever they emphasized about their dilemmas of old age (e.g., frailty and loneliness, in Mo Dickyi's case; the difficulty of relying on paid care, in Mo Tsering's case; and the worry and fear of facing a lonesome death, in Gen Lobsang's case). I let my elderly friends guide the course of our conversations and I often let them carry on in their own flow of sentences, topics, or silences. Many times, when I was thirstier for "hard data," such as verbal statements, I would break the heavy silences and ask questions. But I learned that resting in the silence, or listening to their repetitions, was a much more intimate experience than any replies they supplied to my random questions. Verbal statements do not necessarily provide a truer or more correct understanding of the other. In fact, the most important things are the ones we quite possibly choose to withhold, writes poet and writer Dionne Brand.[86]

That being said, I also know many more details about the lives of my elderly friends than I am willing to write. I have been with them during painful moments; however, I withhold these moments and other details because they are too sensitive to be shared.

With their increasing age, a decline in their memories sometimes presented a challenge. All of my elderly friends, with the exception of Gen Lobsang Choedak and Po Damchoe Ngawang, could not clearly recall the exact year something happened, such as their escape from Tibet, how many years they worked or lived in a particular place, and even their own age. From 2019 onward, there were also times when Gen Lobsang got confused about more detailed matters. Hence, I had to confirm important details about their lives repeatedly with them, their family members, close friends, or neighbors.

Though the chapters of this book focus on specific individuals, my storytelling and analysis is also informed by my observations and conversations with other elderly Tibetans in their homes and public places, such as the circumambulation ground (*lingkor*) around Tsuglagkhang (the main Dalai Lama temple-in-exile), prayer sessions at the TCV old-age home, fieldwork in Boudhanath in Nepal, and my preliminary research period at the TCV old-age home in October and November 2016. My writings also draw upon thirty informal interviews—with the elderly in the McLeod Ganj area, at the TCV old-age home, and at the Jampaling Old People's Home, as well as with workers at Tibet Charity and the TCV old-age home. Three of these interviews were with health-care workers. I conducted additional interviews—with people in charge at the TCV school administration; the Home Department, CTA; and Mentseekhang, the Tibetan Medical and Astrological Institute—and made brief visits to two Tibetan settlements in southern India. These additional interactions provided me with broader insights into aging in other settlements in India, and in McLeod Ganj specifically. The longer quotations in the book, which are often separated from the text, have been transcribed from recorded interviews and conversations. Other statements are from my field notes, which I wrote in English and penned a few hours after an encounter or late in the evening, when I had the time to write. Many times, if important information was conveyed during the massage sessions or if the conversation was heavy, I wrote down words or sentences as I remembered them after finishing the massage.

Finally, this book also draws on my former extended stays in McLeod Ganj, before 2018. From 2015 to 2017, I studied written and spoken Tibetan in McLeod Ganj. The Tibetan language was and continues to be my only medium of communication with my elderly friends. Overall, my experience with the Tibetan exile communities extends over a decade and includes my activism for the Tibetan freedom struggle while in Norway.

Caring: Openings and Limitations

The elderly spoke of the massages as a virtuous action, as a practice of *chö* (the teachings of the Buddha), whereby I sought to benefit them. Massaging Gen Lobsang transformed not only our relationship but also how some of the other elderly at the TCV old-age home perceived me.

After Gen Lobsang spoke about me to others and told them how the massages were benefiting him, I noticed a significant change in the elderly residents' attitudes toward me. The women, who two years earlier had gotten fed up with me, now welcomed me with warm smiles, conversations, and praise. While Genla refrained from touching me, partly because it is considered to be inappropriate for monks, the opposite was the case toward the end of my fieldwork. Whenever I visit him now, he often holds my face between his hands before embracing me with the biggest hug.

My close friendships with the elderly also heightened their expectations of me, as well as my own sense of responsibility toward them. I could not always fulfill their expectations, as my time in the field was divided among several people. There were also times when their actions and opinions troubled me, and I failed to embrace them as persons.

Nor were the massages always motivated out of genuine concern. Giving massages six days a week, running between different parts of the small, hilly town to massage several people a day, attentively listening, and writing field notes every night became rather exhausting over time. Because of this repetitiveness on a daily basis, I came to relate to the visits and massages as a duty—nevertheless, a duty I was committed to fulfilling. On the days I did not want to step out of my room, my obligation to my elderly friends, not my own research, was what pushed me to take the step. I knew that they would be waiting for me, even though their lives moved on and changed independently of mine, whether I was in or away from McLeod Ganj, as mine also did.

Thus, visiting them, including massaging them, was not only a matter of fieldwork driven solely by the desire to collect data; it was equally, if not more, about responding to the ethical demands of our relationship. That was the only thing I felt I could do in return for everything they were doing for me, such as making my fieldwork possible to begin with.

Despite my best attempts at reciprocating their gift, I am also aware that I can never repay everything they have made possible for me, such as the writing of this book.

Their stories reveal a moment we all will face, and I am grateful to be able to share these stories here.

Interlude

What images must have flashed before Gen Lobsang Choedak's eyes on that dreadful 14th day of the second Tibetan month in 1959, when he escaped from Ganden monastery and into exile with four other monks? Did he turn around and take one last look at this precious place before disappearing among the high passes of central Tibet?

When Mo Tsering Wangmo's older brothers left to join the Tibetan resistance in the Lhoka region, and their father to join the resistance at the Norbulingka—the Dalai Lama's summer palace—had they suspected that they would not see each other again? What emotions must have overcome her when she and her younger brother tiptoed among the corpses of men and horses scattered around Norbulingka—some having been eaten by dogs—hoping to locate the corpse of their father?

On crossing the border into Nepal, Mo Dickyi Sangmo and her family had probably not foreseen that they would never cross back to the other side and return to their village in Kyirong. How could they have known that their stay in Nepal would extend to more than a year, before they would carry on to India and join thousands of other Tibetan refugees?

What thoughts must have struck Po Damchoe Ngawang and his fellow fighters in the Chushi Gangdrug guerrilla army when circumstances forced them to give up their eighteen years of military struggle to free their country, fighting first from within Tibet and later from the Mustang region of Nepal? In old age, did he truly believe that their struggles in both places "went to waste in the end"?

None of my elderly friends—the first generation of Tibetans-in-exile—had foreseen the course of history and how it would radically change their lives and the lives of Tibetan generations to come. They had never imagined that they would find themselves aging far away from their precious *phayül* (fatherland, or native land) and have their ashes scattered in a foreign land.[1]

Figure 6: A black-and-white portrait of the 14th Dalai Lama as a young man in 1956, and a later portrait of an older 14th Dalai Lama standing next to the 41st Sakya Trizin Rinpoche in the shrine (*chökhang*) in Gen Lobsang's room. Photo by Harmandeep K. Gill.

CHAPTER 1

Exile

For a brief period, a colorful photo of Mao Zedong used to be taped to the wall in front of my friend Tsering Jamphel's desk. It was the famous photo of Mao wearing the communist military uniform. On his head, he wore a cap with a red star in the middle. His gaze looked away from Jamphel. Next to Mao's photo, with some space in between, hung a photo of Jamphel when he was a small, chubby boy posing proudly next to his mother. His mother's arms were wrapped around him. One of her hands gently rested on Jamphel's small hand in her lap, while the other stretched across his back and held on to the other arm. His mother and the happy and safe five-year-old Jamphel looked directly at the thirty-four-year-old Jamphel. The photo was taken twenty-nine years ago in a studio in Kathmandu, Nepal, after Jamphel's mother made the treacherous journey from Lhasa and across the Himalayas with many others, carrying Jamphel on her back. Soon after this photo was taken, they traveled to Dharamsala in India, where Jamphel was enrolled at the TCV school, like thousands of other Tibetan children have been through the years. And then his mother returned to Lhasa.

Jamphel grew up imagining his parents' presence in such photos, in their handwritten letters, and later through voice messages over WeChat, before losing all contact with them. He still wonders how they must have aged. The connection between Mao Zedong's photo and the photo of Jamphel and his mother is all too clear: the colonization of Tibet that has separated thousands of families. There are many unanswered questions and unfinished stories. The course of history, and that which could have been otherwise, remains unfathomable. A possible life runs parallel to the present.

To be exiled from one's birth place is to traverse a space between dreams and reality, between the present and the possible. It often entails a state of dissonance, one in which the body moves and acts along the materially real, while longing for its most intimate, natural surroundings. To be an exile is to carry on with an unyielding sense of hope, while dwelling in the absences of the "possibles" and the "ifs," drowned for many by an undercurrent of sorrow and loss. Being an exile has "pockmarked our hearts with holes and dug wrinkles around our faces," writes Bhuchung D. Sonam.[1]

The lives of those of the younger generation of exiled Tibetans, like Tsering Jamphel, are reverberations of historical events that began unfolding far back in time before Jamphel's birth, and even before the birth of his parents. But those events happened in the youth of my elderly friends, who bore witness to them.

When the People's Republic of China was formed in 1949, with Chairman Mao Zedong as its supreme leader, Mao publicly announced the "liberation" of Tibet, Taiwan, and Hainan as one of his first goals. The Chinese People's Liberation Army (PLA) marched into the eastern parts (Kham) and northeastern parts (Amdo) of Tibet in the same year. In 1950, officials of the Chinese Communist Party (CCP) and the PLA took control of Tibet in its entirety, including the Tibetan capital city of Lhasa.[2] From 1956 on, things rapidly turned worse, as more aggressive policies came from the Chinese side. By early 1959, around fifty thousand people from Amdo and Kham were camping in and around Lhasa.[3] On 17 March 1959, after an oracle predicted that it was no longer safe for the 14th Dalai Lama to stay in Lhasa, he fled the city on the same evening, dressed as a common soldier.[4] He was escorted into exile in India by the guerrilla army, Chushi Gangdrug.[5] And so began a new epoch in Tibetan history.

Memories from the time of the Chinese invasion and the early period of exile are recalled with great clarity and sadness by the elderly Tibetans with a good memory of the past. When sharing stories about their lives, they often tend to circle back to those early days of exile, when the community was still getting on its feet. They recall times of hardship, as well as of collective strength, as they rebuilt a community from scratch. They share stories of tilling the soil in the high Himalayas in India or Nepal, breaking rocks to build roads and construct buildings, serving in the Indian army, carrying out seasonal winter business across India to sell winter clothes, or working as caregivers of Tibetan refugee children in the Tibetan Children's Village schools.[6] The story of aging and dying in exile cannot be divorced from all of the above. Thus, I start this chapter by fleshing out those early years in exile before providing a brief overview of the present status of the exile community in India, which is crucial for understanding the political, social, and economic conditions that shape Tibetan exiled lives. The coming chapters will often refer back to this one, while Chapter 4 can be seen as a continuation of how Tibet has been reimagined in exile. I conclude this chapter by taking a closer look at the Tibetan community in McLeod Ganj and how its natural and sociopolitical landscape shapes the experience of aging.

Preserving Tibet in Exile

From the border, the Dalai Lama was escorted through Assam, Tawang, and further to Bomdila, which today falls under the state of Arunachal Pradesh in northeast India. Having arrived in Bomdila, he received a telegram from the Indian prime minister, Jawaharlal Nehru, wishing him welcome. Soon after, the Dalai Lama was provided residence in Mussoorie, a former hill station of the British Raj.

On 29 April 1960, a little more than a year after his arrival in India, the Dalai Lama set out for McLeod Ganj in northern India, where he was to be provided a more permanent residence.[7] From Mussoorie, the Dalai Lama traveled by overnight train to Pathankot. Arriving there, he met crowds of Tibetan refugees who were on their way to do road construction work in Dalhousie, another hill station in the north. John F. Avedon writes that people wept uncontrollably. The Dalai Lama told them not to lose courage and that one day they would return to Tibet. From Pathankot, the Dalai Lama was escorted to Dharamsala. In the main market area of Dharamsala, known among locals as lower Dharamsala, thousands of people—hill folks, Sikhs, businessmen, Gurkhas—had lined up to welcome the lama from Tibet.[8]

From lower Dharamsala, the vehicles continued up a steep and narrow hill, through many twists and turns, and finally arrived at Swarg Ashram, the Dalai Lama's new home-in-exile. Swarg Ashram was located in the upper part of Dharamsala, better known as McLeod Ganj, which at the time was covered in dense forest and filled with tranquility. Like Mussoorie, McLeod Ganj had been one of the former summer hill stations of the British. When the British left McLeod Ganj following India's independence in 1947, the small hill station was left more or less empty. Swarg Ashram is today known among local Tibetans as *phodrang nyingpa* ("the old palace"). Soon, construction work to rebuild Tsuglagkhang, the Dalai Lama's main temple-in-exile, began in the lower part of McLeod Ganj. One of Mo Samdrup

Drolma's close relatives had worked on building the Tsuglagkhang, which is equivalent to the Jokhang temple in Lhasa, the holiest temple in Tibet. In 1968, the Dalai Lama moved from Swarg Ashram to the Tsuglagkhang, where a new residence was also built for him.

The Tibetan government-in-exile was reestablished in 1959 by the Dalai Lama, while he was in Mussoorie. It is officially called the Central Tibetan Administration (CTA), and it is regarded by Tibetans-in-exile as a continuation of the Lhasa government that ruled an independent Tibet until its incorporation into the People's Republic of China in 1951.[9] The CTA represents Tibetans from the three main regions of Tibet—namely, Ü-Tsang, Amdo, and Kham—and the four main religious lineages of Tibetan Buddhism: Gelug, Nyingma, Kagyu, and Sakya. The Bon religion, which encompasses the pre-Buddhist or indigenous religions of Tibet, is also represented. The Charter of Tibetans-in-Exile, which was promulgated by the Dalai Lama in 1963, stated that the Tibetan government-in-exile was committed to returning to Tibet. In 1991, the Charter of Tibetans-in-Exile was revised, and democratic governance was pushed forward "through principles of institutionalized separation and balance of powers: it distinguished between the legislative, executive and judiciary."[10] In 2011, the Dalai Lama devolved his political position in an effort to make the governance more democratic.

Another major concern of the Dalai Lama and the Tibetan leadership was to rehabilitate the approximately seventy thousand refugees coming from Tibet between 1959 and 1965.[11] They also saw it important to provide Tibetan children with an education, which was regarded as crucial for preserving Tibetan identity among exiles. To help realize their efforts, the Tibetan leadership received financial support from several governments, including those of India, Nepal, Bhutan, the United States, Switzerland, and Canada.[12]

From the first week that Tibetan refugees began arriving, in April 1959, the Indian government set up camps. Around three hundred bamboo huts were erected in Missamari in the northeastern state of Assam. Similar huts were set up in Buxa, also in Assam. A total of fifteen thousand refugees reportedly arrived in Missamari in May and June of 1959. Many people died and fell ill after the difficult journey across the Himalayas and after exposure to the warm Indian climate. Soon, the refugees were sent off to cooler places in northern India, such as McLeod Ganj, Mussoorie, Dalhousie, and Kullu-Manali. There they took up temporary work as road laborers.[13] In McLeod Ganj, the famous Nauzer N. Nowrojee, a Parsee resident whose family had lived there since the arrival of the British in the early 1860s, tirelessly assisted the Tibetan refugees with everything from blankets to toiletries and cooking utensils.[14]

The first generation of Tibetans-in-exile, including some of my elderly friends, took up work constructing roads in Shimla, Chamba, Kullu, Mandi, and Kangra in northwestern India.[15] In addition, the road builders in the Mandi area also constructed dams and houses in Pandoh, close to the town of Mandi.[16]

Constructing roads in the high Himalayas was dangerous work. Landslides could occur, and many Tibetans lost their lives in various accidents.[17] In 1969, the male workers received two and a half Indian rupees (INR 2.50) and female workers received INR 2.25 per day. The wages were higher for men in the Mandi area, where they received INR 4 a day, while women only received INR 1.75. The wages were higher for both genders in the higher-altitude area of Lahaul Spiti, where men received INR 4 and women INR 3.25 per day.

Early on, the Tibetan leadership recognized that Tibetans could not make a living from road construction alone. It was unstable work that required people to move from place to place, and it posed particular challenges for the old family members of the road builders, and for their young children. The Dalai Lama found it important to rehabilitate Tibetan refugees into more permanent settlements, where they could become more or less self-sufficient and preserve their identity, culture, and language.[18]

The northern parts of India, especially the areas surrounding Dharamsala, did not have much vacant land. With Prime Minister Nehru's help, Tibetans refugees were relocated to the vacant countryside in the state of Karnataka in southern India, where the first Tibetan settlements were established. When Tibetan refugees arrived, the land was a massive wilderness, packed with forest. The toilsome work of clearing the forested land, building houses, reconstructing monasteries and other institutions, and making the land ready for cultivation was undertaken by the first generation of Tibetans-in-exile.

The first settlement was established in 1960 on three thousand acres of land that is, to this day, leased to Tibetans by the state government of Karnataka. It is located in Bylakuppe, approximately eighty-four kilometers from Mysore city. The settlement was named Lugsung Samdupling. In 1969, another settlement was established in Bylakuppe and was called Dickyi Larsoe. Three thousand people were resettled in Lugsung Samdupling in 1960, and two thousand in Dickyi Larsoe in 1969. Today, the Bylakuppe area houses 7,859 people.[19]

Tibetans began growing crops such as maize, potato, lentils, tobacco, and rice, as well as fruits such as guava, mango, and coconuts. Children were taught in bamboo huts in the beginning, and in 1962 the first school buildings were erected in Lugsung Samdupling.[20] The three major Tibetan monasteries—Sera, Drepung, and Ganden, also known as "the three seats/ monasteries" (*densa sum*) of the Gelug lineage of Tibetan Buddhism—were reestablished.[21] Sera is located in Bylakuppe Settlement, and Ganden and Drepung are located in Doeguling Settlement, which was established in 1966 in Mundgod in the state of Karnataka. The resettlement work in Mundgod was the same as in Bylakuppe. The present population of Doeguling Settlement is 8,480.[22]

Tibetan settlements were also established in other parts of India in the early 1960s. Some of these are: Kusangling in Arunachal Pradesh (est. 1962), Dhargyeling in Arunachal Pradesh (1962), Phendeling in Madhya Pradesh (1963), and Phuntsokling in Odisha (1963). Tibetan refugees also began settling in various hill stations across northern India, such as Dalhousie, Shimla, Darjeeling, Mussoorie, and Kalimpong, and in Kathmandu, Nepal. Tibetan refugee help centers were set up in McLeod Ganj, Shimla, Dalhousie, and Darjeeling starting in the early 1960s.[23]

Providing education and care, especially for the many children who were separated from their families during the escape, was another big concern for the Dalai Lama. "The children have been a special anxiety for me; there are over five thousand of them under eighteen," he noted in his autobiography *My Land and My People: Memories of the Dalai Lama of Tibet*, which was first translated into English in 1962.[24] On 17 May 1960, the Dalai Lama's eldest sister, Tsering Dolma, established a nursery for Tibetan orphans that was, at the time, known as the Tibetan Refugee Children's Nursery. After her death in 1964, his younger sister, Jetsun Pema, took over the responsibility for educating Tibetan children. Over the next several decades, with financial support from international aid donations, the school in McLeod Ganj was expanded, and Tibetan schools were also established in other settlements.[25] What began as a nursery for orphans grew to offer a full education to all Tibetan children.

These schools are today known, collectively, as the Tibetan Children's Village (TCV), and they are found in many Tibetan settlements across India. They comprise both day schools and residential (boarding) schools. Several of the elderly Tibetans mentioned in this book have worked at the TCV school in McLeod Ganj, which is one of the biggest residential schools for Tibetan exiles today. The TCV schools have been central in the formation of a homogenous national Tibetan identity in exile and in reimagining the Tibetan nation.[26] Tibetan children (with a few exceptions) are all educated at TCV schools.

The care of approximately three thousand older refugees and disabled individuals posed another challenge. In the late 1960s, with help from the Indian government, a home for old and infirm people was set up in Dalhousie in northern India. The home could house up to 429 people. Other older adults accompanied younger family members to road construction camps, while some were moved to the camp for the old and disabled in Manali in northern India. The United Nations High Commission for Refugees undertook efforts to build old-age homes in both Mundgod and Bylakuppe.[27] Today, old-age homes are found in both settlements and in most of the Tibetan settlements in India and Nepal.

The majority of these homes are run either by the CTA, by private institutions such as monasteries, or by TCV schools. The CTA operates thirteen old-age homes (*gensokhang*) in India and one in Nepal. According to their 2017–2018 annual report, the CTA's old-age homes housed 625 residents in total, 150 of whom resided at the Jampaling Old People's Home in McLeod Ganj. In addition, the report listed 1,525 elderly Tibetans not residing in old-age homes who were provided an "elder's stipend," and 400 ex-army who were also provided stipends of different sorts. In total, 2,550 elderly Tibetans were reported to receive some kind of support from the CTA.

The TCV operates two main old-age homes in India: one in McLeod Ganj and one in Leh in Ladakh. I did my fieldwork at the home in McLeod Ganj, which is located below the TCV school area. In 2020, fifty elderly Tibetans had accommodation there.[28] The home was founded as a gesture of gratitude to the first generation of exiled Tibetans who worked at the school as teachers, caregivers, and cooks. This is the TCV school administration's gift to compensate them for their toilsome work and the meager salaries they received. The elderly residents at the TCV old-age home also receive a monthly pension. Gen Lobsang Choedak, introduced in the opening of the book, used to make bread in the school kitchen, and he receives INR 4,000 on a monthly basis.[29] Some receive less and others more, depending on the position they held. Unlike the old-age homes run by the CTA, which provide residence to those without family and also to the poor (often being the last option for many), the TCV old-age homes are a place of retirement for the first generation of exiled Tibetans who worked for the school.

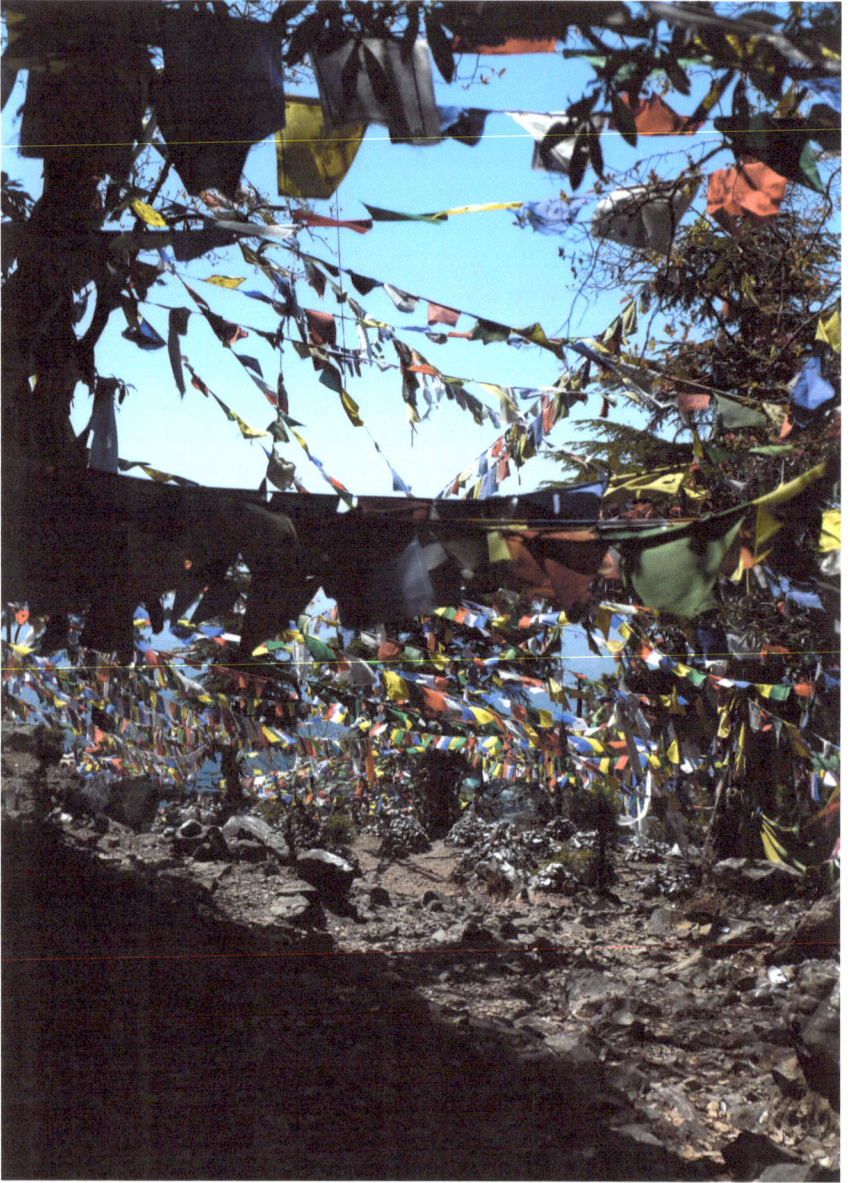

Figure 7: Tibetan prayer flags (*lungta*) in the forest in McLeod Ganj: a common sight in Tibetan settlements. Photo by Harmandeep K. Gill.

In addition to the CTA's services for elderly Tibetans, nongovernmental organizations (NGOs) such as the Tibet Fund, Tibetan Women's Association, and Tibet Charity also run sponsorship programs for poor elderly Tibetans in McLeod Ganj and in other settlements. All three NGOs have their main offices in McLeod Ganj. Among them, Tibet Charity is the only NGO that regularly checks up on old Tibetans. Mentseekhang, the Tibetan Medical and Astrological Institute, also provides free medicine to Tibetans aged sixty-five and older.[30]

Over the years, Tibetan settlements have expanded in size. They house monasteries, TCV schools, Mentseekhang branches, handicraft centers, CTA settlement offices, old-age homes, and local branches of political NGOs, such as the Tibetan Youth Congress and the Tibetan Women's Association.[31]

Today, there are thirty-nine Tibetan settlements across India, stretching from the far northern parts of Ladakh (bordering on Tibet) to southern India. There are ten settlements in Nepal and seven in Bhutan. In India, fifteen settlements are agriculture-based, thirteen are handicraft-based, and eleven are defined as cluster communities. The agricultural settlements are mostly spread throughout southern India, with a few in the northeast and two in northern India. Most of the hill stations, including McLeod Ganj, are defined as cluster communities, meaning that they are also inhabited by local Indians and other foreigners. Internationals do not need to apply for permission at the Dalai Lama's office in New Delhi to visit cluster communities, something that is required to visit noncluster communities, such as in Mundgod or Bylakuppe, which are primarily inhabited by Tibetans. The Tibetan settlement in Boudhanath in Kathmandu, where I conducted ten days of fieldwork in 2018 and have stayed for longer periods between 2013 and 2018, is a cluster community.

All settlements are under the jurisdiction of the CTA. These days, the majority of Tibetans in India make their livelihoods from the seasonal winter business (selling winter clothing) or agriculture (or a combination of both, for those living in agricultural settlements), and other kinds of businesses, such as guesthouses, restaurants, and cafés.

The Present Status of the Exile Communities

Tibetans-in-exile (in India, Nepal, and Bhutan) are first and foremost subject to the laws and governments of their host countries. In India, Tibetans are officially classified as "foreigners" and not refugees, as India is not bound by any international refugee convention. Tibetans in India and Nepal (and also in other places) hold a "Green Book," which is issued by the CTA, and many refer to it as the "passport" of Tibetans-in-exile, because it is a document that asserts their national identity and allows them to claim their rights with the CTA.[32] Green Book holders pay tax to the CTA, and the Green Book is used to vote in the Tibetan parliamentary elections, for admission to Tibetan schools, to apply for CTA's university scholarships, for poverty alleviation programs, and for employment within the CTA or businesses run by the CTA.

The CTA has never encouraged Tibetans in India (or in other countries in South Asia) to take up citizenship, as it is seen to weaken their claims to Tibetan state sovereignty.[33] Apart from a small number of Tibetans who apply for Indian citizenship, mainly to have greater social and economic security, the majority of Tibetans living in India remain stateless.[34] The Indian government grants them a Registration Certificate to stay in India. The certificate has to be renewed annually or biannually, depending on its place of issue in India. This poses great difficulty for elderly Tibetans who have to travel long distances by public transport to other settlements to renew their certificates. In 2018, the renewal period was extended to five years, but only for those who have lived in India for at least two decades.

Despite the expansion of Tibetan settlements, the plan was never to settle in India, but rather to return to Tibet within a few years. In 2024, the Tibetan freedom struggle in exile entered its 65th year. Elderly Tibetans continue to hope and pray that the Dalai Lama and future generations might one day return to Tibet, but they are aware that, because of their advanced age, they will most likely face death on foreign soil. A 2009 demographic consensus by the CTA estimated that 128,014 Tibetans were living in exile in India, Nepal, Bhutan, North America, Europe, and Australia, the majority of whom were in India and Nepal.[35] In 2024, the number of Tibetans living in India and Nepal is estimated to be much lower, in large part because so many Tibetan youths have migrated to North America, Europe, and Australia in recent years in search of more secure and prosperous futures. Some Tibetans (usually people in their twenties to late thirties who escaped from Tibet after the year 2000) have returned to Tibet, but not many. These days, a limited number of Tibetans are escaping into exile.

Work opportunities are limited in the Tibetan settlements. Namgyal Choedup, who surveyed 940 households in the Doeguling Settlement in

Mundgod, reports that in agricultural settlements, young Tibetans do not see farming as a viable option.[36] Fewer than 30 households in the settlement relied solely on farming. One of the younger Tibetans quoted in his article says that farming is more of a hobby for his aging parents and not a real source of profit.[37] As Choedup states, the younger generations seek upward mobility, and for most of them, out-migration has become the main means of achieving this.

However, not all parents in Choedup's study are in favor of out-migration: people comment that the need for out-migration arises out of greed.[38] The elderly I became acquainted with in McLeod Ganj who had children living abroad were for the most part pleased that their children had out-migrated, emphasizing that it had given them greater economic and social security. As a result, these parents were, on the one hand, less constrained by worries over their children's futures and more at peace; on the other hand, they were aging in the absence of their children. For a society that was traditionally guided by norms of filial piety, retirement to old-age homes is considered to be a last option among many Tibetans. Both aging parents and children are stuck in a double bind: if the children stay behind, they risk their own future, and if they leave, their parents age alone and face lonely deaths.

All of my elderly friends, except one, were aging in the absence of children and extended family. But in their case, the reason for this absence was not always out-migration to foreign countries. Two of them never had children, because they were monastics. Others left most of their families back in Tibet, and those who did have family close by did not always enjoy harmonious relationships with family members. However, in all cases and in various ways, their life situations were inevitably tied up with the Chinese invasion of Tibet, which was a watershed moment in the personal lives and the collective history of the Tibetan people.

Dharamsala: The Tibetan Capital in Exile

Dharamsala is located in the Kangra district in the state of Himachal Pradesh in northwest India. Himachal Pradesh borders the state of Punjab in the west and Tibetan areas in the east. Apart from being the location of the Tsuglagkhang, and the Dalai Lama's residence, Dharamsala houses the CTA, numerous NGOs, several monasteries, and central cultural and educational institutions such as the Tibet Museum (est. 1998); the Tibetan Institute for Performing Arts (est. 1959); the Norbulingka Institute (est. 1995); and one of the biggest TCV schools.[39] It also houses the first and main branch in exile of Mentseekhang (est. 1961) and the Tibetan Delek Hospital.

Dharamsala has become the political, cultural, and religious center for Tibetans-in-exile. Being the seat of the Dalai Lama, the CTA, and important religious and cultural institutions, it is also known as "little Lhasa" and is often also referred to as Dhasa. The current Tibetan population of Dharamsala is around eight thousand.

Dharamsala is divided into two areas, lower and upper, the latter being known as McLeod Ganj. All of my elderly friends live in and around McLeod Ganj. The majority of Tibetans live either in McLeod Ganj or in the area between McLeod Ganj and lower Dharamsala, better known as Gangkyi (short for Gangchen Kyishong, "happy valley of snow"). This area also houses the CTA offices, the Nechung Monastery, the Mentseekhang, Delek Hospital, and the Tibet Museum.[40] The main town and markets are located in lower Dharamsala, five kilometers from McLeod Ganj. The drive to McLeod Ganj (through Gangkyi) follows a steep uphill with numerous turns and twists. Reaching McLeod Ganj, one stands face-to-face with the mighty and lush hills typical for the area, with the Himalayan range known as the Dhauladhar range, in the background.

From there, one can reach the wildest, most remote places. In contrast to the British era and the Dalai Lama's arrival in 1960, remote areas are, today, with the expansion of the town and increase in tourism, increasingly distant.

As mentioned earlier, Dharamsala is a place with a history of migration. It has been the home of the Pahari-speaking, mixed-caste, tribal community known as the Gaddi since the mid-nineteenth century.[41] The Gaddis are seminomadic goat and sheep herders, but today many also run guesthouses, restaurants, and taxis. With the arrival of the British, theirs became one of the most vigorous communities outside the cities by the turn of the twentieth century. The church of John the Baptist, named St. John in the Wilderness, was built in 1852. It survived a massive earthquake in 1905, which killed thousands of people. Today, the church and its graveyard, surrounded by the mysterious Deodar forest, are one of the main architectural traces from the British Raj.

The other old architectural treasure of McLeod Ganj is the Nowrojee & Son General Store, founded in 1860 by the Nowrojee family, who in September 2020 sold the property. The store still stands at the main square of McLeod Ganj and sells a few items, such as snacks, drinks, books, and pens.

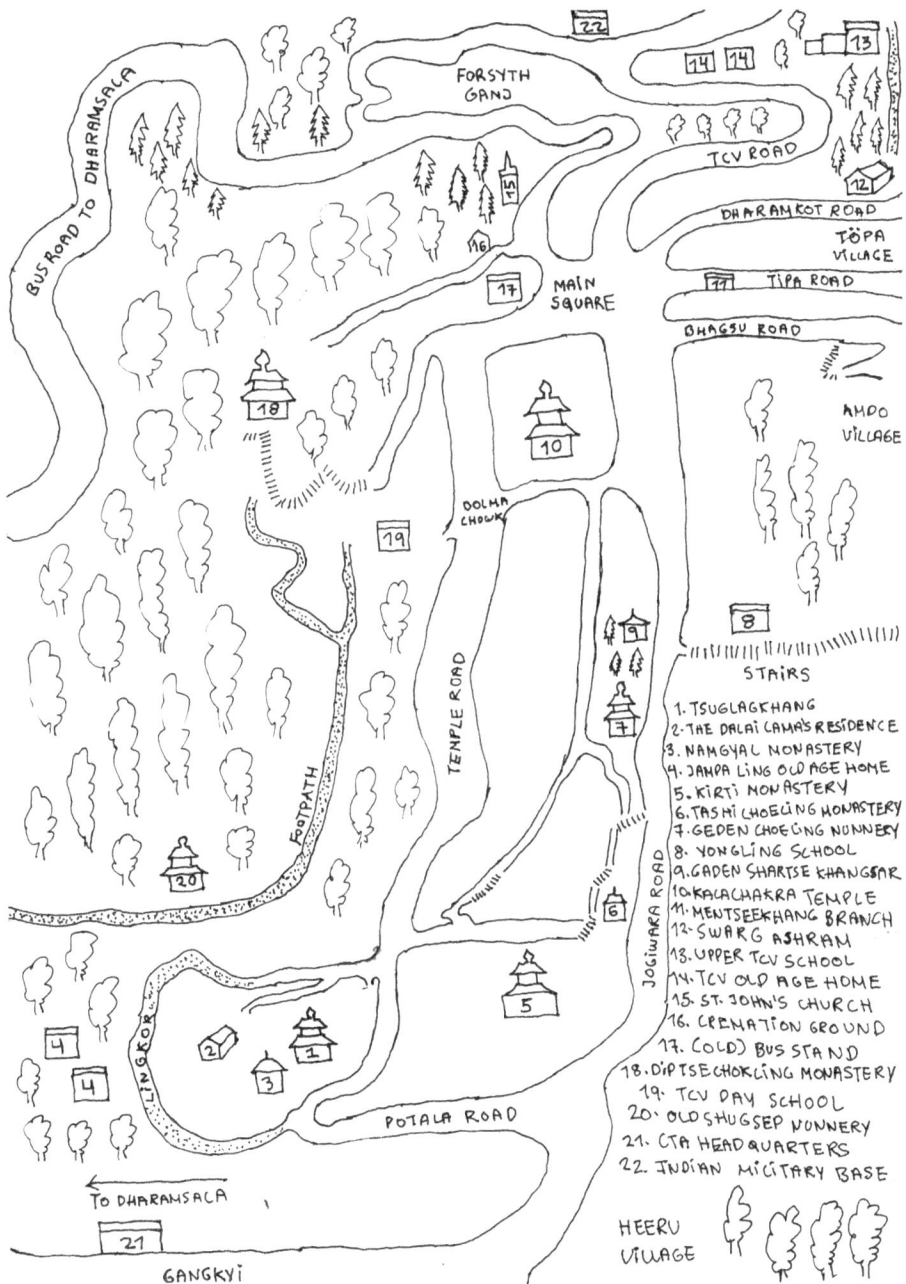

Figure 8: *Little Lhasa*: a simplified view of McLeod Ganj. Illustration by Harmandeep K. Gill.

Following the independence and partition of India in 1947, the Muslim residents of Dharamsala left for Pakistan, whereas the wealthy Hindus, who had vacationed in the hills of McLeod Ganj, returned to Delhi. Ultimately, the population of McLeod Ganj dropped from four thousand to seven hundred between 1947 and 1960.[42] With the arrival of Tibetan refugees in 1960, the town soon transformed into an international tourist destination and a Tibetan "Shangri-la" in exile, attracting hippies and spiritual seekers.[43]

The Tibetan community in McLeod Ganj and the surrounding areas is diverse. It is inhabited by the first generation of Tibetans-in-exile, their descendants, Tibetans who escaped from 1979 onward after the Cultural Revolution had ended, and those who came in the early 2000s.[44]

Exiles who came in the 1990s and from 2000 onward are often referred to as "newcomers" (*sar jorpa*). Nearly all of them left their families back in Tibet, and most of them come from the eastern Tibetan regions of Amdo and Kham. The majority of the younger population in the McLeod Ganj area was not born or raised there. They come from Tibet or other Tibetan settlements across India and Nepal. In general, the Tibetan community in McLeod Ganj, because of its exposure to people from all over the world and being the center for political activities, workshops, festivals, and the like, is more liberal than the closed-off Tibetan settlements in other parts in India and Nepal.

Tourism has completely changed the landscape and mood of McLeod Ganj, especially since around 2014, because of an increase in domestic Indian tourists who visit, in particular, from the Punjab and New Delhi regions.

Newly built guesthouses are increasingly owned by outsider investors from the Punjab, Haryana, and Delhi region, and are often perched unsafely on the hillsides, towering between five to seven floors.[45] The fragile hillsides also hold sacred Tibetan monasteries, nightclubs, numerous cafés and restaurants owned by local Tibetans and Indians, and a few yoga and meditation retreats. The narrow roads of town are filled with honking cars, bikes, and faces from all over the world, which is especially true during the weekends, public holidays, and at the peak of the tourist season in the spring and after the monsoon.[46]

Homeless dogs, cats, cows, and bulls also occupy the streets. Small Asian monkeys are found across town, although most them prefer to live in the densely forested areas surrounding the upper parts of McLeod Ganj. The big cousin of the smaller monkeys, the gentle and shy langur, tends to keep itself at a safe distance from humans. Snow pheasants, partridges, and ravens also share the forest.

Hidden in the dense forest, where Gaddi herders move about grazing their goats, there are leopards, foxes, and bears. Wild hawks and vultures roam high up in the hills, and I have certainly seen the wild hawk on my treks. My elderly friends share that in the past, people often spotted bears or leopards. These days, due to the expansion of the town, increase in traffic, and cars constantly moving between McLeod Ganj and Gallu temple, the highest point accessible by cars and bikes, these animals have moved deeper into the forest. However, leopard and bear sightings, and even attacks by bears, do occasionally happen when these animals descend to the forest area around town during the winter months.

The tranquil sixteen-thousand-foot-high pass of Triund, lying beneath the pinnacle of Mun Peak of the Dhauladhar range and to which the Dalai Lama trekked in 1960, has now been flooded by tourists, most of whom tend to leave behind a lot of garbage.

The steep, incredibly narrow, and broken road up to Dharamkot village, where I have lived since 2015, did not have much traffic in 2015. In 2016, the road was paved, and since then, cars transporting tourists between McLeod Ganj and Dharamkot (a distance of less than one kilometer) and the beginning of the pass to Triund have increased traffic dramatically. During my first longer stay in 2014, Dharamkot was more or less a small village, occupied by the Gaddi community, and had some guesthouses. The increase in tourism has provided new economic venues for the local Gaddis, and today Dharamkot is fully occupied by guesthouses, restaurants, cafés, and yoga and meditation retreats that become lively during the tourist season. Dharamkot also houses the Tushita Meditation Centre.

These days, international and domestic tourists steer away from the hectic McLeod Ganj and prefer to stay in the village of Dharamkot, which offers more tranquility because of its proximity to the forest. During the hectic tourist season in spring and autumn, Dharamkot is also a main hub for Israeli tourists. The local conservative Gaddis now live next door to highly liberal tourists.

Despite the rapid development of McLeod Ganj and its surroundings areas, the town, its forest, and the mountains still captivate people around the world. And even during the busiest of tourist seasons, as a local, one can always find remote hideaways in the dense forest.

But not everything is as harmonious in this tiny hill station as international tourists like to imagine. Apart from the internal political disagreements in the Tibetan community, many conflicts have erupted between the Gaddis

Figure 9: Deodar trees in the early morning light during late spring. Photo by Harmandeep K. Gill.

and Tibetans over the years. For the Gaddis, their homes have been taken over by Tibetan exiles. The latter are also recipients of much international aid, something that rarely reaches the Gaddis.[47] Meanwhile, for the Tibetan residents of McLeod Ganj, especially those who were born and raised there, McLeod Ganj is as much a home to them as it is to the local Gaddis. The latest big conflict erupted after three Gaddi youths stabbed an innocent Tibetan man to death in October 2015.[48] Local Tibetans often worry about their future in McLeod Ganj after the demise of the Dalai Lama, who they feel is keeping conflicts at bay.

Another looming threat in McLeod Ganj is posed by the environmental changes in the region, which affect the local Indians and Tibetans alike. According to the Himachal Pradesh State Disaster Management Plan, the rapid development of the region and change in temperature is leading to more extreme climate events, such as drought, avalanches, landslides, cloudbursts, forest fires, and flash floods.[49] In recent years, people have also witnessed an increased intensity of rain, the latest being during the monsoon of 2023, and fewer and lighter snowfalls, which is causing water shortage in town. In addition, the heavy and irresponsible construction along the fragile hillsides is of grave concern. Furthermore, the hill station and its inhabitants face the looming threat of a major earthquake, which could happen anytime.

For now, the small hill station of McLeod Ganj is shared between the Gaddis, Tibetan exiles, Kashmiri shopkeepers and porters, domestic and international tourists, poor rural migrants, and long-term domestic and international residents. Everything from Buddhist teachings, political protests, and film festivals to beauty pageants, long- and short-term meditation retreats, and parties takes place here. It is the place for traditionally minded elderly Tibetans, more radical Tibetan youths, and everyone in between. It is the place for solitary monks and highly devoted nuns. It is the place for Jack Kerouac's "dharma bums" who seek the spiritual teachings of Tibetan Buddhism, and for those who come to drink and party on the weekends.[50] It is a place where traveling female tourists have flings with Tibetan men, which many times leads to long-distance relationships, and in a few cases to marriage. It is the place for local Gaddi women, covered from head to toe in their colorful *dupatta* (scarf) and *salwar kameez* (dress for women), as well as the liberal females with their naked legs. It is the place journalists, anthropologists, and Tibetologists pass through, and where some stay on, like me. It is the place for those who pass time at cafés, Kunga Restaurant, Moon Peak, The Other Space, Lhamo's Croissant, Woeser's Bakery, or Juniper

Café, and the ones who work tirelessly from early morning until evening in the CTA, NGO offices, shops, and roadside stalls, or in the construction of new buildings. It is the place for those with stable families and for lonely ones. It is a place of lamas and disrobed monks. It is a place for those with visions and those who are lost. Pahari, Tibetan, Hindi, Punjabi, French, German, Japanese, Korean, English, and Hebrew are some of the languages heard. It is a place where children grow up and people fall in love, establish families, make a living, and leave for other parts of India and the world. It is a place where people find freedom and can start anew; it is also a place where people get stuck in circles and then leave to start anew someplace else. It is a place where people age and die. The dense hills of McLeod Ganj, leaning into the mighty Himalayas, hold and embrace them all: the gentle and the cruel, the bravehearted and the scared, the ambitious and the satisfied, the optimistic and the broken. All pass through and stay as long as they like. When they leave, new ones arrive, slightly changing the mood of the city, but the ancient Himalayan range continues to stand as it has for millions of years.

Aging in McLeod Ganj

The landscape of McLeod Ganj is constantly changing with the addition of guesthouses and new restaurants and the continuous influx and outflux of tourists and Tibetans. All of this makes McLeod Ganj a very unstable place to age. Furthermore, Tibetan community networks here are not as strong as in "official," closed-off Tibetan settlements elsewhere, making aging in McLeod Ganj a precarious and lonely life phase for many. In the absence of family, many elderly people often rely on neighbors for help. Whereas people in other settlements, such as in Bylakuppe, Mundgod, or Bir, tend to have good knowledge of the Tibetan families in their camps, and often also of those in the surrounding camps in their settlement, people in McLeod Ganj are more anonymous, with the exception of those living in a few areas in town, such as Kyirong Village and Töpa Village (Chapters 2 and 4).[51] In Bylakuppe and Mundgod, elderly Tibetans also meet for regular prayer sessions in the local monastery of their respective camps. Life there is more stable and bounded.

The mountainous landscape of McLeod Ganj make things harder. The town is a series of steep hills, which makes outdoor movement very challenging for old knees. Nearly all houses are located off the roads and up hillsides, and the only way to reach them is by climbing or descending staircases. Three of my elderly friends had become confined to their homes because climbing up and down staircases was too hard on their legs. One of my elderly neighbors, an eighty-year-old Anila from the Ladakh region of India, walks slowly up the steep hill of Dharamkot Road where we live, aided by her walking stick. She has to repeatedly pause for short breaks before finally reaching home. Taxis and bikes racing up and down the narrow streets make outdoor movement more challenging.

The settlements in other places in northern India (e.g., Bir and Dehradun), as well as in southern India and even Nepal, are on flatter ground. This makes outdoor movement much easier for the old and also makes it possible for them to go for daily circumambulation around the local monastery. In McLeod Ganj, most Tibetans carry out the circumambulation practice around the Tsuglagkhang and the Dalai Lama's residence; this path is referred to as *lingkor*, after the outer circumambulation path in Lhasa. *Lingkor* moves through a dense forest, inhabited by monkeys and dogs. People move, spinning the prayer wheels placed along the route. The last part of *lingkor* is a steep uphill climb, which, as I witnessed, is tiring for both young and old. In Boudhanath, in Kathmandu, where I have lived for longer periods, circumambulation is practiced around the Boudhanath stupa and surrounding monasteries, which are all located on flat ground. The circumambulation path around the Boudhanath stupa is crowded with people during the morning and evening hours. Even the slowest of elders who live close by can make it there, both morning and evening, for religious practice and gossip.

By comparison, the circumambulation path in McLeod Ganj is much emptier, and most elderly Tibetans cannot go there regularly because of the difficulty of walking it. Those who stay close to the main square practice circumambulation around the nearby Kalachakra Temple.

The weather in McLeod Ganj poses another challenge for the old. This small hill station changes with the seasons. Winter used to start in mid-November, but global warming has shortened the winters and pushed their commencement from mid-November forward to December and January.[52] In late October, most Tibetans leave for cities across India for the seasonal winter business and return during the Tibetan New Year, which tends to fall between February and March. In early November, a soft and fresh breeze sets in during the early morning and late evening hours. The snow settles down on the Dhauladhar range in mid to late November, and in January or February, the snow reaches McLeod Ganj, making the hill station more magical.

During my stay in 2014, McLeod Ganj was rather empty in the winter months. These days, more tourists, primarily Indian, visit during the cold winter months. The locals share that the snowfalls used to be much heavier and more frequent in the past. January 2022 saw two heavy snowfalls, but the snow melted by the next day, as has been the tendency over the past few years. The winter season from late 2022–2023 brought the warmest winter I have experienced in McLeod Ganj so far. Despite the beauty of winter, it is nevertheless freezing for the old, as the houses in McLeod Ganj do not have indoor heating. Those confined to their homes remark that their hands and feet are constantly cold. Nonetheless, most people, young and old, use electric heaters these days.

Spring is one of the best seasons for my elderly friends, and in 2023 it arrived as early as February. The weather turns warmer, and the sun shines most days. The forests burst with life. Birds sing. The rhododendron trees bloom bright red and pink. These days, one can also witness them blooming in the warmer winter months, a sight that would have been unlikely more than ten years ago. Monkeys sunbathe on the roof tops, plucking and eating lice from each other's backs. Kittens, puppies, and baby monkeys explore the world that opens up to them. The nuns from Geden Choeling nunnery gather on the rooftops for their evening debate classes that continue until night. Tourists pour into town, and closed-up cafés and restaurants reopen. The annual Tibetan Opera Festival (also known as *zhotön*), celebrating Ache Lhamo, takes place at the Tibetan Institute for Performing Arts, and Tibetans from settlements across India and Nepal arrive to participate.[53] Many elderly Tibetans, like Ani Jamyang Choedon, attend the festival. The weather turns warmer in May/June, melting away most of the snow on the Dhauladhar peaks. That is the time when my Tibetan friends head for picnics at nearby waterfalls on Sundays or other days to cool off.

In the beginning of July, the monsoon sets in and brings the bustling streets of McLeod Ganj to stillness for long parts of the day. The world closes once again for both people and animals. July and especially August and September are months with heavy downpours of rain. People say that there is nothing like the Dharamsala monsoon. Thunder roars with such intensity that it feels as if the sky itself would collapse. The forest goes wild with bushes and turns intensely green. The bloodsucking leaches reappear and are found throughout the forest. One can witness the marvelous shows of thick clouds floating and reforming above the Kangra Valley. The circumambulation ground turns emptier than in the rest of the seasons. One has to seize the

Figure 10: Monsoon fog in McLeod Ganj. Photo by Harmandeep K. Gill.

rain breaks to buy groceries, run from one place to the next, or go for a walk. The worst thing about the monsoon is the dense humidity. Wet clothes are hard to dry and the humidity settles into clothes, walls, and untouched objects, threatening to ruin them with a heavy odor and extreme moisture. Landslides also occur during the monsoon. The monkeys take shelter in empty buildings, or in between trees, tucked tightly together. For some elderly confined to home, the monsoon and its thick fogs make the loneliness worse.

When the monsoon finally ends at the end of September or beginning of October, it is as though a burden has been lifted from everyone's shoulders. Once again, the world opens up for both people and animals. The leeches disappear. The sun returns. Film festivals and Miss Tibet pageants take place.[54] The old can slowly make their way to town and the Tsuglagkhang without the fear of rain. The few old men and women who gather at what the local Tibetans call *Jütog kubkya* ("the gossip chair") in the main square can enjoy cups of chai from the local *dhaba*—a Hindi word for roadside tea stalls and restaurants in India—on the TCV road. One of my neighboring *ngagpa* (a nonmonastic, tantric practitioner) walked down to town aided by his younger wife. The two Pola who sit outside the meat shop on Tipa Road could be spotted there on a daily basis, reciting mantras in each other's company and keeping themselves occupied with the familiar and unfamiliar faces moving up and down the street.

For those who are confined to their homes, being alone is made easier with the sun's presence. At the end of October, the heat begins to subside and the colors of autumn reappear in the forest from about mid-November onward. When the snow settles down on the Dhauladhar peaks, a soft and cool breeze returns.

The landscape and the weather do not make McLeod Ganj an easy place to age. But it is still considered an auspicious place to age and die because it is the location of the Dalai Lama's main temple and residence in exile. The elderly can make offerings at the Tsuglagkhang; attend the Dalai Lama's teachings, which usually take place in the busy tourist months of spring and after the monsoon; get a glimpse of the Dalai Lama when he leaves and returns to McLeod Ganj in his car; and simply be blessed by his presence in town.[55]

An elderly couple I met had moved to McLeod Ganj from the Tibetan settlement of Phuntsokling in Odisha in eastern India to be closer to the Dalai Lama. Their children had moved to the United States and Europe, and they could no longer farm the land in the settlement by themselves. Likewise, another elderly man had left his home and land in Doeguling Settlement in Mundgod to spend the last phase of his life in McLeod Ganj. In an interview with a representative from the home department of the CTA, I learned that many elderly people who apply for residence at the CTA's old-age homes wish to be granted residence at the Jampaling Old People's Home in McLeod Ganj, which is located in the circumambulation ground surrounding the Tsuglag-khang and the Dalai Lama's residence.

Thus, despite its downsides for the elderly Tibetans, McLeod Ganj is also a culturally appropriate and auspicious place to age and die. When aging and dying in one's own country is not possible, it is at least comforting to die close to the Dalai Lama, who, as the patron deity of Tibet, is also the heart of the body of exile.

Interlude

Mo Dickyi Sangmo wears her warm UGG boots, gifted to her by a sibling who lives in Europe. They are easy to slip off.

I take off her socks and then her leg warmers. Mola is wearing two sets of pants underneath her *chupa* (Tibetan dress). She lends me a hand in pulling her pant legs above her knees. Mola makes a face. The cold is getting to her. She firmly holds on to the woolen shawls covering her thighs. I pour some Mentseekhang massage oil onto one leg.

"Achoo," she says, a sound Tibetans make when they are cold.

I promise her that I will warm up her legs in no time. A doubt arises in me as I touch the ice-cold sole of her foot and toes. I start massaging her foot. My forever-cold hands do not make it easier to warm her up.

Slowly, I move up the leg. "Achoo," Mo Dickyi says again. Her legs are much thinner than those of her older sister, Ani Jamyang Choedon. What little flesh Mola has hangs down from the bone like an empty sack. Anila's legs are not too thick or too thin. And they are wonderfully soft. Her feet are not as cold as Mo Dickyi's. I massage around Mo Dickyi's knee but never on the top, where she says it hurts.

As always, she pokes her finger at the spot where it hurts, as if to make sure that the pain has not gone away. She cries in pain, "Arraa!" The pain is still there.

Mo Dickyi has several small burn scars on her knees. These were left by a Tibetan medical therapy known as moxibustion, which involves burning a small cone of dried herbs on certain points of the body. Mo Dickyi, like her sisters, underwent this treatment a long time ago, thinking it would provide relief from joint pains and muscle stiffness.

Mola rarely seems to enjoy the massages. There are always a lot of "achoos" during cold weather. She neither tells me that the massages are helping nor tells me to stop, except on occasion, when the weather is so cold that she cannot stand the thought of undressing her legs and feet. Perhaps she finds it soothing to have someone connect with her through a caring touch? She seems relieved as I pull down her pant legs, put her leg warmers back on, then her socks, and finally her boots, after finishing. She tells me to wash my hands. Slowly, she gets up from the bed to make us chai.

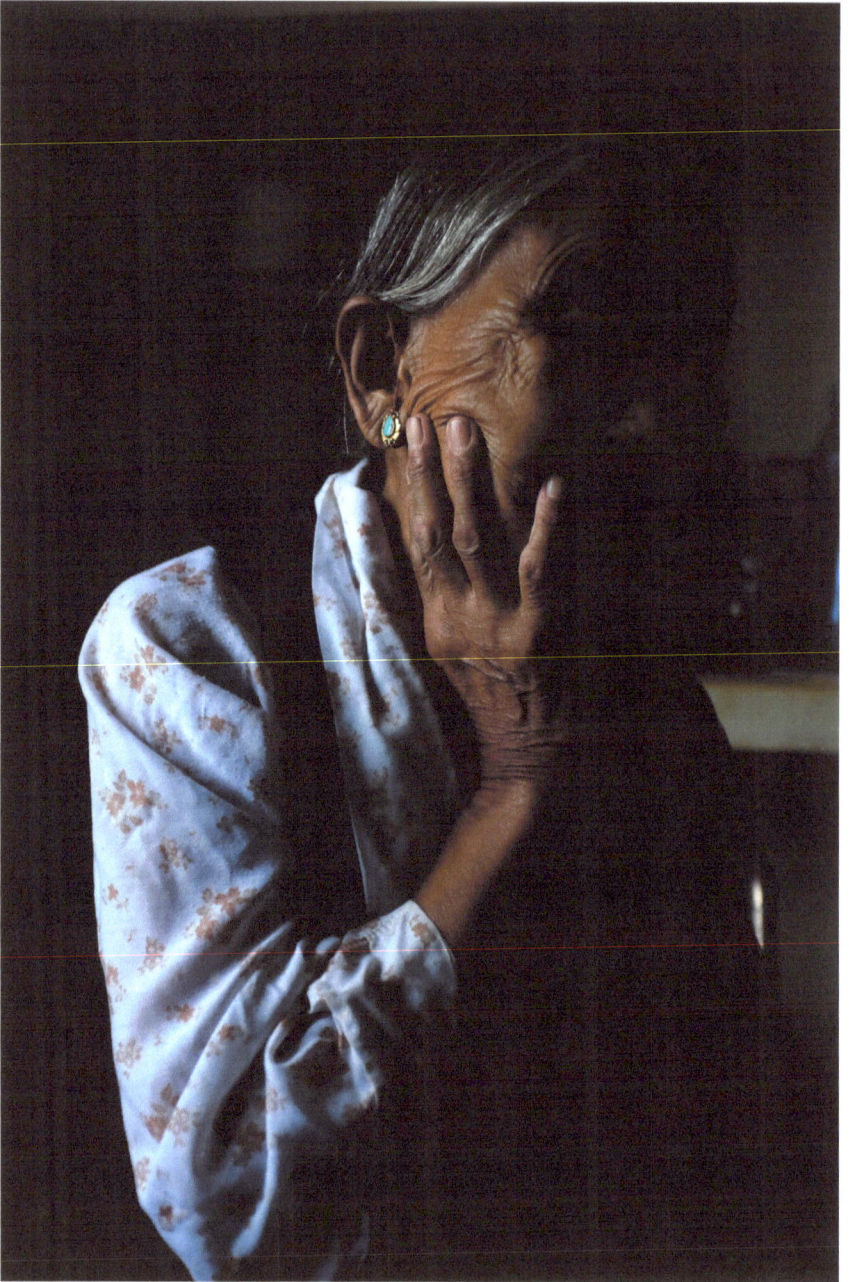

Figure 11: Mo Dickyi Sangmo. Photo by Harmandeep K. Gill.

CHAPTER 2

Melancholia

M o Dickyi Sangmo had a melancholic heart, engulfed by a deep longing for that which was not. I still see her sitting by herself on the bed placed in front of the kitchen window, silently looking out, her focus seemingly zooming in and fading away. In the background is a yellow, faded wall with several open shelves filled with big and small plastic buckets. Most of the buckets are empty. Others hold wheat flour, roasted barley flour, or rice. Two clocks are placed on the lower shelf. The big one stands still at 4:00. Only the small one ticks as Mo Dickyi sits in front of the window from morning until evening.

Unless she was busy with her daily routines of clearing the water-bowl offerings (*yönchab*) from the shrine (*chökhang*), cooking lunch, making tea, or watching the television, Mo Dickyi faithfully sat in front of the window, sometimes while reciting Tibetan Buddhist mantra.

Mo Dickyi's stiff composure would come to life as she stretched and turned her neck to get a good glimpse of people moving about on the road below. The window provided her daily contact with the outside world. It was from the window that light entered. From here, she kept an eye on her neighborhood of Kyirong Village (*drongseb*) and her fellow Kyirong-wa, who, like Mo Dickyi, descend from the Kyirong region of Tibet. She carefully observed them from a distance as they occasionally moved about on their rooftops, checking the water tanks or enjoying the sun. Aside from Mo Dickyi's memories of her native region of Kyirong in Tibet, Kyirong Village in McLeod Ganj was one of her last remaining links to the life she used to live there before the Chinese colonization of Tibet. It was also from the window that she witnessed the shifting landscape of McLeod Ganj, with more and more autorickshaws transporting tourists back and forth between Dharamkot and

McLeod Ganj. The window gave her access to the other residents in the building as they passed through the main gate. From here, she also kept an eye on one of her elderly sisters, Ani Jamyang, as she moved between town and her residence one floor above Mo Dickyi's.

Glimpses of her fellow Kyirong-wa and others moving down below on the road also varied with the seasons. While there was a steady flow of both people and traffic during the lovely, sunny days of spring and autumn, as well as the winter, during the monsoon this usually came to a halt for large parts of the day. Her daily company during the monsoon was the heavy downpour of rain, leaving the hill station of McLeod Ganj in a thick blanket of fog. Her kitchen turned dark and humid. The color of the walls faded some more, and the dark spots on the wall behind the kitchen counter, the corners of the door, and the curtains turned even darker. The wetness gave rise to bedbugs and insects. Mo Dickyi's arms itched constantly. The monsoon also made the loneliness worse, and I witnessed her descent into a heavy and annoyed silence.

Mo Dickyi told me that she liked spring best. Although she glimpsed strangers passing by during autumn and winter, she missed the presence of her fellow Kyirong Tibetans, who left for the seasonal winter business at these times. I could not fully comprehend who it was that she missed. Most of the Tibetans in Kyirong Village were elderly people, and like Mo Dickyi, they stayed put during every season. By spring, all of the Kyirong Tibetans would return to town. She never met them, but it was comforting for her to know that they were present in Kyirong Village, somewhere in their homes or around town.

It was not easy to be in Mo Dickyi's company. Although she said that she had everything she could ask for in life, emphasizing material possessions such as food, clothing, and a home, she kept complaining about most things: the weather, the other residents in the building, the vegetables, the milk, the monkeys, and all the rest. During winter, she longed for spring, when Tibetans would return to town and the weather would be warmer, but when spring arrived, she would be consumed by another absence.

The melancholic side of Mo Dickyi was prominent during my return in September 2019, when the monsoon entered its third month. After many visits with a heavy atmosphere, on one occasion I took the liberty of reminding her of advice from the 14th Dalai Lama to maintain an open mind and vast mind (*gu yangpo*).

She nodded in agreement, "Yes, that is what Kundun [the Dalai Lama] also says, that we should have an open mind." Mola silently pondered the advice, but then came an outpouring of her frustrations. "But my whole body is ill. It pains here, here [pointing at different body parts]. . . . Neither can I go out."

Once again, her situation dawned on me. And as Mo Dickyi implied, how can one be light in one's being and thrive when one suffers from multiple health problems and, as a result, becomes imprisoned behind a window? How can one accept that one's body and life keep falling apart?

This chapter delves into the interdependencies of body and mind, and how the body is constituted of other bodies. In Tibetan medicine, bodily disorders are caused by the environment, which consists of social relationships to both human and nonhuman sentient beings.[1] Moreover, as Vincanne Adams notes, the physical body is the site for relationships among people who are connected together, as a physical prior to a sociological fact. This means that "the Tibetan body must be seen as physiologically constituted as a multitude of beings."[2] I will not expand on the Tibetan medical specificities here; for the purpose of this chapter, it is sufficient to remark that in Tibetan Buddhist epistemology, the body is constituted by other bodies, which also has ramifications for how we think about selfhood.

The interdependency between self and others is also echoed in Maurice Merleau-Ponty's phenomenology of experience and subjectivity, noting that it is through our bodies that the world comes into being, and our being-in-the-world is completed by our surroundings.[3] Thus, body and world are always in a process of becoming, mutually defining, and responding to one another. Building on the Tibetan medical and phenomenological approach to the body, I ask: What happens to our inner world when our body, which is our access to others and the world, begins to fall apart? How might the emotional absence of bodies that constitute one's body affect or "in-complete" one's sense of self? Thus, I understand the body not merely as a biological entity but also as an affective map of our relationships, life history, and hopes or imaginaries, which make us into specific persons. The aim of this chapter is to meditate on the complex interrelations of body, self, and world, and how these are disturbed in old age.

I take inspiration from the writings of Tibetan Buddhist practitioners, specifically Menriwa Lobsang Namgyal, who descends from a linage of medical practitioners, and two phenomenological thinkers, Drew Leder and Lisa Guenther.[4] Whereas both Lobsang Namgyal and Leder consider our existence through a focus on the physical body and how it is altered by the onset of illness and old age, Guenther pays attention to the constitution of the body by other bodies and what happens in their absence. Following Lobsang Namgyal and Leder, I too begin with the physical body before I build on Guenther's work to reveal that the body is held in place by a series of "hinges," such as a nexus of relations and hopes. And in their absence, one stands to become unhinged from one's own sense of self.

The Body Closes Itself Off

In old age, things take longer. Slowness, accompanied by pain, illness, or both, gives the body a presence it does not have during days of health and vitality.[5] Getting up from the bed in her kitchen to reach the stove or the bathroom could be quite an ordeal for Mo Dickyi.

First of all, she put the woolen shawl covering her knees onto the bed and then pushed her right hand against the bed in an effort to lift herself up slowly. She then supported herself with her left hand on the kitchen shelf as her stiff knees loosened up and she prepared herself to take one step further. Sometimes she would cry "*Arrraa!*" or "*Ama!*" because of the pain. When the pain settled and her legs seemed firm enough to move, she would move slowly toward the kitchen counter. Her right hand would support her slightly bent back. Mo Dickyi moved as if her joints were glued together, and there was always a break of a second or two between each step. She had been confined to her home for more than six years because of worsening knee problems.

The only time she would walk down to the main road was when she needed to see a doctor or a dentist. On such occasions, she was accompanied by me or her relative, Tenzin. A taxi always waited for her down the staircase. Whereas Tenzin and I could easily make our way down to the main road in about a minute, the ordeal would take Mo Dickyi ten minutes at the least. Sometimes lacking time or patience, Tenzin often chose to carry Mo Dickyi on his back.

The absence of daily movement had taken a toll on Mo Dickyi's knees. The building she stayed in was located up a hillside. The only way to get there from the main road below was through a long, narrow staircase. Whereas Ani Jamyang, who is two years older than Mo Dickyi, still managed to make her way up and down the stairs, Mo Dickyi chose not to. According to Anila, Mo Dickyi's knees would be in a better condition if she walked up and down the stairs at least a few times a week. As I was informed by the elderly

Tibetans who were still able to move outdoors, the only way to avoid rapid decline of the knees was to keep walking on a daily basis. Mo Dickyi on the other hand, chose not to move outdoors because it was too burdensome and painful for her, especially following more than six years of home confinement.

I also understood that Mola's deliberate decision not to go outside was motivated not only by the hazards of moving up and down the staircase but also, it seemed to me, by her silent wish to hide from the world. This was clear to me during the numerous times I suggested I take her for a trip down to lower Dharamsala. She always responded that she did not have any wish to go out. When I insisted on knowing her reasons, she would reply that she was too old and sick and could not enjoy herself because of the state of her body. Another time, I suggested that we attend a teaching by the Dalai Lama at the Tsuglagkhang. Mo Dickyi replied that she did not want other acquaintances to see her in her current state, old and frail. "What will they think?" she said, expressing shame over her physical condition.

Mo Dickyi was usually hesitant to sit out on the balcony. During days of sunshine, I would insist that we sit outside. From the balcony, she also had a better view of Kyirong Village. We could see the house of her *Acha* (elderly sister), Samdrup Drolma, whom she had not seen for a long time. In fact, I could even spot Mo Samdrup Drolma sitting outside on her balcony. Because Mo Dickyi was unable to see that far, I would act as her eyes and tell her about Mo Samdrup's movements: whether she was staring down below the balcony wall, chasing monkeys with her walking stick, or just sitting in silence.

Family members tended to comment that Mo Samdrup was the stark opposite of Mo Dickyi. She remained optimistic and joyful even at the age of ninety-three; but then again, in contrast to Mo Dickyi, she was well respected by other family members and also admired for her generous personality. Unlike Mo Dickyi, Mo Samdrup had also been receiving full-time care by their relative, Tenzin, since 2020. Tenzin's help certainly made Mo Samdrup's everyday life much easier and more comfortable.

Besides their family bonds, what the sisters shared in common was that both of them had been confined to their homes for years. For Mo Samdrup, her balcony was her window onto the outside world, and, unlike Mo Dickyi, she could always be found there from morning until evening on sunny days. For Mo Dickyi, the sun only shone on her balcony for a brief hour or so in the morning, which was also why she refused to sit outside.

But I suggest that the lack of sunlight was not the only reason. It was more as though Mola dreaded sitting outside, for fear the other two residents on

Figure 12: Mo Dickyi's kitchen door. Photo by Harmandeep K. Gill.

her floor might come outside onto the balcony to wash their dishes, as if they would be disturbing her with their presence. Whenever I suggested we sit outside, she would insist that it was too cold, even during the warm months of April and May. Sometimes, she would suggest that we go up to the rooftop instead, where we would be all alone. Even though Mo Dickyi desired the company of others, it also appeared as though she wanted to be left alone, at least by certain others.

In November 2021, because of her increasing frailty, Mo Dickyi moved in with Mo Samdrup, but only after much persuasion from family members. However, for the entire period that Mo Dickyi stayed at her sister's place, she desperately wanted to return to her own place. She constantly worried about thieves, or about how the Buddhist deities on her shrine were not made offerings; an omission that could bring her harm.

After one and a half months at Mo Samdrup's place, Mo Dickyi finally returned to her home. "I am so happy to be back," she said with a big smile. Although the kitchen made her feel lonely and cut her off from her surroundings, that was where she preferred to be, embraced by that dark, yet familiar space.

Impermanence and the Body

In Tibetan Buddhist literature, the old body is a common metaphor for impermanence.[6] The great abbot of Ngor Monastery, Ngorchen Konchog Lhundrub (1497–1557), elaborates in his book, *The Beautiful Ornament of the Three Visions* (1991), various forms of human suffering (of birth, illness, old age, and death).[7] Regarding the sufferings of old age, Konchog Lhundrub writes of the body turning ugly and waning in strength and of the disappearance of brilliance and, finally, the snatching of one's radiance.[8] Apart from the physical sufferings of an aging body, articulated in his writing on the waning of strength, alienation from what one has become is another form of suffering, especially as the body turns ugly. This second form of suffering is a result of holding on to one's youth and not embracing one's impermanence, which, in contrast to one's younger days, manifests itself through the aging body. On the body becoming ugly he writes: "Changing from what one was before, one becomes bent and crooked, one's hair turns white or becomes bald, and so on."[9] In addition, one is accompanied by loss of brilliance. Whereas one was praised and honored by others in younger days, in old age, one is subject to ridicule by others, even by one's children.[10] The shame and alienation associated with an aging body that wanes in strength, beauty, and brilliance is something that I clearly sensed in Mo Dickyi's attitude toward her own body.

The decline of old age was not easy for her to accept. By 2019, she was suffering from multiple illnesses. Her teeth were falling out, the skin around her eyes had darkened, and her eyes were shrinking deeper into the skull. She would worry over her loss of hair, thinking there would soon be nothing left. Her figure was shrinking. Her many *chupa* and *onju* (blouses) no longer fit her shape and had become too large for her. She also told me that she found herself dizzy and tired. If she did not have to get up early to make water-bowl offerings in the morning, she said that she could sleep on.

As expressed in the words of Konchog Lhundrub and other Buddhist teachers, such as Patrul Rinpoche and Gungtang Rinpoche, who comment on the experience of old age for laypeople, Mo Dickyi felt that because of her decline in old age, the world was no longer hers to take.[11] Her body came across as alienating, not only because it was actually falling apart but also because of the absence of her youth. In her youth, she was not only healthy and beautiful but also honored by others, and, unlike in old age, the world lay open with endless possibilities. The aging body brings about a decline of social status, as well as a decline of choice. For Mo Dickyi, it was as though her life was, in her words and the words of other elderly Tibetans, "finished" (*tsar*).

Mo Dickyi's alienation from herself in old age was strikingly present during one incident, when I showed her a photograph of her younger self. The picture is in black and white and was taken not long after Mo Dickyi, her siblings, her mother, and her grandfather escaped into exile and arrived in India (in 1965). The photo belonged to her sister Samdrup Drolma. I obtained a digital copy of the image from one of their relatives who had digitized a number of Mo Samdrup Drolma's family photographs.

In the picture, Mo Dickyi is accompanied by her sisters Mo Samdrup Drolma and Ani Jamyang Choedon, as well as Samdrup Drolma's late husband and an unknown nun. No one is smiling, and they pose rather stiffly (as one did in those days) while holding lotus flowers in their hands. Mo Dickyi could not recognize the image. Neither could she remember when it was taken. I had to point out who she was in the photograph.

Mo Dickyi stared at me in disbelief. "This?" she said pointing at her younger self. "Yes," I insisted several times. Mo Dickyi was silent for a few seconds before giving a small laugh. When she spoke, all she could say was, "*Ama*," which was the most common phrase Mo Dickyi used in situations of surprise or disbelief. Although she kept staring at herself and the others in the picture, she was unable to recognize herself. The contrast between her appearance in old age and youth was for her too stark. They might as well have been strangers.

Mo Dickyi had a similar moment of disbelief whenever I showed her photographs I had taken of her. She would examine them with a similar misrecognition. However, pictures of her current self were not taken as a nice surprise, and "*Ama*" was followed by a clicking of the tongue, as an expression of disbelief. As described by Gungtang Rinpoche, it was as though she could not comprehend her own old age. In his words, it was as if old age were "a total mystery" to her.[12] Who is this? Mo Dickyi wondered, taken back by the young and the old woman, as if disconnected from herself.

Such moments made apparent the alienating presence of the aging body and the disorientation old age had brought. They seemed to confront her with her present appearance and the fact that there was no escape from the reality of old age.

I recognized the shame and alienation associated with the aging body, as described by Konchog Lhundrub, in another elderly friend of mine, the eighty-year-old Mo Tsering Wangmo (Chapter 3), who had been more or less confined to her home since 2010 after a hip fracture. She relied on a paid caregiver for almost everything, sometimes even for intimate tasks, such as urinating. Mo Tsering said that she had no freedom (*rawang*) because of her body and regarded her condition as a form of death in life. With Mo Tsering, because of her bodily condition, I found a more striking form of alienation from the body and what it had reduced her to in the gaze of others, to the extent that she wanted to be freed from it.

Among the many episodes in which Mo Tsering's helplessness against her physical condition stood out, the one that has become imprinted in my mind is the time she was unable to make it to the toilet and defecated on the kitchen floor. I was in the middle of eating chow mein (fried noodles) when Mo Tsering began the process of getting up from her chair. "Do you need to pee?" I asked. "I will try to go to the toilet," she responded while pushing herself up from the chair.

"Do you need help?"

"No, you eat," Mola told me, not wanting to burden me.

Mola continued struggling. When she was finally up, she attempted to find stability on the ground by holding on to her walker. Her right leg trembled and so did her arms. Still, unlike most other days, she succeeded in getting up on her own. Slowly, she walked past me and entered the kitchen, which was only about five or six steps away from the chair in the other room. I followed behind her to get myself more chow mein. Mola's steps seemed steady, and I thought that I would not need to follow her to the toilet. As I was putting more chow mein on my plate, I heard a large fart, mixed with the sound of liquid feces. My movements froze. I gathered the courage to look to the floor. There were drops of feces on the floor and on the side of my left foot. It was not a lot, but knowing that it was feces panicked me. Mola, too, stood completely still. I noticed that it was a disturbing event for her: a senior woman who had just defecated on the kitchen floor in front of someone else.

Because Mo Tsering's helper was not there, I was the one who would have to clean up. My appetite vanished. Despite the discomfort I felt, I had to act before Mo Tsering's skirt became drenched with feces. There was no way she would make it to the toilet. I stepped out of my frozen state and ran for her urine tray in the other room, and placed it on the bed in the kitchen, which is where her caregiver also slept. Mola hurried as best she could with her slow body. When she finally reached the bed, which was not more than three steps away from where she had defecated, I lifted up her skirt and she fell down on the urine tray. She looked relieved. And so was I. I left her to defecate on the bed in the kitchen.

Later, when I had cleaned the floor, changed her skirt, and helped her back to her chair, I noticed that Mo Tsering struggled to look me in the eye. She threw some fleeting glances my way and seemed to have difficulty letting her eyes rest on my face. Mola even suggested that I not massage her legs (something she rarely did) because she had put me through enough trouble for the day. It was more than clear that Mo Tsering was disturbed by the turn of events. I did my best to communicate that it was no trouble to me, and I massaged her in spite of her inclination.

Alienation from an Aging Body

In old age, the body emerges as something strange and familiar, simultaneously. It is neither experienced as fully alienating nor completely oneself. Even though the dichotomy between the physical and the spiritual has rightfully been deemed irrelevant for approaching Tibetan medical notions of the body, as for example argued by Geoffrey Samuel, I also suggest that things get more complicated when we move beyond Tibetan medical texts and into people's everyday lives, especially in the context of aging, illness, and disability.[13]

"The Questions and Answers of the Weak and Old Man," a poem written by the famous aristocratic monk official Menriwa Lobsang Namgyal of Tashilhunpo Monastery in Tibet, offers an illuminating dialogue on the experience of living with an old body and on the general dilemma of attempting to accept one's own impermanence while also wanting to secure a continuity with what one used to be.[14] The poem seems to be a question-and-answer session between Lobsang Namgyal and his reflection in the mirror, which I choose to call his younger voice. The poem is a refreshing take on impermanence because it brings a first-person experience of impermanence and the struggle of coming to terms with it. Furthermore, unlike Konchog Lhundrub, Lobsang Namgyal does not dismiss the sufferings of old age (of not accepting one's impermanence) as ignorance only. On the contrary, he seems to acknowledge that humans, even a monk official, have a basic urge to hold on to themselves. The dialogue of the poem opens with the young voice describing the physical features of the aging body. He describes how the wrinkles on the face "resemble a pond blown by the wind." The saliva dripping from the mouth (referred to as a net, imprisoning his face) makes it hard to see the rough and wrinkled face. Finally, the graying of the hair, "white like camphor" (*gabur*, a medicinal herb), competes with his whitening beard. "When did you come to me? You, the old, who has a different/unprecedented character," the young voice questions, expressing a certain alienation, not only from the aging body with new physical attributes, as those pointed out by Konchog Lhundrub, but also from the person he has become.

In answer, the old voice emphasizes the gradual coming of old age. It is not something unprecedented or unknown, like the young one expresses. Instead, he is the same person now, facing the decline of old age. In fact, old age or impermanence was always there, but the younger one was too busy in his worldly pleasures to notice it. Now that old age has arrived, it is not possible to ignore it, like the young one used to, since it is "pressing the back of the neck." The younger voice has the understanding that an old body is accompanied by an entirely different persona from the one accompanying the healthy and younger body.

When the dialogue returns to the young voice, he compares old age to clouds that are covering the face of the sun, and then to the suffering of hell.

He further tells the old one to leave on his own. Otherwise, he will have no choice but to banish or drive him out.

The old voice laughs at these words and tells the young one to stop speaking nonsense, as there is no way he can return or go away. Moreover, death is just behind him. He is followed by the Lord of Death (Yama Dharmaraja):[15] "I am like a flower that has been touched by frost."

In the words that follow, the old one also seems to be saying that he is death itself, as he is not only the flower touched by frost but also the frost itself that withers away the flower.

In the words of the old voice, I also see an attempt to reconcile with impermanence. The difference between the experience of impermanence in one's younger days in contrast to old age is that it becomes all too visible in old age, to the point that it cannot be ignored anymore. The poem makes a crucial point that I see reflected in both Mo Dickyi's and especially Mo Tsering's relations to their bodies. Like the old man in the poem, they too were accompanied by two different voices, one that attempted to identify with the old body and tried to come to terms with who they had become, and the other one, who felt alienated from what old age has reduced them to and how other people came to see them as a result.

However, this alienation from one's body is due not only to an altered physical appearance but also to what can be described as a rift between the body and mind.

Edmund Husserl's phenomenological approach to the relation between consciousness and the body can be helpful in understanding this rift or disruption that both Mo Tsering and Mo Dickyi lived with in their everyday lives. As in Buddhist epistemology, which sees the "human organism as a unity,"[16] in the phenomenological tradition of philosophy, the mind and the body are not regarded as the two separate entities, as they are in a dualistic Cartesian view. Neither can the body or the "self" be separated from the outside world. Instead, the complex interrelatedness of oneself and the world is at the basis of a phenomenological approach to experience. To give an example on the wholeness of the body and consciousness, Husserl writes that the experience of my left hand touching the right, or my legs moving in synchronization with another, sets in motion a nexus of bodily interrelations. These interrelations are experienced by the individual in their totality.

For Husserl, because of the whole set of interrelations that one single movement unfolds, one cannot regard the body "like a marionette controlled by a puppeteer mind."[17] Rather, the body itself permeates consciousness. We

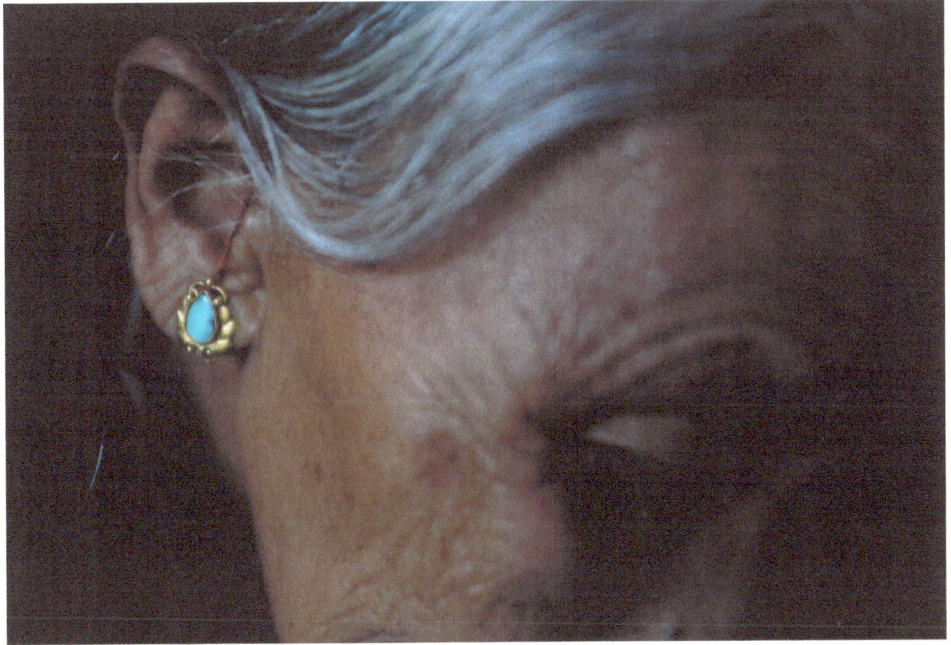

Figure 13: Mo Dickyi lost in thought. Photo by Harmandeep K. Gill.

do not even need to think when performing basic movements, such as moving our hands or legs. In old age, by contrast, I suggest that even these basic movements become disrupted, as it was for both Mo Dickyi and Mo Tsering. They needed to think and plan before getting up from the bed or walking. This is when what Husserl refers to as the "kinesthetic" unity of consciousness and the body becomes disrupted, and the body becomes experienced more like an outside object to be "manipulated, or moved by a separate or disjointed consciousness"—for example, as when Mo Tsering was unable to make it to the toilet or whenever I attempted to help her lift herself up from the chair.[18] In spite of her will to move and the immense physical energy she put into moving, her lower body was many times simply unwillingly to move. We had to make several tries before succeeding. On the days when she had high blood pressure, her legs would shake beyond her control, while they would move slightly up and down on their own when I massaged her each day. In these moments, in the incident described earlier, and in Mo Tsering's own words, I see the disruption Husserl describes. Moreover, the experience of the body as an outside object is made ever real by the dependence a disabled body forges onto other bodies, even in such basic tasks as getting up. Because she lacked control over her own body, Mo Tsering, like the old man, did not fully identify with her body. This complicates how we understand the interplay of body and mind, which in the context of aging and disability appears to be a struggle between the physical and the spiritual.

Drew Leder's reflections on the body provide a further elaboration on the disruption described by both Lobsang Namgyal and Husserl. In his book *The Absent Body*, Leder provides some provocative reflections on how our bodies are essentially characterized by an absence in our day-to-day life.[19] Although he, like other phenomenologists, recognizes that the world comes into being through the body, he also problematizes to what degree the body itself is "the thematic object of experience."[20] When I am walking down a road, my consciousness does not abide in the movements of my legs or arms; instead, I am, as usual, engulfed in multiple streams of thoughts or external observations outside my body. This is what Leder refers to as the absent body.

For Leder, the body remains absent not only because of the natural flow of my movements but also because when my body functions normally, I find myself out there in the world, in the midst of everything that binds me to others or my surroundings. A disruption, on the other hand (e.g., pain), draws my attention back to my body, in here.[21] Following Leder's point, I argue that this is when the body closes itself off. It sheds light on Mo Dickyi's statement that it would not be possible for her to enjoy herself, even when outside on a picnic or at a teaching. Although she would be outside among others, her access to the surroundings would be constricted, as her attention would be constantly directed toward the pains of her body and the worries it gave rise to. Furthermore, witnessing the youthfulness and health of others also turns attention inward to one's impermanence. The body is constantly present; however, it emerges through what Leder identifies as "an alien presence."[22] The pain makes the body present, but pain also causes a certain alienation from the body, as described by the younger voice of the old man in Lobsang Namgyal's poem. As Leder writes, one usually refers to the pain as "it," as if separate from the "I." Similarly, Mo Dickyi expressed the different pains as, "this is paining, this is paining," while pointing at different parts of her body. Leder argues that pain changes our relation both to ourselves and the world.[23] The alienation of the body is taken to a different stage during cases of disease or severe illness, since it gives rise to dysfunction in the body, when "the 'I can' of bodily ecstasis is disturbed."[24] Disease renders one disabled: "Abilities that were previously in one's command and rightfully belong to the habitual body have now been lost," such as with Mo Tsering's inability to do even the most intimate physical tasks on her own.[25] Or when Mo Dickyi in her final months suffered from a severe constipation, to the point that she would deny her body food as a final attempt at exerting some command over her own body.[26]

It is in light of the disruption of one's habitual body, and the alienating presence of the body during illness, that one has to understand Mo Dickyi's choice to stay indoors or Mo Tsering's statement about having no freedom from her body or how she preferred death over being alive in her condition. Furthermore, the alienation of the body also has to be considered from an intersubjective perspective, as already pointed out by Konchog Lhundrub. The awareness of our bodies is, as Leder suggests, "arising out of experiences of the corporeality of other people and of their gaze directed back upon me."[27] The gaze of the other also contributes to alienation, since, as Lobsang Namgyal notes, the appearance of the old or disabled body does not express, to borrow words from Leder, "one's own wishes or personality."[28] Looking at photos of herself in the present, Mo Dickyi could not recognize, neither fully reconcile with how she was seen through the gaze of others, made visible by my camera.

However, in contrast to Leder, I do not suggest that the body is experienced as only alienating. Both Mo Dickyi and my other elderly friends also identified with their bodies as their own—for example, through caregiving practices, such as massages or the intake of medicines. Mo Dickyi's refusal to eat during episodes of constipation was also an act of care for her body, not to trouble it or make it heavier than it already was. Instead, I suggest that in the aging body, the unfamiliar and the familiar are present simultaneously. One is left in an in-between state, never being fully home with oneself. This is the dilemma of old age expressed by Mo Dickyi and Mo Tsering, something the words of Lobsang Namgyal capture so well.

An alienation of the body can unsettle one's sense of self. When healthy, the body is absent by virtue of its disappearance; during illness or disease, the body becomes alien by virtue of what Leder calls its "dys-appearance."[29] Thus, according to Leder, in illness the body is not as alien as it is forgotten: where our attention is directed to the world, instead it is alien, as remembered, "a sharp and searing presence threatening the self."[30]

Following Elaine Scarry's and Christina Crosby's insights on pain, the remembered body is thus characterized by a constant "present-ness."[31] There is no getting away from it. Mo Tsering said that the only times she could get a break from her condition was in the presence of others, which provided momentary relief by giving her a chance to be in touch with a different side of herself. In the absence of others, time stood still for her. The chronic condition of Mo Tsering's body and Mo Dickyi's various illnesses and bodily pain resulted in their withdrawing from their surroundings, against their own will; but in Mo Dickyi's case, she also withdrew partially by self-choice, as if wanting to hide from the world.

It is in light of this searing presence of the body—through pain and illness, and an altered physical appearance or disappearance of youth—that I suggest we must understand one aspect of the alienation or "in-completeness" that Mo Dickyi experienced in old age. There is a "disruption" or dissonance between the body and mind, through pain and illness and through an altered physical appearance, which is hard to identify with. Mo Dickyi Sangmo was not completely home with herself. The dys-appearance of the body (by its falling apart) unsettled her everyday life. It reminded her of who she no longer was, leaving her on a precarious ground where she became a stranger to herself. The strangeness encountered with oneself in old age was also echoed by others, such as Gen Lobsang Choedak who used to say that old age had reduced him to half of a person. At the age of ninety-five, he says that not much remains of him, as if parts of him are evaporating day by day.

Another aspect of the alienation that Mo Dickyi experienced was connected to the lack of affection and emotional support from family members, who could help her to be home with herself in spite of physical decline. I suggest that significant others are essential for withdrawing from the constant present-ness of the body, as Mo Tsering articulated herself. In the next part of this chapter, I locate Mo Dickyi's body back in her home, where she was surrounded by other people. Is it really the case, as Leder suggests, that the alien body—as remembered, or constantly present—is the main thing unsettling one's sense of self?[32]

Despite having a phenomenological orientation to his analysis, Leder does not explicitly pay attention to our relation to others or problematize to what degree our subjectivity is first and foremost dependent on biological functions or comes prior to intersubjectivity.[33] By contrast, I suggest that we also need to turn our attention to the social space the body finds itself in, as also emphasized in Tibetan Buddhist epistemology. By this, I am specifically referring to the emotional or loving support that was available to Mo Dickyi and Mo Tsering in handling the sufferings of physical decline. The gaze of the other to which Leder refers can also be supportive and loving, and not only alienating.

Whereas I sensed Mo Dickyi as distant and melancholic, this was not the case with Mo Tsering, who suffered from a more severe condition. Mo Dickyi seemed to be dissolving further into the annoyed silence inside her, as if the life force (sog), which Tibetans identify as the "spark" that brings a life into being, was being extinguished by the day.[34] Mo Tsering, by contrast, had a strong presence that I picked up on through her talkative and engaged nature. I suggest that one of the main reasons for this is that, unlike Mo Dickyi, Mo Tsering had a supportive daughter, and she also enjoyed the company of friends on a regular basis.

In the next part of this chapter, I provide the wider context through which I understand Mo Dickyi's melancholic mood, by bringing to the fore her reminiscences of her life in Tibet and family relationships.

The Hinged Body

"There are many ways to destroy a person, but one of the simplest and most devastating is through prolonged solitary confinement," writes Lisa Guenther in her book *Solitary Confinement: Social Death and Its Afterlives*, which

explores the effects of long-term solitary confinement on how prisoners relate to self, world, and other.[35] Prisoners describe various symptoms, including paranoia, hallucinations, perceptual distortions, and anxiety. Others
describe solitary confinement as a form of social death.

Based on the testimonies of prisoners, Guenther argues that solitary confinement results in prisoners becoming "unhinged" from reality and from
themselves. By arguing that we do not exist as atomistic individuals, but in
a complex interrelation to others and to situations we find ourselves in, Guenther suggests that in the physical absence of others, the self can become
fragmented. What is more, in the absence of such hinges to others, one even
stands to lose oneself. Guenther remarks that "becoming unhinged" is thus
not merely "a colloquial expression; rather, it is a precise phenomenological
description of what happens when the articulated joints of our embodied,
interrelational subjectivity are broken apart."[36] As remarked by Buddhist
philosophers, relationality is the ontological structure of the self and life itself. Thus, we need others not only to sustain our sense of self, but to be sane
and sustain our basic sense of reality.[37] Moreover, Guenther argues that our
consciousness is thus constitutive of the bodily presence of others.

Building on Emmanuel Levinas's philosophy of solitude, Guenther argues
that prolonged, enforced solitude is a form of violence, because solitude is
not experienced as singular but as a dual phenomenon. This means that to
be alone is to be alone with oneself with the risk of turning against oneself.
Guenther follows Levinas's argument further to suggest that the only escape
out of the solitary existence is the face of the other (or voluntarily relations
with others). What prisoners seek is an ethical escape and not an ontological
one: "The main thing that my body gears into is not a thing at all; it is the
body of another person, another 'here,' another starting-point for the experience of the world."[38] It is only through ethical relations with others that we
can escape ourselves and give meaning to our precarious individual lives.[39]
Hence, the body is not merely a biological mechanism that can be sustained
with food, shelter, or exercise. Instead, from birth, we depend on support and
protection from others.[40]

From a Buddhist and a phenomenological perspective, consciousness is
not complete in itself; it is, instead, a relation. Similarly, the body, which permeates consciousness, is not complete in itself but is a relation between "in
here" and "out there." While the world comes into existence through us (our
bodies are our only access to the world), simultaneously, our existence is
informed by and hinged to others. This is what I bring to the fore in the

Figure 14: Mo Dickyi in front of the kitchen window. Photo by Harmandeep K. Gill.

following, by turning my attention to the lack of affection and emotional support from significant others in Mo Dickyi's everyday life.

But first, there is an important distinction between Mo Dickyi and prisoners in solitary confinement. Unlike prisoners, Mo Dickyi is not locked up in a cell. Neither is she completely deprived of human contact. Even though Guenther's reflections are grounded in radically different circumstances, nonetheless, I find them useful because they take my thinking one step further than Leder does, through her attention to relationality and how it can be supportive or destructive for selfhood.[41] Guenther builds further upon the classical phenomenological view that an individual is a relation, as Leder also does, but she takes distance from the absolute priority of subjectivity above intersubjectivity as proposed in the phenomenology of Husserl.[42] In other words, while Leder explores the interrelations between the "in here" and "out there" for sustaining a person, Guenther pays more attention to the "inter" of interrelations between self, others, and world. Whereas Leder takes biological processes such as pain, illness, and death as his starting point to look into the interrelations between body, self, and world, Guenther takes relationality as her starting point. Following her, I turn my attention to the "inter" of intersubjectivity that, in Mo Dickyi's case, seemed to unsettle her sense of self instead of complete it.

Hinges to ethical others are visible in terms of socially defined roles. Mo Dickyi is also someone's daughter, sister, wife, and mother. In the absence of these hinges, the aging body becomes like a prison, also rendering Mo Dickyi incomplete, to the point of depleting the *sog* that keeps a human being alive, spiritually as well as physically. Like the prisoners, she too sought an ethical escape: an affectionate face, another "here," who could support and protect her in the face of physical decline.[43] Before delving into her relationships with family members, I turn to Mo Dickyi's reminiscences of the past in Tibet, another "hinge" that informed her sense of self but remained absent.

The Absence of Kyirong

Mo Dickyi's mother gave birth to twelve children, but only eight survived. These were Samdrup Drolma (female, age ninety-three), Ani Jamyang Choedon (female, age ninety), Dickyi Sangmo (female, age eighty-six), Dawa Lhamo (female, age eighty-five), Dhondrup (male, age seventy-nine), Penpa Kyipa (female, age seventy-six), Tsering Choephel (male, age seventy-two), and Tenzin Dhargye (male, age sixty-nine). While five of the siblings—Samdrup Drolma, Ani Jamyang, Dickyi Sangmo, Dawa Lhamo, and Dhondrup—lived in McLeod Ganj, the remaining three were well settled in Europe and Canada. All of them (except Ani Jamyang) escaped from Kyirong in 1963, accompanied by their mother and grandfather. Their father passed away when they lived in Kyirong.

Before 1959, Kyirong was a district-level administrative unit, *zong*, under *Ganden Phodrang*, the Tibetan government in Lhasa. Most Kyirong-wa were classified into two categories. The first were "taxpayers" (*khelpa*), who were granted the heritable right to farm land. Their tax obligations included unpaid labor, such as for the local monastery, and an annual grain payment. The second category consisted of "small householders" (*dü chungpa*), who did not own any land and worked for taxpayers, who in turn provided them with shelter and food.[44] Mo Dickyi's family was a taxpayer household that farmed a specified amount of land. One of her younger siblings, *Akhu* ("uncle") Dhondrup, explained it as such: "So, we *khelpa* worked for the monastery, by transporting their goods from place to place and by taking care of their cattle. Those who were *chungpa* had to pay tax to Kyirong *zong*. The taxes were in the form of whatever harvest they had, barley or anything else. But for us [*khelpa*], it meant providing [the monastery] with work. For instance, if the monastery called for work in their fields, we had to send one person. The monastery would buy the rations, barley or millet, from the Kyirong capital, and we were responsible for picking it up and transporting it to the monastery."

Both Mo Dickyi and her eldest sister recalled their life in Kyirong—the name meaning "happy" village—as the happiest period of their lives, despite all the hard work they undertook. There was always plenty of work in the fields, with herding animals, and in the household. The sisters also recalled the huge amounts of work for their village monastery. They would reminisce about the loads they carried on their backs up the steep uphill to the monastery, located at the top of the village. Mo Samdrup, the eldest of all the siblings, remembered that the monks would call her "the girl from the big household," because they were one of the wealthiest families in the village. Despite its arduous nature, Mo Samdrup recalled the work for the monastery with great joy and as an act of immense merit.

Mo Dickyi's and Mo Samdrup's most cherished and frequently mentioned memories were from their trips to Kathmandu with their father and siblings. Kathmandu was a popular place for pilgrimage and trade for the Kyirong

Tibetans, even before the coming of exile. In fact, Kathmandu was in closer proximity to the Kyirong region than was the Tibetan capital of Lhasa. While Mo Dickyi undertook several trips to Kathmandu before escaping into exile, she never made it to Lhasa. According to Mo Samdrup, the journey from their village to Kathmandu was a nine-day journey by foot. Every time she spoke about the journey, she would hold up ten fingers, while clearly exclaiming, "Nine days down and nine days up." And then summing up the journey, she said, "Eighteen days." Mo Dickyi insisted that Mo Samdrup remembered incorrectly because of her declining memory, and that the journey one way took four or five days at the most.

Their main destination in Kathmandu was the Boudhanath stupa, where Mo Dickyi and her siblings would help their father sell goods such as wool on behalf of Tibetan traders. Many Kyirong Tibetans undertook such paid work for Tibetan traders who had made their way into Kyirong. Upon their return from Nepal, they would buy rice from local traders at the Nepalese border, often trading for it with salt from Kyirong. The coming of exile forced a split of their large family. It changed everything for them.

On their arrival in McLeod Ganj in 1965, the custom was that all newly arrived Tibetans in India received an audience with the 14th Dalai Lama, which is still the case today. At the time, he had his residence at Swarg Ashram. It is also around this area (on Tipa Road) that the first Tibetans in town built their houses, including Mo Samdrup and her deceased husband, as well as their younger brother, Akhu Dhondrup. Today, the majority of the Tibetans living in this area descend from the Kyirong and Töpa part of Tibet. Most of Mo Dickyi's siblings, such as Mo Samdrup, Ani Jamyang, and Dawa Lhamo, still live here, in close proximity to one another.

When the Chinese soldiers first entered Kyirong, Mo Dickyi and her siblings took up work in road construction initiated by the Chinese Communist Party. Ani Jamyang, on the other hand, escaped into the Hyolmo region of Nepal with her fellow nuns from their nunnery before the Chinese entered Kyirong. According to Mo Dickyi's younger brother, Akhu Dhondrup, the younger members of their family worked for the Chinese for about two years. However, the work was not stable. They shifted between constructing roads and selling wood to the Chinese soldiers. Regarding road construction, Mo Dickyi would tell me: "We did not work well because we did not like the Chinese. It was just to pass the time, and then we would go back home."

When the family had finalized their escape plans with the other families in the village, they decided to escape during the night. On reaching the

Nepalese border, they were met by a friend of Mo Samdrup's late husband. Mo Dickyi recalled:

> We felt pity for the animals. Tears come to my eyes when I think of our animals. I had milked them. We got so much milk from *zomo* [a crossbreed of a cow and a yak]. We took the animals with us and we came to Nepal's border. My *Acha* [Samdrup Drolma] had a husband, who is no more. He had a friend at Nepal's border. We gave all of our animals to him. When I think of our animals, tears come to my eyes. I pity them. They were like human beings. They can't talk, but they remember everything. I feel so emotional thinking about them. We gave all of the animals to this man. His home is at a place called Briddim, close to the Nepalese border. We gave the animals to him for free. We didn't take a single coin from him. I pity those animals. We fed them well at our home. We got good milk and butter from them.

Mo Dickyi had shared a strong bond with the animals. They were the basis of their livelihood and for Mo Dickyi, an important part of their household. When she complained about the butter or milk in India, her point of comparison was always the rich butter and milk they sourced from their animals in Kyirong. Life in Kyirong always served as the reference for what Mo Dickyi perceived to be a good life and what remained absent in the present.

From the Nepalese border, they left for a place called Tirseli in northern Nepal, where many Tibetans had been sent by the Tibetan leadership in exile to construct dams. The times at Tirseli were hard. Many of the elderly got ill and passed away in a matter of days. Mo Dickyi recalled the sight of dead bodies. She also fell ill. Mo Dickyi said, "There were many old people. In a day, three or four persons would die. Each day two or more people died. *Ama!* So many people died then. I fell sick many times, but I didn't die. I went to a hospital in Nepal and I slowly recovered. . . . We had Tibetan doctors. I also had a severe headache which made me sleepless. After consulting the Tibetan doctor, I got better." The family stayed in Tirseli for about a year and a half before seeking refuge in India. Mo Dickyi recalled: "We arrived in Dharamsala on the 27th of the 12th month. On the 29th, we went to get blessings from *Kundun* [the Dalai Lama], who used to live in the old palace up on the hill. On the 30th, my father's father passed away at Forsyth Ganj. We lived in tents then. Our grandfather died. We stayed in Dharamsala until the third month

of the following year. Then we went to Pandoh. We worked as laborers, building houses. We stayed at Pandoh for nine or ten years. We left Pandoh and
came to Dharamsala. Then we stayed in Dharamsala and went to sell
sweaters."[45]

On their arrival in exile, the siblings became scattered to different parts
in northern India. Life in exile changed many things, but most importantly
it shattered the web of caring relationships that Mo Dickyi had with neighbors, monks at the village monastery, extended family, animals, and the land
itself. In India, they faced an unknown way of life, where their family life
would not return to what it had been in Kyirong. By the time of their arrival
in northern India, Tibetan refugees were constructing roads in northern India. While Mo Samdrup and her husband, *Pa* ("father") Ngodrup, were stationed in Shimla—the former hill station capital of the British—the rest of
the family were sent to Pandoh in northern India, where they built houses
for about ten years.

In the late 1960s, Mo Samdrup and her husband moved to McLeod Ganj
and built their house in the area below *phodrang nyingpa* (the old residence
of the Dalai Lama). Soon thereafter, the rest of the family followed. After moving back to McLeod Ganj, Mo Dickyi met an older Tibetan man, Pa Lobsang, who had three children from a previous marriage. They began a
relationship and moved in together in the Forsyth Ganj area in McLeod Ganj,
where she stayed until his death in 2008. Together, they traveled around India
for the seasonal winter business: "We went everywhere, Kashmir, UP [Uttar
Pradesh], Gujrat, everywhere in India. I think there is no place where we
didn't go. Slowly, we learnt new languages and slowly we learnt to do business." In those years, Mo Dickyi's life was marked by stability, and she recalled those years with joy. Accompanied by her husband and siblings, she
traveled to different pilgrimage sites across Nepal and India, such as Bodhgaya in the state of Bihar, where Siddhārtha Gautama (Buddha Śakyamuni)
attained enlightenment under the Bodhi tree, and the three big Gelug monasteries of Ganden, Sera, and Drepung in southern India.[46] The family and
fellow Kyirong Tibetans in McLeod Ganj also enjoyed regular gatherings.

Her old age, since home confinement, was characterized by an absence
of all this. The death of Mo Dickyi's husband marked a new period in her
life. She stopped participating in the seasonal winter business, both because
of old age and because she considered traveling alone to be dangerous. Mo
Dickyi's younger brother, Akhu Dhondrup, offered her a residence in the
building he owned in Kyirong Village where she would be closer to her sisters

and have free accommodation. In old age, Mo Dickyi lived close to her siblings, but emotionally, they seemed rather distant. She only met Anila and Akhu Dhondrup on a regular basis, as Mo Samdrup had been confined to her home for years; and the youngest of the sisters, Mo Dawa Lhamo, had also become more or less confined at home because of worsening back problems. Since the death of her late husband, Mo Dickyi did not have much contact with her three stepchildren. They did visit her once or twice a year, but they did not offer any help or assistance. Her own son, Tashi, was no exception.

The Absence of Affection

Tashi, Mo Dickyi's only child, was born while she was in Kyirong. After their escape into exile, Tashi was separated from her and raised by Mo Samdrup and her late husband. Perhaps as a result of living apart from his mother during his childhood, Tashi did not have a close relationship with her, as I witnessed when I first met him, in April 2022. During the four years I knew Mo Dickyi and spent time with her, he only visited her twice, and only one of these times was voluntary.

It would not be an exaggeration to state that the mother-and-son relationship was completely absent from Mo Dickyi's everyday life. When she fell seriously ill during my fieldwork, in April and May 2018, none of the family members called Tashi. They did not even have his phone number. Mo Dickyi herself preferred not to bother him, although he lived only one day away by bus from Dharamsala. "He is busy with his family. He has small children," she would say. Or, "He is away for winter business." This is how she excused his absence. Tashi did not pay many visits to Mo Samdrup either, even though she had, in fact, raised him. Ani Jamyang expressed her disappointment in him countless times. "He does not benefit us. He does not look after Dickyi or Acha Samdrup. It is the same as not having [a child]," she would say. "Does she mention him?" Anila asked me another time.

As I would learn upon meeting Tashi in 2022, he had his reasons, which are too sensitive to be disclosed. It is sufficient to say that life had not always been kind and just toward him. When I met him, I was struck by the facial similarities between him and his mother. He had the exact same eyes, the same smile, the same face. Just like her, he had a composure that seemed somewhat defeated by life. It was hard to fathom that two people of the same flesh and blood, so similar in their appearance and ways of being, could grow so far apart.

Occasionally, Mo Dickyi expressed disappointment over Tashi: "What is there to miss about him? He does not benefit me." But she also kept photographs of Tashi, his wife, and their two children neatly tucked into a photo album. I could sense her affection for Tashi and his family when she once showed me their pictures. When I returned to McLeod Ganj in July 2019, Mo Dickyi's relationship to Tashi had grown tense. In June 2019, she fell ill again with the stomach pain that had troubled her in 2018. Once again, she was hospitalized, this time for two weeks. While I and her relative, Tenzin, helped her during a one-week hospitalization at Delek Hospital in 2018, and later with the follow-up rounds to the hospital, in 2019 both of us were out of town. As a result, she had to rely on Akhu Dhondrup. Mo Dickyi's other siblings (Anila and Mo Dawa Lhamo) were too frail to keep visiting or accompanying her to Delek Hospital. Even Akhu Dhondrup, who was in his late seventies and in frail health himself, chose to step back when the doctor recommended that Mo Dickyi should be taken to Chandigarh (close to New Delhi) for a biopsy during the worst of the summer heat. That is when Akhu Dhondrup decided to contact Mo Dickyi's son. Tashi and his wife had visited her earlier in the year, in February 2019, during a lifelong empowerment ceremony for the Dalai Lama at the Tsuglagkhang. During his visit, he had gifted a substantial amount of money to both Mo Samdrup and Mo Dickyi. But Tashi stayed with neither woman during his brief visit, instead choosing the accommodation organized by the Tsuglagkhang.

When Akhu Dhondrup called Tashi, he was nonetheless quick to come to McLeod Ganj, but Mo Dickyi did not find him particularly caring or helpful. He was hesitant to take her to Chandigarh, partly because Mo Dickyi was reluctant herself, just as she had been the previous year when I offered to accompany her. She still feared the heat in the lowlands, the hospital expenses, and whether all the hassle might bring her an early death (Chapter 5). Tashi accompanied her to Delek Hospital for two days, before he "got eager to return," Mo Dickyi told me. Moreover, one of Mo Dickyi's relatives who accompanied them on hospital visits told me that Tashi expressed some annoyance over Mola's behavior, something he was not alone in feeling. I had heard similar comments about Mo Dickyi from neighbors and her siblings. Something had not gone right, so when I asked Mo Dickyi whether it made her happy that Tashi helped her out, she did not have anything

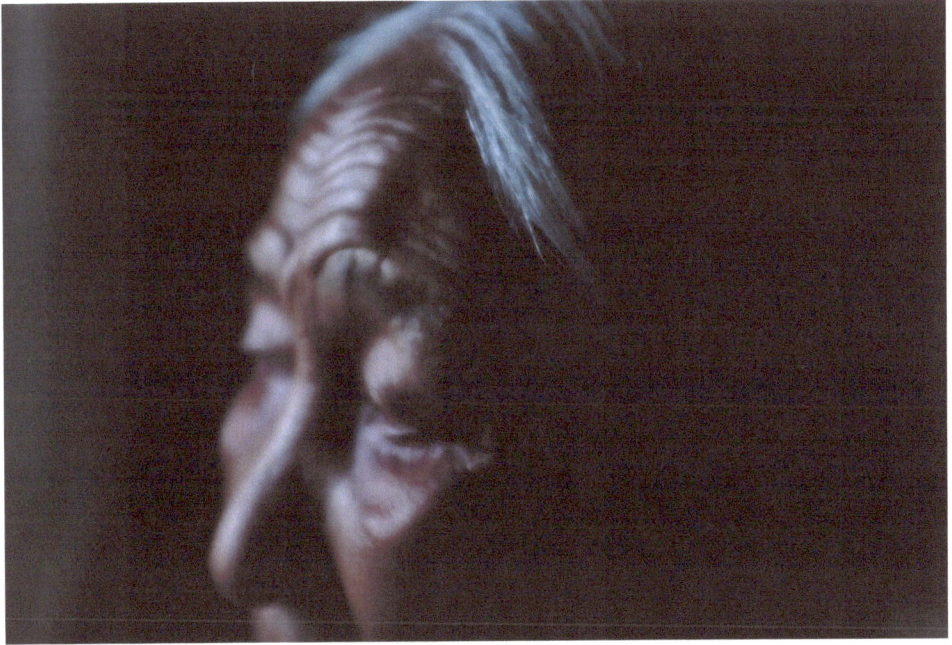

Figure 15: Mo Dickyi lost in thought. Photo by Harmandeep K. Gill.

positive to say. "He was in such a hurry to return. He left after two days," she complained before adding, "Evil behavior (*chöpa ngenpa*)."

Mo Dickyi's words made clear that she had sensed an absence of affection and care in Tashi. Despite coming to her assistance, he had not lived up to the expectations she had of him. However, despite being unable to refrain from voicing her annoyance with Tashi that one time in September 2019, I also sensed that she cared for him as deeply as before. He was her son, her own flesh and blood, after all.

Yet, when Mo Dickyi thought ahead into the future, to a time when she might not be able to look after herself, she did not rest her hopes with Tashi. "Who knows what will happen?" is what she said instead.

On several occasions, Mo Dickyi could be so absorbed by her melancholic mood, which enclosed her in a dark shell, that she would not even greet me. Even if she wanted to, it was as though she could not bring herself to reach out to others, show affection, or make herself vulnerable. And a few times, when her mood was an undeniable test of one's patience and it seemed impossible to reach her, I would massage her legs and feet in silence and then leave her. During such moments, and still, I wonder what had become of Mo Dickyi. Why was she so distant and her body so closed off to others? All that seemed present during most days was an unappeased and closed-off figure, seemingly residing in the absence of all that had been and could no longer be.

It was not only Mo Dickyi's relationship with Tashi that was marked by the absence of affection, but also her relationships with Ani Jamyang and Akhu Dhondrup, who were the only family members she met on a regular basis. Ani Jamyang, who had to encounter Mo Dickyi regularly, was not fond of her complaints, stubbornness, or perceived lack of gratitude. Anila raised many complaints about Mo Dickyi, such as how she did not devote more time to religious practice: "She is always looking out the window or watching TV." Unlike my other elderly friends, who did ten thousand recitations a day of the mantra of Avalokiteśvara—the Bodhisattva of Compassion—combined with other mantras, Mo Dickyi did two thousand recitations daily.

Anila would also complain about Mo Dickyi's weekly washing of her hair. "She is of old age now. Old people shouldn't be so concerned with how they look."[47] Anila perceived her sister's weekly hair washing as an attachment to physical appearance. Most of Mo Dickyi's ways of being and acting in the world were considered unsatisfactory, and perhaps even unvirtuous, by Anila.

Moreover, Anila experienced Mo Dickyi as *gusu dogpo*, someone who is narrow-minded and (constantly) bothered by minor things. And Anila was not entirely wrong. There was indeed always something that was not quite right for Mo Dickyi. She seemed fed up with the food she ate. The vegetables were always slightly overcooked, to the point that the dish tasted as if it were a day old. Anila's dishes by contrast, made of the same type of vegetables, tasted delicious. Unlike Mo Dickyi, she put her heart into cooking. The only times I witnessed Mo Dickyi relish a dish was when I brought her meat dumplings (*momo*) on Fridays or other juicy meat dishes, or fruits such as mangoes, which were her favorite fruit.

Her annoyance with others and everything appeared to overflow at times, like when she would not even spare the rare, white butterflies that fluttered around on the balcony during late spring. She cursed them and chased them away, complaining that they would fly into the shrine room. I failed to understand how she could be bothered by something so beautiful and harmless as a butterfly.

Mo Dickyi's closed-off figure, accompanied by many complaints, was perhaps one of the reasons behind her sometimes-troubled relationships with both Anila and Akhu Dhondrup, who regularly visited his sisters. Mo Dickyi exhibited a type of behavior that the older generation of Tibetans do not find to be culturally appropriate, especially for women. One is expected to be grateful, satisfied, and immersed in Buddhist practice from morning until evening, ideals that Mo Dickyi was not considered to live up to.

While Anila and Mo Dickyi at least had some contact and occasional sisterly conversations, I never witnessed Akhu Dhondrup sitting together with Mo Dickyi in her kitchen. We would see him walk straight up to either meet Anila, check the water tanks, or collect the rent. If I happened to be massaging Mo Dickyi as Akhu Dhondrup walked up the stairs, she was always quick to cover her knees, and I had to stop the massage. She seemed very shy of Akhu Dhondrup, perhaps even scared, despite being much older than him. Mo Dickyi's complaints about other residents in the building (e.g., their excessive use of water or electricity) was of grave concern to Akhu Dhondrup, who relied on the rent. Mo Dickyi could cause them to move out, and some residents had indeed shared their complaints over Mo Dickyi with Ani Jamyang. This had even pushed Akhu Dhondrup to suggest that Mo Dickyi move in either with her son or with Samdrup Drolma.

The loving bonds Mo Dickyi had shared with her siblings in their youth in Tibet, and later during the early period of exile in India, were missing in old age. Whereas Anila regularly visited one of their younger sisters, Dawa Lhamo, just for the sake of her company, this type of sisterly affection was absent with Mo Dickyi. From Mo Dickyi's numerous remarks, I learned that she was somewhat jealous of their affectionate bond and bothered by their unintended exclusion of her. Ani Jamyang and Dawa Lhamo simply happened to be each other's favorites, as often happens in all large groups of siblings. Anila also embraced me with warm smiles and gently slapped my cheeks as one does with a child, but with Mo Dickyi she always kept a serious face. Both of them avoided looking into each other's eyes. I never witnessed them laugh together, as Anila openly laughed with me.

On several occasions, even Mo Dickyi would break out in laughter in my company. Such moments took me by complete surprise. I could not stop staring at her, trying to catch the woman appearing before me, before breaking into laughter myself, usually at the sight of her laughing while making fun of other people.

In Anila's company, and especially in Akhu Dhondrup's company, Mo Dickyi was closed off, and dismissive, as evidence by her constricted face expressions. To be fair, this did not make it easy for her siblings to reach out for her. In return, they were also not open to letting her in. Mo Dickyi's body did not open up much in my presence either—for example, she never stretched out with her hands to greet me, like Samdrup Drolma, Tsering Wangmo, and my other elderly friends did.

Mo Dickyi's siblings tried their best to help her. Ani Jamyang, for example, always made sure to share offerings of snacks she received while attending prayers or teachings at the Tsuglagkhang, and she also shared with Mo Dickyi any fruits she bought in town. And despite the emotional distance between Akhu Dhondrup and Mo Dickyi, he had nonetheless aided his sister immensely by letting her live rent-free. He had perhaps expected some gratitude from Mo Dickyi, and she had maybe failed to make it clear to him?

Akhu Dhondrup and Anila did care, although in a silent and distanced way, and perhaps even in an obligatory rather than in an affectionate way, which was also the case with Mo Dickyi.

Although Akhu Dhondrup and Mo Dickyi continued to share a life in the early years of exile—when they, along with Dawa Lhamo, Penpa Kyipa, Tenzin Choephel, Tenzin Dhargye, and their mother built houses in Pandoh for ten years—in old age, they came across as strangers. I witnessed a widening gap between them, a gap neither of them seemed to know how to overcome.

"The World Has Turned Upside Down"

Mo Dickyi's everyday life was unsettled not only by the alien presence of a body affected by decline and illness, but also by a "thinning-out" of family bonds. The hinges that once had informed her sense of self and held her world together—such as health, youth, and beauty, or her beloved homeland in Tibet—were absent in old age. And even though she was someone's daughter, sister, and mother, and had been someone's wife, these relations had become invisible in the present.

Although her siblings and she had together worked for a common household in Kyirong and were united by a common goal, in exile their lives went in separate directions, as old age made especially clear. Mo Dickyi's son, Tashi, was completely absent. His absence did not erase the fact Mo Dickyi was his mother, but her motherhood was incomplete. The ethical escape, another "here" that could have provided orientation in old age, was missing.

Mo Dickyi often expressed that nothing was the same anymore, from her own body and the weather to relations between people. "Times have changed. How [strange] is the weather . . . in winter, it is raining like summer, no? Everything is upside down. Bad times have come. Earlier, times were good. Good people, good times. These days people are hard to understand. The world has turned upside down," she said.

Everything that had once made the world sensible and familiar to Mo Dickyi was falling apart, leaving her in an in-between state, never fully at home with her own body or the world. And with her world turning upside down, Mo Dickyi's inner world, like her physical body, seemed to be disintegrating, unhinging her not only from others but also from her own sense of self. I felt the split in her sense of self many times (as when she looked at photographs of her present self). Such moments signaled an incoherence or uncertainty about who she was, her place in the world, or what it is that would make her happy in life. Her mind, instead of being *gu yangpo*, seemed to close up like her body, shutting others out and leaving her engulfed in a state of melancholia.

Yet, I also sensed that Mo Dickyi was not ready to give up on what used to be. In fact, she longed for it deeply and held on to it stubbornly. It was almost as if all the absences in her life ran parallel to the materially present, like a possible reality. Maybe this was her way of hinging herself to something? Holding on to what used to be might have opened up imaginations of a possible future, one in which her body was not falling apart in loneliness but was supported by more moments of loving togetherness with Ani Jamyang, or by the care of her son Tashi. In the imaginary life, from another time, that was present despite its absence, Mo Dickyi Sangmo maybe imagined herself back to the time she was an attractive and strong woman, to the time she was still someone's beloved daughter, sister, wife, and mother. And if Tashi and she had a loving relationship, she could have been a real grandmother too.

As Mo Dickyi's days moved in between these real and imagined spaces, there were also moments that offered her a withdrawal from her habitual life. These moments came when I massaged her legs and feet, when she visualized the paths in their village in Kyirong, or when she made fun of other people. They also occurred when we sat outside on the rooftop on the sunny, warm days of spring and autumn and she sunbathed her cold feet and hands, or when I returned to McLeod Ganj in the end of December 2020 after eleven months and she allowed herself to smile, commenting that seeing me was like a dream. During such moments, sometimes intentionally created by me as an act of reaching out for Mo Dickyi, she seemed to emerge to life, so unguarded that a different side of her—open, accessible, and light, as if about to bloom—came to the foreground.

January 2020

I had known Mo Dickyi Sangmo for almost two years. As I was on my way to her apartment, I recalled her mood during my last visits in September 2019. I was excited to see her after more than three months, but a part of me also dreaded it. I could clearly sense the discomfort of facing her closed-off figure.

But Mo Dickyi surprised me with a shy smile. While massaging her legs, I noticed that they were slimmer, and her knees were bonier than before. She only had one neighbor now, Pasang, who had stayed there for years. The other, a monk whom I met in September 2019, had moved out some time earlier. I found Mo Dickyi to be more open and calmer than during all of my visits in 2019. My follow-up visits also had an ease about them. As a result, I also took the freedom to be more open around her and make more jokes. The laughing did her good.

When leaving her house one day, Mo Dickyi, like she had done many other times, stood at the balcony and watched me walk out and down the stairs. I had declined to have sweet biscuits and chai (which I had been overloaded with on my visits to other elderly friends that day), and as I stepped down the stairs, she gently complained, "What is this, you don't eat, you don't drink?"

I laughed. *"Momo* [grandmother], seeing you has filled my stomach," I sincerely replied, in a joking manner. To my surprise, Mo Dickyi gave in to a short, sharp laugh. She even forgot to cover her mouth as she always did when laughing. I think I saw her teeth clearly for the first time in two years.

I was not the main reason for Mo Dickyi's lighter mood in January 2020. It was her younger sister, Penpa Kyipa, who had come from Canada to McLeod Ganj for three weeks of holiday. She had arrived a week before me. Penpa Kyipa and Mo Dickyi had reunited after several years. During her brief visit, she diligently looked after her elderly sisters Mo Samdrup, Ani Jamyang, Mo Dickyi, and Mo Dawa, lending a particularly helpful hand to Mo Samdrup and Mo Dickyi, who were confined to their homes. Penpa Kyipa also supported her sisters financially, especially Ani Jamyang, who, as a nun, did not have a source of income. And occasionally, the other siblings who lived abroad also provided care for Mo Samdrup and Mo Dickyi from afar by sending them money.

The white tiles of Mo Dickyi's kitchen counter shone brighter than ever. "Penpa Kyipa cleaned them," she told me. Mo Samdrup also appreciated Penpa Kyipa's assistance in cleaning and cooking, but more than anything, she appreciated her sisterly company. She even encouraged Penpa Kyipa to retire to McLeod Ganj so she could spend the last phase of her life with her.

During my return trips in 2019, I had sensed a widening gap between Mo Dickyi and me, as if she was disappointed that I could not be present as I had been during my fieldwork in 2018. She kept asking whether I would stay longer than only a few weeks. When my answer disappointed her, she would inquire whether I planned to return after finishing my studies.

Days after Penpa Kyipa left, Mo Dickyi said, "With Penpa Kyipa gone, my heart is empty," as she sat behind the window. Once again, her heart—identified by Tibetans as the seat of the mind—was filled with melancholia. She then counted the days since Penpa Kyipa had taken the night bus to New Delhi for her flight back to Canada, and concluded, "She must be back in Canada by now." The distance was beyond her comprehension. She carried on speaking about Penpa Kyipa, how she had worried about her long flight, and all the necessary precautions she had told her to make as an elder sister. Penpa Kyipa had certainly left an absence in Mo Dickyi, but her presence and care

Figure 16: Mo Dickyi searching for something from the rooftop. Photo by Harmandeep K. Gill.

also seemed to have breathed life into the memories of their shared history and family bonds, lightening Mo Dickyi's spirit.

Penpa Kyipa's company was transient, like all other phenomena, but memories of her would continue to stay with Mo Dickyi. They were fragments of the good that made the loss more bearable. Once again, there was the hope that, although the world had turned upside down, there would be times when she would feel more at home with herself and her surroundings. Penpa Kyipa was gone, but I was still there. I would also leave, but her fellow Kyirong Tibetans and others in the surrounding area would return from the seasonal winter business in a few weeks. Soon, another winter would end, and once again spring would bring the promise of life.

Interlude

Lunch will take some time, Pasang-la tells us. So, I get down on the floor in front of Mo Tsering Wangmo to massage her legs and feet. Her legs are hard as wood, the right leg slightly worse than the other. This is the one she wants me to massage for longer. Her feet are swollen and heavy. There is no gap between her toes. They seem glued together.

"Don't put too much oil," Mola insists. Sometimes, I accidentally pour too much, and then I have to massage until the oil is soaked into her skin and her legs are dry enough to put on the leg warmers.

After the oil, I squeeze a pain-relief cream onto her leg. I mix the oil and the cream and spread it around her knee, leg, and foot. Her legs and feet are pale, but her feet are not cold like Mo Dickyi's. But it is far more challenging to massage Mo Tsering's heavy legs. The flesh is hard and thick, so much so that I cannot poke my fingers into the skin. It is difficult to wrap my hands around her leg.

I softly press my fingers onto her skin and work with the flesh like a piece of dough. After some time, my hand and arm muscles seize up. It is a relief when the flesh loosens. Mo Tsering compliments that I massage for a long time. This means that I have to massage each leg for about half an hour (the right one slightly longer), making for one hour of massage in total.

As I massage, Mola keeps moving between topics. She often says that I do not talk much, just like her daughter. "She also likes to listen," she has told me numerous times. Only Acha Dolkar, who is also fond of gossip and has an opinion about everything, is able to keep up with Mo Tsering's conversations. I find it hard to massage and listen attentively. Mo Tsering is rarely quiet.

I am relieved when the hour is almost up. Mo Tsering is pleased and grateful as always, but she does not tell me to stop.

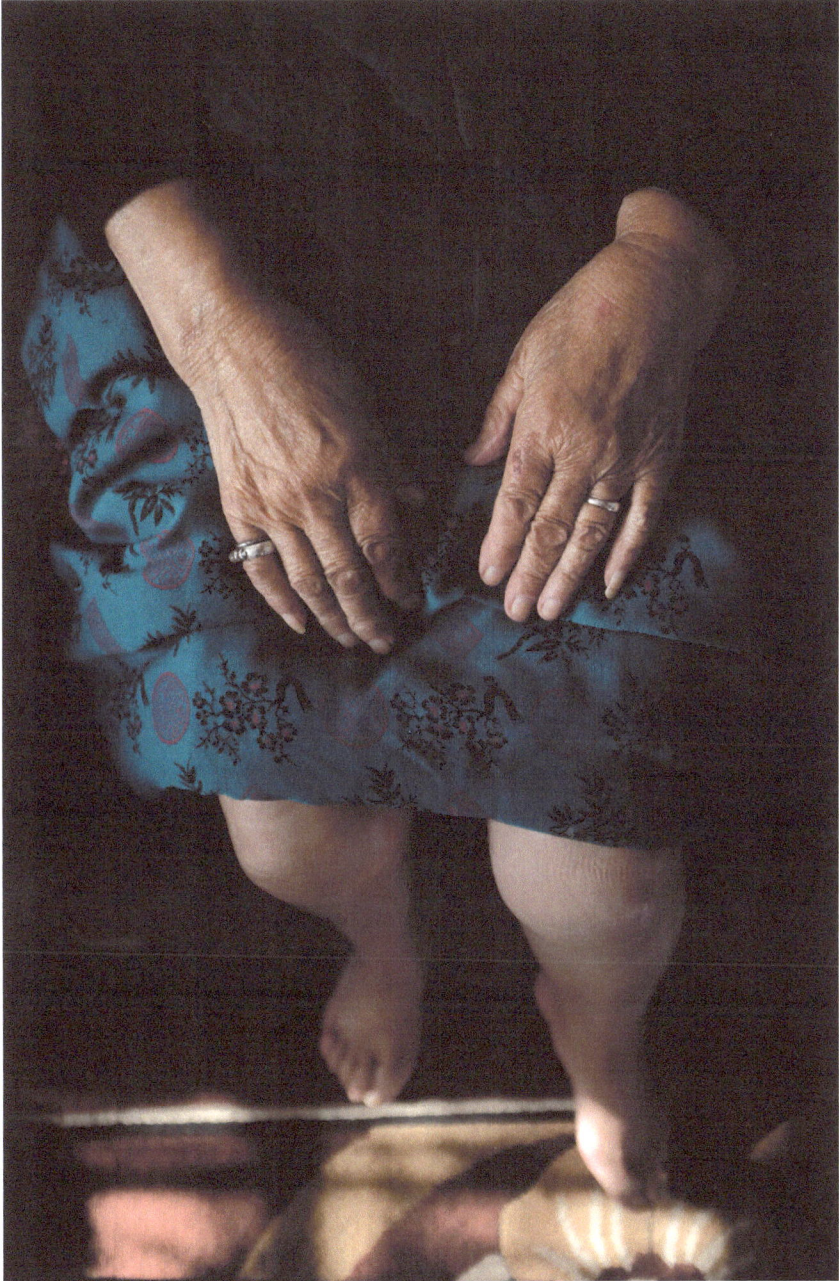
Figure 17: Mo Tsering Wangmo. Photo by Harmandeep K. Gill.

CHAPTER 3

Desperation

It was a sunny morning. Spring was just around the corner, and McLeod Ganj bustled with life. But for Mo Tsering Wangmo, it did not make much of a difference. She was confined to her chair, just as in the other seasons. The promise of spring did not bring any more life into her compound. It did not lift her spirits (as it usually would have done). And there she was, seated, arms resting on the arms of the chair, and staring into the empty room surrounding her. The television was off. It was comforting for me to know that at least the morning sun was peeking through the windows and keeping her company. She turned her head slowly and greeted me.

"Come in," she told me politely.

Greeting her back, I walked to the kitchen to check if Pasang-la, her caregiver, was there. The silence surrounding Mo Tsering was not enough to tell me whether he was present. "Pasang-la doesn't talk. He is always busy on his phone," Mola had complained to me more than once.

The kitchen was empty. Mola told me that he had gone to town for some work. It was soon lunchtime, but Pasang-la had not prepared any lunch before leaving. Not knowing whether he would return on time, I offered to do it instead. Mo Tsering hesitated and ordered me to sit down, to relax and eat *khapse* (a fried Tibetan snack) that Pasang-la and Mola had made during the Tibetan New Year.

Mo Tsering no longer dressed in the traditional *chupa* with *onju* underneath, like other elderly Tibetan women that I knew. She wore an oversize T-shirt, with a purple vest on top. A woolen skirt covered her lower body. But she still wore her long hair in the distinct Khampa hair style: two plaits braided into two separate blue or red ribbons and wrapped around her head.[1] The only jewelry she wore was a ring on her right little finger and another one on her left ring finger. She was a tall woman with big and heavy hands. It was hard to believe that someone like her could one day be at someone else's mercy, as she was now.

Mo Tsering was more patient with Pasang-la's delay that day, because he had gone to do some important work. Yet that day was no exception when it came to her daily complaints about him. She shared the same story I had been listening to for a month. It was her daily catharsis. I tried my best to listen with patience and let her empty her heart.

In between her complaints, she shared some news about Tenzin Tsomo (a distant relative of hers who had arrived back in the United States) and a phone call from her daughter, Tenzin Jigme, before returning to the subject of Pasang-la. I felt terrible thinking about how restless her mind was. One thought only provoked another.

How will she find relief, I wondered, when her thoughts are constantly sinking her deeper into unrest, making her heavier, like that unmoving body of hers? What is the solution?

While she continued speaking, I got down on the floor to massage her legs and feet. Her feet could not properly stretch out on the ground. If her toes touched the floor, her feet were always hovering above the ground, never getting a proper rest. I took off her socks and leg warmers and lifted up the thick woolen skirt. As I rubbed a mixture of massage oil and pain-relief cream onto her leg and began the massage, Mo Tsering told me about the solution.

She lowered her voice and whispered to me, as if the echo of her words would linger around until Pasang-la's return, "I am looking for a new caregiver. Don't tell Pasang-la."

The news surprised me. I knew that Mo Tsering had the option of getting a new caregiver, but she had previously announced that she would get one only when Pasang-la moved away from Dharamsala. He had told her numerous times that he would stay with her until he left. But now Mo Tsering had decided to fire him, much earlier than planned.

"He doesn't stay here much anyway," she defended her decision. Mo Tsering mentioned how he left to wander around town after preparing breakfast, returned to make lunch, left after lunch to wander around some more, and then returned to make dinner before he took off again, only to return around 9:00 or 10:00 P.M. to sleep. "What if I fell down while he is out? Sometimes my legs go completely stiff; you know that. I am old. I need assistance," she said.

I wondered whether Pasang-la would be more present if he were paid more. Mola had told me that he often complained about his low salary; and although he had offered to stay with Mo Tsering for a few more months, he had also threatened to leave.

Mola carried on, "It's better I die. It's better to die than to sit in this chair always, isn't it? I have to always stare at others' faces and say 'please, please.'" The fact that she always had to ask other people for help and assistance exposed her vulnerability, leaving her in a state of desperation, always seeking relief. All she sought was to be seen and for her suffering to be recognized.

In 2010, Mo Tsering Wangmo accidentally slipped in her kitchen. She fractured her right hip and was forced to undergo surgery. Since then she became confined to her home. After recovering from the hip surgery, she managed her everyday life on her own for a few years. She could slowly move around in the apartment and cook by herself. But since about 2014, she had become completely dependent on paid care, sometimes even for intimate tasks such as urinating and defecating. When I met Mo Tsering in January 2018, the condition of her legs was always uncertain. Even her daily toilet visits would be impossible without her walker. She never knew how her legs would react from one day to the next, and even from one part of the day to the next. There were days or moments during the day when her legs turned completely stiff and she was unable to make her way to the toilet. These were the desperate moments when she could not even urinate on her own. On other days, she was surprised at how flexible her legs could be. These were the more hopeful days, when she took the courage to walk a few meters back and forth on the terrace. Her everyday life was pervaded by uncertainty about her own body and the nonkin networks she relied on in the absence of her daughter, who migrated to Europe in 2008.

This chapter reflects on Mo Tsering Wangmo's search for care in old age. Through her story and the stories of others, I consider the new forms of relationality that elderly Tibetans engage in and rely on in the absence of family. By tuning into these nonkin networks of support, I attempt to make sense of what Mo Tsering regarded as good and bad care, and what she looked for in the various nonkin others in her everyday life. In an effort to better understand what was at stake for her, I further engage with the mutuality of being by turning to the ethics of care articulated by the philosophers Emmanuel Levinas and Knud E. Løgstrup, for whom such ethics is grounded in interdependence. Finally, I turn to a feminist approach to care, which fleshes out the abstract and idealized ethics of care proposed by Levinas by considering the structural constraints that shape one's ability to care.[2] Even though the face of the other might evoke an infinite responsibility, as suggested by Levinas, in real life, care also has a limit. This chapter builds on the notion of hinges introduced in the former chapter by turning to the ones Mo Tsering found important in enduring the struggles of old age.

From Lhasa to McLeod Ganj

Mo Tsering's family hails from the Kham region of Tibet, where she was born and spent her early childhood. She did not remember much from the years they lived in Kham. All she recalled was playing around and not having to do any work, since she grew up in a wealthy household with servants. The family had a trading business and moved to Lhasa when Mo Tsering was a small child. Having grown up in the Tibetan capital and lived there until adulthood, she proudly identified as a Lhasa-wa more than a Khampa. Her affinity with Lhasa was undeniable in her sophisticated Lhasa accent and her use of honorific verbs and nouns when addressing others.

Mo Tsering would recall that her father and two elderly brothers who did the trading business were absent during most of her childhood. She grew up with her mother and younger brother and spoke very fondly of them. Mola described her childhood as the happiest period of her life, a happiness that was later shattered by the Chinese invasion of Tibet. When the People's Liberation Army took control of Lhasa, Mo Tsering's family, like other wealthy and aristocratic families in Lhasa, lost everything they owned. She recalled: "Everything was taken away from us, everything . . . our horses, money, home. They turned us into complete beggars. . . . We barely had enough to wear and eat. Our clothes were full of patches. We didn't even have shoes. Because they labeled us 'bad people,' they wouldn't sell us shoes. . . . We were banished to a poor house. We lived at an uncle's home earlier. We had a good house. But then later, when they labeled us as bad people, we were kicked out of our house and were put in an old, dark house. That's where I stayed until I came to India. I heard later that the house was destroyed."

These memories pained Mo Tsering deeply, even in old age. Having grown up in a wealthy household, the poverty and humiliation that followed was horrifying.[3] At the time, her mother had passed away. Her elder brothers joined the Tibetan resistance in the Lhoka region, while their father joined the resistance at Norbulingka. Mo Tsering Wangmo and her younger brother stayed back in their home but were later banished from it. She never saw her father and two brothers again. Her uncles in Lhasa were imprisoned, but Mo

Tsering and her brother were spared because they were young, she told me. The time after the invasion was for her the most painful period of her life:

> The air was filled with the sound of guns [firing] and bombs. I saw a man who was being eaten by dogs. It was so scary. My sister would cook something for us and we would go to Norbulingka, carrying a stick with a white cloth on top. Dogs would attack us. They ate the corpses. We were eight people. I was the youngest in the group. We went to Norbulingka to search for my father. There were so many injured men. Some were medicating the injured. There were piles of human corpses and of dead horses, burning. Some were floating in the river. We went searching for my father day after day. We would run away when the Chinese started shooting. It was so sad. Never have I lived through more difficult days than those.

Some years after the Chinese colonization of Tibet, Mo Tsering found work in road construction that had been initiated by the Chinese Communist Party in and around Lhasa. Mo Tsering was sent to a place that was a day's journey from Lhasa.

Even though she could clearly visualize the events from her past, time seemed to have become a blurry concept for her in old age. She could not recall the exact year she started working as a laborer or how long she worked in one place. After some time, she found employment at the Mentseekhang in Lhasa. The work was easier, and she made enough money to get by. Life got a little better for Mo Tsering.

When she was in her late thirties, Mo Tsering gave birth to a daughter and named her Tenzin Jigme. The father of the girl met another woman while Mo Tsering was pregnant, a betrayal that still angered Mola in her old age. Mo Tsering's experiences with the men in her life had, for the most part, been negative. She spoke of her father with some disdain too. He was not only physically and emotionally absent from her and her mother's lives but also too fond of drinking, as was the man who made her pregnant. In the absence of a husband, Mo Tsering raised Tenzin Jigme with the help of her younger brother. When Jigme was old enough, and in accordance with the practice of Tibetans living in Tibet at the time, she took Jigme into exile in India and enrolled her at the TCV school in McLeod Ganj. There, Jigme could live in close proximity to the Dalai Lama and enjoy the kind of freedom that Tibetans were denied under Chinese rule. For Mo Tsering, her daughter was the

Figure 18: Mo Tsering's living room. Photo by Harmandeep K. Gill.

center of her world, and she made sure to visit Jigme several times after returning to Lhasa. In 1990, Mo Tsering returned to India to attend the Kalachakra initiation led by the Dalai Lama and decided to stay there.[4]

She settled down in McLeod Ganj, and like most Tibetans living in India and Nepal, she made a livelihood through the seasonal winter business. When I met her in 2018, she was once again alone in life, separated by thousands of miles from her daughter who lived in Switzerland, from her homeland of Tibet, and from her younger brother, who still lived in Tibet. Mo Tsering's daughter covered all of her mother's living expenses, including the salary of the caregivers. In the physical absence of Jigme and close family members, Mola's fate was tied to strangers, often the norm for a life in exile.

A Multitude of Caregivers

It did not take long for me to discover that Mo Tsering did not have an easy relationship with her caregivers. Her complaints about Pasang-la and subsequent caregivers focused on their neglect of her needs and their disrespect. Having experienced disobedience and dishonesty from many caregivers over the years, Mo Tsering had learned not to trust them. In fact, from the moment a new caregiver started the job, Mo Tsering expected that person to turn out to be just like the rest. She perceived their care practices as not genuinely motivated by a desire to help her. From the caregivers' perspective, however, it was not an easy job, and Mo Tsering's mistrust of them made things harder.

In June 2018, about a month and a half after Mo Tsering decided to fire Pasang-la, she got a new caregiver—an Indian woman in her late forties who spoke Tibetan like a native. She also had a Tibetan name, Bhuti. Unlike Pasang-la, Bhuti-la seemed to have a calm and gentle nature. Not being familiar with Mo Tsering's history with caregivers at that point, I felt hopeful that she would satisfy Mo Tsering's needs. But Mo Tsering was not very hopeful: "Now she is good, but who knows what will happen later." Having had enough experience with various caregivers, she knew that after a month or so, the harmony would be disrupted. And things did, indeed, soon take a turn for the worse.

Her first complaints about Bhuti-la began three weeks into the arrangement. Mo Tsering complained that Bhuti-la did not listen to her and purposely ignored things she told her to do. In addition, she accused Bhuti-la of lying about the cost of groceries and taking money for herself. I felt that Mo

Tsering was being unjust. Bhuti-la stayed with her throughout the day, something Pasang-la never did. She did all the work on time, and also helped Mo Tsering to urinate and even massaged her legs on most mornings, for half the salary Pasang-la was paid. I also felt that Mo Tsering looked down on her new caregiver in a way she had not done with Pasang-la, who was both a male and a fellow Tibetan.

By contrast, Bhuti-la was a poor, illiterate woman with a dark complexion. She had grown up working as a servant for Tibetan families in a Tibetan settlement in central India. Bhuti-la did not know her age, but she must have been in early or mid-forties. As a result of malnutrition and the hardships of life in her youth, many of her teeth had fallen out. I describe Bhuti-la's physical appearance because, like most Indians, most Tibetans-in-exile too equate physical appearance with a specific class or caste. Mo Tsering and some of my other elderly friends were no different in this regard. Whereas Mo Tsering had addressed her male Tibetan caregiver with the honorific suffix *la* ("Pasang-la"), she referred to Bhuti-la simply as Bhuti. It also took a while before she began calling her by her name instead of just addressing her as "girl" (*bumo*), "my worker" (*nge leka chekhen*), or "my helper/assistant" (*nge rogpa chekhen*). It was clear that Mo Tsering did not consider her an equal. An acquaintance of Mo Tsering's said that this might be because Mola had belonged to a rich family of traders and had grown up with servants in her household.

Even though her family lost everything they owned after the Chinese colonized Tibet, their aristocratic ways of dealing with servants were still evident in Mo Tsering's attitude toward her caregivers. She provided them with everything—food, shelter, and, occasionally, pocket money—and was often generous with them, but she never confided in them. In return, Mo Tsering expected them to be accommodating and obedient. Although Bhuti-la and some of the other caregivers accompanied her in all her daily activities, Mo Tsering did not consider herself to be *champo* ("friendly," "warm-hearted," or "close") with them. Being *champo* with someone involves a two-way process of giving and receiving care. The relationship between Mo Tsering and her caregivers was clearly hierarchical, and its degree of intimacy seemed to be dependent on the gender and social class of the caregiver in question. As a male, Pasang-la was given more respect than the female caregivers, and Bhuti-la was treated worse than the Tibetan female caregivers.

As time passed, the relationship between Mo Tsering and Bhuti-la grew steadily worse, and after two months, it seemed unlikely that their relationship had any future. Whenever Bhuti-la stepped out of the room to do some work, Mo Tsering would immediately begin to gossip about her. Once again, uncertainty and desperation regarding the future took her over. Mo Tsering told me that Bhuti-la had started answering back in a rude manner on a regular basis, and that her calm composure during my visits was nothing but a pretense. I did not know what to believe. Had I been so wrong in understanding Bhuti-la, or was Mo Tsering exaggerating in a desperate effort to be understood? Mo Tsering's hostility toward Bhuti-la became so strong that she even accused Bhuti-la of deliberately trying to hurt her. One incident that she brought up regularly was that Bhuti-la once forcefully bent her leg when putting on Mola's shoes. This was an accusation she had also directed at Pasang-la.

Shortly after, she also began accusing Bhuti-la of stealing money. Distrusting her with money, Mo Tsering requested that a distant relative purchase medicines for her and also accompany Bhuti-la in buying groceries. A Tibetan acquaintance of Bhuti-la's, who had secured her the job, visited Mo Tsering several times to settle disputes between them. But Mo Tsering had made up her mind, and in October, four months after Bhuti-la started working, she decided to get a new caregiver. I never got the chance to ask Bhuti-la about her version of the story, because she and Mo Tsering were always together. Moreover, interviewing Bhuti-la could shatter Mo Tsering's trust in me, and if she found out, it would have hurt her deeply. Thus, my ethical obligations to Mo Tsering demanded that I take her version of events as the truth, although I now regret not hearing Bhuti-la's side of the story.

Bhuti-la was replaced by a younger caregiver, a Nepalese girl in her early twenties named Sarasvati.[5] Sarasvati, who only knew a few phrases in spoken Tibetan, seemed very shy, obedient, and adaptable. She carried out the same tasks as Bhuti-la for the same salary. In addition, she was an excellent cook and served Mo Tsering delicious food. Once again, I was hopeful that things would work out. In particular, I expected the age gap to reduce the number of confrontations between them. Also, because they spoke different languages and could not carry on a conversation, perhaps Mo Tsering would not complain to Sarasvati and Sarasvati would not answer back. I encouraged Mo Tsering to praise Sarasvati, especially because she was a shy and reserved person. Mola agreed to this and added, "If she is good to me, I will, of course, be good to her." Sarasvati was a petite woman with a small appetite. Mo Tsering would affectionately nag her to eat more, just as she did with me. I noticed that she was also getting tired of changing caregivers.

But by that point, I had gotten to know Mo Tsering well, so when her first complaints about Sarasvati began shortly thereafter, I was not surprised. She told me that the young Sarasvati had a bad temper: "She gets very angry, and whatever I say, she does not respond to me." Once again, I was left to listen, nod, and try to understand.

Sarasvati was still with Mo Tsering when I left McLeod Ganj at the end of December 2018. I had grown fond of Sarasvati, and when I left, I gave her some gifts in Mo Tsering's presence, also in the hope that she would continue to do Mo Tsering good. When I called Mo Tsering about a month later, during the Tibetan New Year, she informed me in a panic that Sarasvati had run off with her salary and a few things from the house. I was surprised by the turn of events and was disappointed by my own naivety. Simultaneously, I also wondered whether Mola's choice of words was exaggerated, and that instead of "running off" all of a sudden, perhaps Sarasvati had informed Mola about leaving the job.

"Do you know she was planning to get married? She ran away to get married," Mo Tsering told me. This was something Sarasvati had told me before I left. "Bad girl," she kept repeating. At the time, Mo Tsering did not have a new caregiver and was being taken care of by a distant relative.

When I returned to McLeod Ganj a few weeks later, she had a new helper. This time it was a Tibetan woman in her mid-thirties, who also happened to be from the Kham region. But I had missed out on the initial "glory days" of the relationship, and by the time I arrived, Mo Tsering's complaints about the new caregiver had begun. This time, she complained that her caregiver did not have good speaking manners, and that when she went out, she stayed out for a long time, just like Pasang-la.[6] Once again, she expressed the need for a new caregiver.

Dependence on Others in Old Age

On nearly all of my visits to Mo Tsering, I entered her room with a greeting and then asked her if she was feeling well. I cannot recall her ever replying positively. Instead, she would often laugh at my question, finding it ridiculous to ask this, given her bodily condition. Regarding her happiness, she said: "I am not happy. I am disabled. I can't do anything on my own. Tibet Charity takes me to hospital. The helper cooks for me. As long as I can't do things by myself and have dependency on others, I am not happy. If I could do things by myself even while using the walker, just to get by, it would be good, you know. There would be some freedom in that."

Moreover, she told me that she was always waiting for death: "In this condition, I am dependent on others. I wish to die. Relatives from Gangtok and Bhutan came to take me with them, but I didn't go. I want to die here. I know my condition. I am not able to work, walk, or cook for myself. I am dependent on others, and that's difficult. If I die, it will bring an end to all this. I wish to die. Others tell me not to think like this, that even an extra day in life is worth living, because one can say *mani*. But I think it's better to die. I am not afraid of dying. One has to die anyway." The main reason Mo Tsering wanted to die was that she had no freedom. Dependency on others made her feel helpless and vulnerable.

I have struggled to understand Mo Tsering's problematic relationship with all her caregivers. Were they all so bad? They were people with different personalities, yet she did not get along with any of them.

Having reflected on Mo Tsering's statements about her caregivers and her own condition, the main reason for her difficulties with her caregivers seemed to be how she saw herself in the relationship: reduced to an old and dependent woman. She felt that she was not respected as an elderly person with authority and wisdom. Her bodily condition had come to define her, and she had no freedom because of her body. She also felt that the caregivers ignored her sufferings of living with a disabled body.

Despite obvious cultural differences, Mo Tsering's experience of old age corresponds well to Simone de Beauvoir's writings on old age.[7] Although Beauvoir's rather negative attitude toward old age does not correspond to Tibetan Buddhist notions, it does speak well to Mo Tsering's experience of being seen as nothing but an old body. Moreover, as Beauvoir points out, the real death for her is old age itself. It would not be too far off to state that, to some extent, Mo Tsering felt the same way. Old age had taken away her independence, leaving her at the mercy of strangers.

Mo Tsering and another elderly friend, Mo Sangye (age sixty-five), who also relied on paid care, both stated that good care can only be provided by one's own children. Mo Sangye was also from the Kham region of Tibet and escaped into India in 2004. Both of them had daughters who lived abroad. Relying on strangers, even when they were paid, made them uncomfortable, and they both found it hard to trust their caregivers. Mo Tsering once said, "My daughter is my own," unlike the paid caregivers or someone like me. Could it be that she was trying to convey that for her own daughter, she is not merely a dependent and old body? For Tenzin Jigme, she was a mother who had sacrificed much for her in the past. She was also the main person who could see the continuity of Mo Tsering's life and recognize her for the singular person she was.

Mo Tsering sought a type of response from the caregivers, from me, or from others, which is usually typical for parent-child relationships. The relationship is not simply an exchange, as she perceived her relationship to be with the caregivers or other nonkin networks of support. I will return to this later, but first I will elaborate on certain notions of care for aging parents in Tibetan Buddhist communities that are helpful in making sense of Mo Tsering's expectations.

Care in Tibetan Buddhist Communities

Filial piety among exiles is taking on a new form, in which more and more children mainly provide financial support for aging parents.[8] Likewise, Tenzin Jigme covered all of Mo Tsering's living expenses. She also tried to be present for her mother through weekly phone calls. Retiring to an old-age home has never been an option for Mo Tsering. Not only would it take away the freedom she enjoyed in her own home, but it would also spread gossip about her daughter and her among relatives and acquaintances.

For centuries, and even as recent as a decade ago, the norm in Tibetan and other Himalayan communities was to designate at least one child to be a nun or a monk, a decision which would not only bring merit for the family but also secure a caregiver for parents in old age.[9] Through his work in a small village in Nepal, Geoff Childs learned that an unmarried daughter, such as a nun, was often considered "as the most suitable to provide old-age security, for she can still reside in her natal household until her parents die."[10]

In other cases, even when parents designated their child to be a monk to secure care in old age, it was not guaranteed to work out in practice. The norm in Tibetan Buddhist villages in the highlands of Nepal is that monks leave for bigger monasteries in Kathmandu or other monasteries in the Tibetan exile communities in both India and Nepal. Hence, it is sensible to designate at least one daughter to be a nun. Other literature, such as "Externally-Resident Daughters, Social Capital, and Support for the Elderly in Rural

Tibet," also suggests that daughters, especially unmarried ones, are often thought of as the ideal caregivers for aging parents.[11]

Building on interviews conducted in rural Tibetan communities, Geoff Childs, Melvyn Goldstein, and Tsering Wangdui argue that rapid modernization in Tibetan areas does not necessarily pose a threat to traditional family-based care systems.[12] Instead, they see it as opening up new opportunities for aging parents to send their daughters away for education and work. In this way, daughters represent a form of social capital in old age. If coresident children do not treat parents well, aging parents can find alternative accommodation or invest in caregiving services. One man who was interviewed stated, "Daughters are better because they give good care."[13] Another expressed, "When parents become invalids or are dying, then daughters are important because they can care for the elderly. Parents are happier if a daughter is nearby during their dying days."[14] Such opinions were also expressed by the elderly I knew in McLeod Ganj.

Both Mo Tsering and Mo Sangye were lucky to have daughters who cared a lot for them. Mo Tsering in particular expressed much pride over her daughter, Tenzin Jigme. She was managing her career and her newly married life, while also providing her mother with both financial support and emotional support through weekly phone calls. Mo Tsering shared: "My daughter is very good. I never ask her to send me money, but she always does. Her aunt always advises her not to send me too much money, since I will spend it on offerings, prayers, and other things. But she is always concerned about me and never listens to her aunt." Mo Sangye's daughter, too, had an active concern for her mother's well-being and tried to visit her mother at least once a year. As in the case of rural Tibet, parents in exile encourage their children to migrate, not only because they worry about their children's futures but also because they have financial concerns for their own futures. Children living in the West are a stable source of social capital for aging parents, as Mo Tsering's case exemplifies, and they can also increase one's social status.[15] But even though filial piety is taking on new forms in the exile communities today, I found that it is still grounded in the same old idea that children have a moral obligation to their aging parents. And one way of fulfilling that obligation is by providing for them from a distance.

Moreover, neglecting old parents is also considered to be bad karma. As expressed by my elderly friends, taking care of one's parents is the foremost practice of *chö*. On a regular basis, Mo Tsering encouraged her daughter, Jigme, who is a nurse, to provide good care for the elderly she worked for.

She repeatedly shared the story of an old man who had expressed a lot of gratitude for Jigme's good care.

Mo Tsering also made sure to ask whether I had called my own mother:
"You have to remember to call your mother. No one loves like a mother."
In accordance with her own life experience—a father who was absent during most of her childhood and later a man who left her while she was
pregnant—Mo Tsering had come to believe that fathers were incapable of
caring for children in the way mothers do. Having raised Jigme on her own
and having made many sacrifices for her also steered her expectations of
Jigme, something I believe her daughter knew.

If Jigme failed to call for a week, often because she was consumed by work
or other duties, Mo Tsering found this hurtful. An elderly nun, Ani Tenzin
Pema (age ninety-one), a resident of the TCV old-age home who was provided
for financially by her nieces in England, had on one occasion said to me, "If
the legs stop working, what can one do with money alone?" As her statement
makes clear, financial support alone is sometimes not enough.

Above all, parents wish to be taken care of by their children, but in wanting to secure better futures for them, they have to settle for long-distance financial support and rely on hired caregivers or other nonkin. The pain of
separation can be ameliorated to some extent through weekly phone calls,
which both Ani Tenzin Pema and Mo Tsering desired. Emotional and moral
support through regular phone calls, visits, or assistance during periods of
illness is equal to, if not more important, than financial support, which alone
is not considered to live up to Tibetan Buddhist virtues.

Tibetans, like people in other Asian contexts (e.g., in India), believe that
daughters are more capable of providing care that lives up to Tibetan Buddhist virtues. Daughters are understood to have the ability both to nurture
and to sacrifice themselves for loved ones. According to a Tibetan proverb,
"On the morning of birth, [one prefers to have] a son. On the morning of
death, [one prefers to have] a daughter."[16]

Daughters are believed to be better able to provide what Elana Buch calls
embodied care: to "inhabit and reproduce the sensorial and social worlds."[17]
Through this process, the caregivers or daughters incorporate the needs of
the cared for into their own bodies, sustaining the way of life, independence,
and personhood of the cared for.[18] This is exactly what Mo Tsering sought in
her caregivers and in others who tried to support her in her everyday life.
Good care for her was thus not only financial and supportive care, such as
cooking, washing, or help with more intimate bodily tasks; it also involved

emotional and moral support, sharing her troubles and joys, being listened to and embraced by others.[19]

The Singularities of Mola's Life

Mo Tsering's expectations of care—from her daughter and others—were also grounded in the singularities of her own life: the hardships she had faced in life with poverty, illness, raising a daughter on her own, and most importantly, the way she herself had treated others. Whenever Mo Tsering spoke about the importance of helping others, she mentioned her own experience of helping others in need, such as poor people in Lhasa and the case of a poor elderly Tibetan man she used to meet in the circumambulation path around the Tsuglagkhang in McLeod Ganj.

One example of Mo Tsering's generous nature is when she badly wanted to help a teacher who she felt had been subjected to unfair treatment by the TCV school. Mo Tsering shared the news about the teacher shortly before I left in December 2018. She came to know of the teacher through her daughter, who knew her from her former studies at the TCV school. The old teacher was asked to retire from the TCV school, something she was unwilling to do because the few thousand rupees of pension from the school would not be sufficient to cover her family's living expenses. After her retirement, the school had not offered her free accommodation at their old-age home, and her drug-addicted son made things worse.[20] Mo Tsering emotionally shared the teacher's story with me. She insisted that I try to obtain the teacher's phone number so she could offer her some financial help, despite not knowing her. Neither Mola nor her daughter could remember the teacher's name, which made it rather difficult for me to locate her, and in the end, I was unable to help. The way Mo Tsering had responded to others throughout her life informed her own expectations of the type of care she deemed honorable. Finally, having been raised in a wealthy household with servants also had an effect on how she expected the caregivers to behave toward her. Her expectations of care were informed by the life she had lived.

It is in light of all the above that we must make sense of Mo Tsering's problematic relationships with the caregivers. I suggest that in these relationships, Mo Tsering saw a particular version of herself, which was nothing but "the body that is dependent on others."[21]

Figure 19: Mo Tsering sitting in her chair. Photo by Harmandeep K. Gill.

This image reduced her to a category of the old and disabled and over-shadowed who she believed herself to be and all that she endured in life.

Back in the day, Mo Tsering was a very attractive woman. An acquaintance of hers from Lhasa said, "Everyone would notice her coming, such height and beautiful face *Acha* had." Mo Tsering had an exceptional height for a Tibetan woman. Looking at an old photograph of hers that used to hang in front of my desk, I was always reminded of the gorgeous Tibetan actress, Lhakpa Tsamchoe, from the movie *Seven Years in Tibet*.[22]

Her tall, slim figure, that attracted people's attention in her youth became a hindrance in old age. Like Beauvoir, Mo Tsering led an independent life. She told me that she used to be fearless, once even confronting an Indian rickshaw driver with a knife when he threatened to rob her.[23] When Mo Tsering acted out the scene, she pretended to hold a knife against her own throat and repeated the exact words she had uttered to the rickshaw driver.

She had traveled all over India, from the farthest Tibetan settlements in the northeast to the biggest ones in the south. These solo travels were her fondest memories from her life in India. "I went everywhere, and now I can't even go to the toilet," she once said.

In spite of being confined to her home for years, Mo Tsering was the most engaged and outgoing among all my elderly friends. Despite not being able to step out of her home for years, she had maintained an impressive social network around her. She knew a lot of gossip about people in town, including my former landlady, whose relatives come from Lhasa. Mo Tsering also had an interest in everything from Bollywood actors to international politics. When the legendary Indian actress, Sridevi, passed away all of sudden on 24 February 2018—leaving Indians in a state of shock—Mo Tsering was even up-to-date with the possible reasons for her death. She had picked up the news through the Indian channels and inquired about it from others who visited her. The reports speculated that Sridevi had died of a heart attack because she was filling her body with various substances to stay looking young. This is, at least, what Mo Tsering told me. Meanwhile, my other elderly friends had no idea who Sridevi was or that she had passed away.

When Mo Tsering and I watched television together, she would cheer, cry, and sometimes even be on the brink of shouting. Connecting with these different sides of her was one of the reasons Mo Tsering and I became close. Our relationship opened up the possibility of her world being otherwise. My presence, or the presence of the nurses from Tibet Charity, was not the only daily outlet Mo Tsering had to transcend her bodily condition and be more like herself. Television was another.

In the following, I unfold Mo Tsering's relationship to a different kind of ethical other in her life: TV personalities. Her relationship to TV personalities points to several things: (1) her continuous engagement in the world despite being confined to her home; (2) how her engagement with them provided an example of what good care meant to her; and (3) how the television offered the possibility of transcending her bodily condition, reminding her that she was also a moral person who could care for others.

TV Characters as Ethical Others

Watching television with Mo Tsering was always an exciting experience. I witnessed a range of emotions in her, depending on what show we were watching. She was almost jumping up and down in her chair, shouting with desperation, "Go, go, go!" when an Indian girl in the famous Indian reality-based program *Crime Patrol* attempted to escape from her kidnapper. Another time, I witnessed her anger during the live sessions of the Tibetan parliament. She laughed mockingly at one of the parliament speakers; when she could no longer bear to listen to him, she pressed the "off" button on the remote control as hard as she could, telling the speaker to "eat shit" before throwing the control onto the bed.

Her favorite show was a Bhutanese singing competition for young students, a show Mo Dickyi Sangmo also enjoyed watching. Mo Tsering watched it with great passion. When the young singers received negative feedback from the judges, Mo Tsering was easily moved to tears. "It hurts them. They are so young," she would say. She was highly suspicious of one of the male judges who had a reputation for being overly critical. During the show's 2018 season, she grew particularly protective of one male contestant who was the most destitute person on the show. Throughout her life, she had felt strongly about destitute people, perhaps because she had the experience of being one herself after the Chinese took control of Lhasa. It was moving to witness her compassion for disadvantaged people (which unfortunately never included her caregivers). She was easily moved to tears by others' sufferings, as if her heart, despite its courageousness and strength, was actually broken.

Mo Tsering began referring to the young boy as her "male friend" (*drokpo*). She wanted him to win, but, in the end, he only placed third. Still, Mo

Tsering did not feel too badly about it, because he won a large sum of money. And she was quite fond of the boy who won, anyway. To my surprise, Mo Tsering suddenly turned hostile toward one of the contestants on the show. The victim of her hostility was the person who came in fourth, a young girl who was very disappointed with the outcome and openly proclaimed that she should have won instead. "What a greedy girl," Mo Tsering repeated several times with a great deal of annoyance, even a week after the show had finished. She seemed unable to accept that the girl wanted to win over the poor boys, especially her *drokpo*. Mo Tsering had a deep empathetic concern for the Bhutanese youngsters that was hard to find in her relationships with her caregivers.

She cared in a similar way for a Tibetan female singer who died in a tragic car accident, leaving behind her child and husband. When a monk acquaintance lent Mo Tsering an iPad for a week, she requested that we play the songs of the deceased singer. Because she did not know how to use the device, she would ask anyone who happened to be present to play them for her. She felt sorrow over the fate of the singer's young child, worrying what would become of him without the love of a mother. At other times, the television brought her too close to her own life, even keeping her up at night. "That Chinese man cheated on his wife. I got so mad. I couldn't sleep at night," Mo Tsering told me about one of the characters in a Chinese drama series she followed, dubbed in a Lhasa-Tibetan accent.

Television enabled her to engage with the world outside her four walls and to be someone who could care for others. As Andrew Irving remarks, a disabled person is not merely a passive entity but can also "retain a sense of social and existential continuity amid the disruption of illness by listening to the radio, making conversation, and forming relationships."[24] Through her connections to the TV personalities and by acting on their situations, Mo Tsering regained her sense of being a moral person who was invested in the world. The TV personalities were also a face of the "other," in Levinasian terms, calling her to responsibility; and in her response, she also gained her own singularity. They did not react back or recognize her humanity, but her own investment in them made it possible to see another side of herself and retain a social and existential continuity. Television was the interruption in her daily life that offered the possibility to be someone else—someone who was not simply a burden but who could care for others.[25]

Witnessing Mo Tsering's level of engagement with the young Bhutanese singers helped me to realize what good care meant to her. It was a form of care that, in the words of Arthur Kleinman, meant to recognize the other's sufferings and engage in practices, through words and emotional states, that attended, supported, and collaborated with the contestants, the kidnapped Indian girl, or the Chinese woman whose husband had cheated on her.[26] Mola's happiness for their success was genuine, and so were her tears for their setbacks.

Good care for Mo Tsering was, thus, not merely defined by the fulfilment of an obligation or a duty. She had the same need as elders in Elena Buch's article: to be "treated like a person and not as a piece of furniture."[27] Mo Tsering sought the latter, which seemed to be informed by how she had responded to others in life and was also grounded in Tibetan Buddhist ethics.

Good Care: Responding to the Other in Their Singularity

The literature on care suggests that morality is a central component in our understanding of care.[28] Kleinman understands the work of doing good to others and oneself as the central commitments of caregiving.[29] This commitment or responsibility to the other is what makes us human, he suggests.

Rebecca Thornton's fieldwork among socially abandoned elderly people, and her involvement in the life of one elderly woman, offers an excellent ethnographic example of attempting to respond to the commitment we face on meeting people in vulnerable life conditions. Thornton suggests that care for these people involves "someone who recognized their existence and tried to honour their personhood," something that can also be understood in Kleinman's words as "doing good" to the other.[30]

Thornton's conceptualization of care as a form of recognition of the other's existence and personhood also goes hand in hand with Janelle Taylor's explorations of care for elderly people with dementia, which are first and foremost informed by the ethnographic case of her own mother.[31] Her interest in the term *recognition* is triggered by people's constant questions about whether her mother recognized her. Drawing on Paul Ricoeur's work on recognition, Taylor explores the linkages between recognition and care and how claims to social or political recognition are connected to the cognitive ability to recognize phenomena.[32] She suggests that the loss of normal cognitive abilities often leads people to stop recognizing and caring about elderly people with dementia.[33] Furthermore, following philosophers such as Charles Taylor and Nancy Fraser, she argues that to deny others recognition and care is also to deny them their selfhood, as selfhood is not inherent in individuals themselves, but "is distributed among networks, sustained by supportive environments, emergent within practices of care."[34]

The work done by Kleinman, Buch, Thornton, and Janelle Taylor takes seriously the togetherness of our lives. This complicates the distinctions between self and others, and the way in which we think about care. To examine this, I now turn to the ethics of Levinas and Løgstrup, both of whom have written about an asymmetrical ethical relationality and the importance of responding to whatever the other brings forward.

According to Løgstrup, we self-surrender to the other in any type of encounter. Thus, regardless of whether we want it or not, we have a certain power over the other's state of being.[35] In any type of encounter with the other, one is exposed to a certain extent, because one is present with a body or a face.

In contrast to Løgstrup, Levinas gives particular significance to the face in his ethics.[36] It is not merely the features, or an object we perceive. The face is present with a certain expression, a nudity and vulnerability.[37] Michael Morgan, who has written extensively about Levinas, compares Levinas's understanding of the face with Bernard Williams's "thick" moral concepts, in which one cannot separate the descriptive and prescriptive dimensions.[38] Similarly, the face makes an appeal (with its vulnerability and nudity—e.g., needs or desires) and, simultaneously, a demand. Likewise, for Løgstrup, in the self-surrender to the other lies a similar, silent demand or plea to the other to respond.

Løgstrup, however, differentiates between three ways of exposing oneself to the other: (1) through glance, expression or tone; (2) through emotions or expectations of the other; and (3) through any state of needed help or despair, in which one is at the mercy of others' assistance, which unlike the first two cannot be concealed. In all three forms, there is an appeal to me to embrace the other, "to take care of that part of the other's life that is within my power, and which I therefore am responsible towards," regardless of whether they are loved ones or strangers.[39] This is what Løgstrup conceptualizes as the ethical demand, which gains significance through the basic condition that our lives are hinged to the lives of others.[40] It demands that one protects that part of life that has been delivered "into the hand of another."[41] According to Løgstrup, the most important aspect of our lives is where we stand in this type of mutual self-surrender to the other. We constitute, in the words of Løgstrup, "one another's worlds and destiny."[42]

Despite certain differences (e.g., Levinas's notion of the face and alterity), the philosophical starting point for both Løgstrup and Levinas is the ethical obligation we hold toward others. These obligations demand that we take responsibility for and respond to what the other has dared to come forward with.[43] I suggest this is what Mo Tsering sought in those around her—namely, care and compassion for her frail condition. More importantly, Levinas highlights that we must respond to the other in the other's singularity, and refrain from responding in a way that reduces the other to a category of difference, such as old age or physical disability, which is what Mo Tsering felt her caregivers did.

As it is for Løgstrup, the ethical is, for Levinas, at the starting point of all interaction. Moreover, our own singularity, which Mo Tsering wanted recognition of, is according to Levinas interlinked with the other, in the self's responsibility to the other, which takes shape in the nudity and command of the face, or the claim (e.g., needs) the other makes on the self.[44] Thus, Levinas is not concerned with an individualistic singularity that exists prior to our relations with others, if at all, but rather as arising in response to the other. The starting point for Levinas is not concepts or categories of people, but the meeting between two particular individuals.[45]

The ethical responsibility that for Levinas and Løgstrup acts as a guiding force for human interaction is also emphasized in Tibetan Buddhist ethics that inform Mo Tsering's expectations of good care. In Tibetan Buddhist ethics, motivation is what differentiates a virtuous action from an unvirtuous one, and compassion counts as one of the highest virtues. Engaging in a morally defined action cannot in itself bring merit and improve one's karma. As highlighted by the Dalai Lama's numerous teachings, the right motivation is also necessary. A common example given by elderly Tibetans is that it is of no benefit to recite mantras or read Buddhist texts if one does not hold good thoughts about others. Repetitive, ritual practices alone cannot bring merit and ensure a good rebirth. Likewise, Mo Tsering's complaints about her caregivers were centered on a strict Tibetan Buddhist view of motivation. For her, they were only providing care because she paid them to and not because they were sincerely trying to fulfill an ethical obligation. Thus, responding to the ethical responsibility of the relationship seemed for Mo Tsering to be dependent on virtuous motivation.

Even though Levinas and Løgstrup give us a vantage point from which to engage with Mola's complaints and what she perceived to be good care, their arguments, like Buddhist ethics, remain limited to an ideal world. They imply that we meet the other without considering categories of difference and their inherent judgments, and that those giving care are not blinded by whether the other is a parent, friend, stranger, or rival. As remarked by Lisa Guenther, in meeting and responding to the other, we do not meet a naked or a vulnerable face in the Levinasian sense, but a face with specific features, such as the color of the skin, or a body in a certain physical condition, or dressed in a certain fashion.[46] These features guide our responses to the face and also add to the face's vulnerability. Furthermore, another problem with Levinas's thinking is that every single encounter with another person seems to carry a demand or plea, and thus an inescapable responsibility.[47] This is impossible to honor in practical terms because we are entangled in responsibilities to multiple people, which imposes a limit on our ability to take full responsibility for each and every one. In caregiving work, as argued by feminist thinkers, such as Chloe Taylor, the ethical responsibility toward the other is put under pressure because of hierarchical relations and the physically and emotionally draining nature of care work.[48] This adds to the difficulty of responding to Mo Tsering in her singularity—especially because she failed to respond to the caregivers in their singularity (e.g., their needs, life histories). She also reduced them to a category or "token of a type"—namely, "workers" or "helpers." She felt that if they ignored her humanity, she would treat them similarly: "If they are good to me, I will also be good to them."

Like others, the caregivers offered real gestures of care, especially at first, such as cooking delicious food or doing as they were told. But these actions were rarely actively appreciated by Mo Tsering. It was almost as though she had chosen to put up a barrier between a potential caregiver and herself from the start. Occasionally, she sympathized with certain incidents in the caregivers' lives; but on the whole, she did not allow herself to invest in them, or to care for them as she cared for her TV characters, the nurses, or me.

So far, I have focused on what Mo Tsering sought in care relations: she was in search of someone who would listen to her, recognize her sufferings, and honor her for the person she was. For her, being recognized and honored for her wealthy family background, her generous and outgoing nature, her struggles in life following the Chinese colonization of Tibet, her caring and intelligent daughter, and her status as an elderly person with authority and a lifetime of wisdom were vital components of who she perceived herself to be. In other words, she sought care practices that took seriously the ethical demand of the relationship by responding to her in her singularity, and not only as a category of difference.

With these thoughts in mind, I turn to my own relationship with Mo Tsering, first to exemplify what good care meant for her and, second, to show how her relationship to me (and the TV personalities) enabled her to establish herself as a moral and independent person who could influence the world around her. Last but not least, my presence was also used to deepen the hierarchical relationship to the caregivers. Unlike her relationship to the caregivers, our relationship was nurtured with kind words, praise, and care.

Mola and I

"If I could only walk on my own to the toilet, I would be happy. I just want to be able to go to the toilet without the fear of falling. It's too difficult like this," Mo Tsering said countless times, often following up with an expression of her appreciation for my care. "The way you look after old people—massaging my legs will bring you merit (*gewa*). You will be happy in life." She would tell me that she prayed for me and shared her praise of me with the nurses from Tibet Charity and her daughter. If I happened to be present during her daughter's phone calls, she would hand me the phone.

Though a Tibet Charity representative tried to visit her every week, those visits were not always reliable, and Mo Tsering never knew when to expect them. After concluding my volunteer period with Tibet Charity, I started visiting Mo Tsering on my own. For several months, I massaged her legs for up to fifty or sixty minutes each day, from Monday to Saturday; but in the second half of my fieldwork, I had to cut it down to thirty minutes, three times a week, due to exhaustion. This served as an important lesson in the often-depleting nature of caregiving.

Mo Tsering insisted that I eat my lunch with her during my visits. I believe it was her way of doing something for me and caring back. If I ate too little, she would scold me like a mother. When Pasang-la was her caregiver, he would occasionally prepare dumplings for lunch. Despite her love of meat, Mo Tsering would ask Pasang-la to prepare vegetarian dumplings out of consideration for me. On these occasions, Mo Tsering would make sure to call me in the morning to urge me to show up on time so we could enjoy the dumplings while they were still warm. When I felt tired from my walks between different households and massages, she would affectionately tell me to rest and sleep. And sometimes I did. Over a short period of time, Mo Tsering and I became rather close. She could count on my presence on a daily basis (except Sundays) and began dreading my departure from McLeod Ganj. "When you leave, I am done," she would say. "Who will massage my legs like you?" In the beginning, I often also stepped in for other things in Pasang-la's absence, such as serving food, helping her to the toilet, washing her hair, and performing other minor tasks. Mo Tsering referred to our relationship as *champo*. Occasionally, she even likened it to a mother-daughter relationship. What fostered this intimacy between us?

One of the main reasons Mo Tsering and I became close, I believe, was the massages. Although she faced a bleak future, the massages offered her the hope that, if they continued, perhaps she would be able to make her way to the toilet on her own, without relying on her walker and without the constant fear of falling. She had suffered some minor falls on her way to the toilet, and a few times when her caregivers had been absent, no one was there to help her up. Her hopes for a better life were invested in her legs. Furthermore, having me or the nurses massage her legs also offered a sort of intimate presence: the relief of not being alone with her body but rather sharing it with another, in the sense that the other carries some of the burden temporarily. Mo Tsering perceived the act of massaging as an act of (good) care, because it recognized her sufferings. By massaging her legs, I temporarily lifted the burden of having to bear them alone, and I participated in her hope for a better future. I believe that we became close because I responded to Mo Tsering's ethical demands of our relationship by embracing the most vulnerable part of her (her legs), which she literally had placed in my hands.[49] For her, I responded to the appeal or demand she had put forward with my commitment to massaging, and I also massaged in the "correct" way. She would often contrast my massages with Bhuti-la's or Sarasvati's massages: she said that they put in no effort, as she made a face.

She described their massages as too slack and short, saying once again that they were merely doing it out of obligation and not out of genuine concern for her well-being.

I, on the other hand, massaged for a long time and with a powerful force, Mola would comment. I believe that in that effortful touch and my commitment over time, she sensed my recognition of her sufferings. I had responded to her in her singularity.

The role of touch, thus, needs to be understood within the context of Mo Tsering's everyday life, and we must also take into consideration its

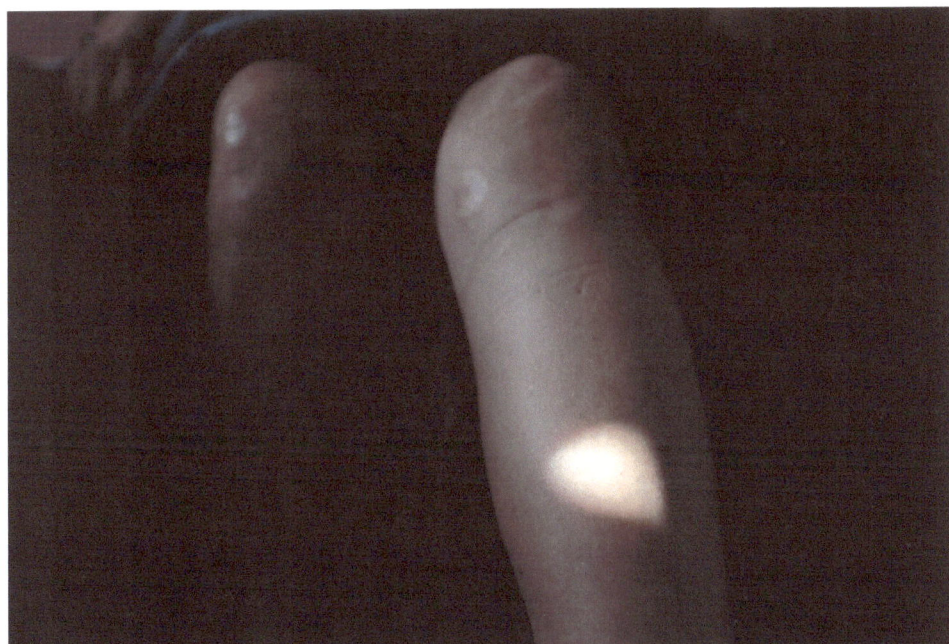

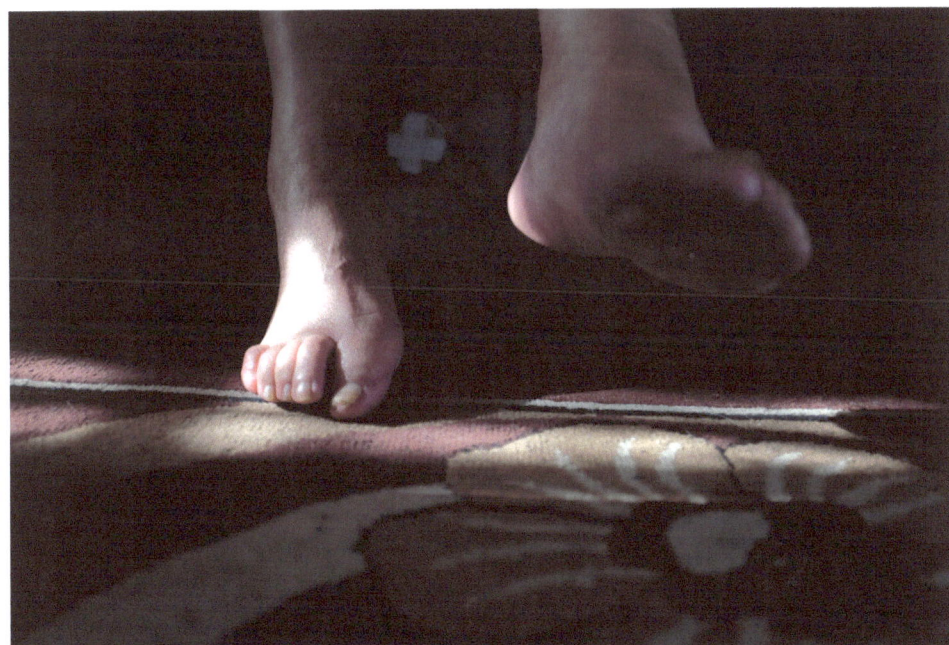

Figures 20 and 21: Mo Tsering's legs and feet. Photo by Harmandeep K. Gill.

significance in the Tibetan context.[50] Giving massages to elderly people is considered to be an honorific act among Tibetans. During my rounds around McLeod Ganj with Tibet Charity, the nurses were usually stopped by many elderly Tibetans who greeted them with gratitude. Their occasional massages and small donations of medicines were immensely appreciated. The act of massaging an elderly person is also understood to be a virtuous action, motivated by compassion. It would not be incorrect to say that I was acting as a virtuous Tibetan Buddhist for Mo Tsering. This was clearly stated when she said of the act of massaging, "This is *chö*," as I was massaging her legs. Thus, when Mo Tsering and my other elderly friends referred to the act of massaging as *chö*, they were attributing certain (virtuous) motivations to it and, therefore, also commenting on what qualified as good care for them.

Caring in Return

In her article on gift exchanges between older adults and home caregivers in Chicago's home care industry, Elena Buch points out that elderly people regard monetary-exchange relations entering the home space as problematic, because they are part of the capitalist care provision, in which care is provided as a form of commodity.[51]

As Anna Tsing argues, a commodity system is driven by different values from the moral values of social and gift relations: "Value in a commodity system is things for use and exchange. Value in a gift system is in social obligations, connections, and gaps."[52] Following Buch, in a capitalist market system, care has been purified from its initial gift relation, guided by certain values, and has been transformed into a commodity, with a different set of values, although these boundaries become more complicated when care is delivered in practice. The elderly people in Buch's Chicago study attempt to surpass the capitalist-driven care provision and build more intimate relationships with their working-class caregivers—for example, by giving informal gifts of money. For the elderly, it is an act of showing appreciation and care for their caregivers.

The relation of monetary exchange was an issue for Mo Tsering. In both her and Mo Sangye's cases, it created a degree of distrust from the beginning and led to certain judgments about the caregivers. For Mo Tsering, their care practices were only a job to them and not motivated by the moral obligations and connections that Tsing would describe as typical in a gift system. My relationship with Mola, by contrast, was not defined by the values in a mone-tary exchange, meaning that she was not paying to have me around. My role was neither prescribed nor fixed by Mo Tsering, as the role of the caregivers was, making the relationship between her and them more unequal. That be-ing said, Mola was well aware that our relationship was also a form of ex-change, but it was a type of exchange grounded in the moral values of social and gift relations. By this I mean that our relationship came with obligations and intimate connections that involved more freedom and flexibility, mak-ing us more equal, at least compared to her relationship to the caregivers.

Moreover, ours was a relationship in which Mola could give me the "gift" of her care. Being cared for by others is not the only component of care; en-gaging in and caring for others is equally important in sustaining oneself, as argued by Arthur Kleinman and Sjakk Van der Geest.[53] In addition to the caregivers from Tibet Charity and the TV personalities, I also offered a pos-sibility for Mo Tsering to assert herself in everyday life as a moral and independent person.

Mo Tsering cared for me by insisting on feeding me on a daily basis, med-icating me during illness, telling me to rest when she could see that I was tired, and reminding me to call my mother.

She sought to influence the world around her and engage in it, despite her impairment. This was apparent to me in her level of engagement with the Bhutanese singers, other people, and me. Not being able to reciprocate made her feel like a burden, even in the case of her own daughter: "It's dif-ficult for my daughter too [that I am unable to manage on my own]. She called the other day and told me that she was on night duty. She went to drink coffee and then called me, *nyingje* ['poor thing']." Mo Tsering went out of her way to make life easier for her daughter, such as by choosing to pay low salaries to the caregivers. Even though Tenzin Jigme insisted on paying them higher salaries, Mo Tsering declined her request in order to save her daughter money.

Moreover, Mo Tsering even prohibited Jigme from visiting her, fearing that it might jeopardize her new job, where she only had a temporary con-tract: "I told her that if you come, do not come here and stay with me. Go and stay somewhere else." At the end of the day, Mo Tsering felt that it was better for Jigme to focus on her new married life and said that she did not mind dying without ever seeing Jigme again. What Mo Tsering did not know was that Jigme had secretly paid both Bhuti-la and Sarasvati additional sala-ries through the nurses from Tibet Charity and, at other times, through a monk acquaintance. Knowing her mother too well, and the hardships of care-giving work (she is a nurse herself), Jigme had chosen to keep it a secret.

My presence, and the presence of others, such as the nurses form Tibet Charity, was also crucial for Mo Tsering in her effort to assert her independence from the caregivers. Keeping us around was one way she communicated to the caregivers that, although she was dependent on them, she still had a net-work of friends who cared for her. Her destiny, in other words, was not bound to the caregivers, something that to me seemed to became particu-larly important for Mo Tsering to assert once the relationship turned prob-lematic. I understand this not only as an attempt to assert her independence but also as a strategy to keep the hierarchical relationship to the caregivers intact. It was a habit of Mo Tsering's to praise me in the presence of the caregivers—a gesture that made me uncomfortable—which I understand as her deliberate effort to put them down, by emphasizing all that they were not in her eyes. This was also her way of communicating to them what good care meant for her.

For Mo Tsering, her engagements with various significant others and car-ing for them, such as her beloved daughter, TV characters, nurses from Tibet Charity, and me, enabled her to temporarily transcend her physical condi-tion, reconnect with different sides of herself, and imagine her world being otherwise, albeit temporarily. Through her multiple opinions and our con-versations, she could be more like the person she believed herself to be: a person with authority and wisdom, a person of high social status, and a strong woman who had endured much suffering in life.

I have so far reflected on how Mo Tsering wanted to be cared for and what was at stake for her. In the next section, I consider why she was not cared for the way she wanted. What types of constraints hindered the caregivers from fully embracing her?

The Limits of Care

An important critique that has been directed at Levinas by feminist ethicists is that he overlooks political contexts and the suppression of certain groups of people. Chloe Taylor, drawing on the works of prominent feminist think-ers such as Claire Elise Katz and Joan Tronto, argues that Levinas is over-burdening certain groups of people, usually women—and in the case of Mo Tsering, her caregivers.[54] Feminist theorists of care argue that these factors have to be taken into consideration to appreciate that ethical responsibility also has limits.

Although there are points of divergence between the ethics of Levinas and feminist ethics, Taylor also highlights points of connection. One of the most important is that both approaches see ethics as coming *before* being.[55] Thus, in contrast to mainstream continental philosophical ethics, in which the self is theorized prior to relations, both Levinas and feminist ethicists emphasize autonomy as relational and responsibility above freedom.[56] Taylor remarks that, because Levinas redefines subjectivity as relational, marking a break with continental philosophy, his ideas can actually further feminist theories.[57] But Levinas and feminist ethics take us in separate directions because the latter, in contrast to Levinas, aims to "*alleviate* the burden of responsibility on specific selves," in order to hinder the physical and emotional fatigue that caregiving can give rise to.[58] Even though "the other" is a feminine other in Levinasian ethics, he is still writing from the point of view of a masculine and privileged subject.[59] Despite paying attention to justice to the self in his ethics, Taylor notes that self-love and self-preservation in the underprivileged or economically marginalized, such as the helpers of Mo Tsering, are underdeveloped.

Instead of overburdening one person with an infinite responsibility, feminist thinkers argue that the such responsibilities should be distributed among "thirds" or "fourths" which can be men or government institutions.[60] Mo Tsering's daughter, Tenzin Jigme, who is familiar with the exhaustive nature of care work, tried her best to distribute the obligations of caregiving among several people, for example, through her generous donations to Tibet Charity and her repeated gratitude to me every time we spoke.

Both Mo Tsering and her caregivers each had commitments beyond their relationship to each other. Like the caregivers in Buch's study, the helpers were also responsible to family members or friends, and those responsibilities shaped their responses to Mo Tsering.[61] Likewise, Mo Tsering was pulled by her responsibility to her own daughter, which was the reason she paid low salaries to the caregivers. However, something she did not admit to others, but was nonetheless aware of, was that her troublesome relationship to the caregivers was actually burdening Jigme with more worries and guilt.

Pasang-la's mood swings and his limited ability to clearly demonstrate his care for Mo Tsering were affected by several factors: his own past as a former political prisoner; his present-day struggle to provide for his wife and child; and his frustration over not obtaining a visa to move abroad.

In my own case, I sometimes failed to embrace Mo Tsering because that meant rejecting her caregivers. At other times, I chose to prioritize other elderly friends or myself over her. Thus, the other might raise an ethical demand, as asserted by Løgstrup; their face might also evoke an infinite responsibility, as argued by Levinas; but in the real world, people remain limited by personal, situational, or structural constraints, and they respond accordingly.

This also means that exposing oneself to others always comes with a great risk, which I believe Mo Tsering was aware of. When the other is unable to elicit a desired response, it also serves as a grave reminder of our solitude and vulnerability. This is perhaps the saddening aspect of our interconnectedness with others, which can become particularly dreadful in the decline of old age, accompanied by disability. Mo Tsering was clearly agonized by her dependence on others. I noticed how she always had to exaggerate her sense of gratitude for every small gesture, something that pained me. When she expressed that all she could do was stare at others faces and say "please, please," her desperation over subordinating to nonkin was undeniable. She was angered not only by her dependence on the caregivers but also by her dependence on others, such as the nurses from Tibet Charity and me. Waiting for our visits left her in a state of limbo, dominated by uncertainty and desperation. All she could do was wait and hope, which on certain occasions resulted in disappointments. As an act of desperation, she would sometimes call me several times to tell me to hurry for lunch, as if she could not stand the waiting or was unable to trust that I would show up when I said I would.

I could sense Mo Tsering's disappointment in me more than once—for example, when I failed to be on time for lunch, when I insisted on having dinner in my room instead, when I sometimes left too quickly, or the few times I failed to show up. But because of the dependency on me (for the massages and company) that she had forged, she often needed to downplay her disappointment, perhaps out of fear that I might stop visiting. Similarly, her disappointment with the nurses from Tibet Charity was also undeniable. During each visit, she would mention whether Tibet Charity had dropped by or had failed to do so for several days. Normally, they visited once a week. Other times, even a week could pass without a visit from them. I know that Mo Tsering found this very disappointing, but when the Tibet Charity nurses did come, she would hide her disappointment behind praise and hospitality. If she had to comment on the infrequency of their visits, it had to be done gently.

Dependence on nonkin in old age, especially in cases of disability, was dreaded by all of my elderly friends. Despite her high expectations of others, Mo Tsering was also aware that investing in others came with a price. While relationality helped her endure the sufferings of living with a disabled body and presented a new possibility in the world (as argued by thinkers like Løgstrup and Levinas), it also meant that, without others to whom she felt her destiny was hinged, she felt stuck in time (as she said herself). Moreover, if the other failed to respond, she also stood the chance of losing herself, or the person she believed herself to be.

Without relationality, or the face of the other, we are caught in a searing solitude, as suggested by Levinas.[62] Only by holding on to others can we hold on to ourselves. And thus, we must make ourselves vulnerable again and again, and along the way, also risk losing ourselves.

July 2019

When I visited Mo Tsering again in July, a few months after my previous visit, a new caregiver had started a day earlier. The previous caregiver from Kham, who was there during my visit in March, had been fired after little more than a month. The current caregiver was a Tibetan woman in her early forties. Things seemed to be going well, but it was only her second day of work.

Many things were the same. Mo Tsering wore a large T-shirt with a purple vest on top. Inside her shoes, she wore the leg warmers I had bought for her before leaving in December 2018. The room had lost more patches of color but was otherwise the same. She was still very fond of pork (and then felt bad about eating meat), and the Bhutanese singing competition had returned for a new season. Her nights were as before, sleepless. Jigme's phone calls were still regular.

But things had also changed. Her eyesight had worsened. Mola's voice was lower than I recalled, more fragile. She told me that the condition of her legs had worsened, and she could not always make daily toilet visits. Tibet Charity had bought a portable toilet chair for her. It was placed on her terrace, hidden under a large, blue plastic cover. Some days she defecated outside. On other days, inside. I assumed that this made the caregiver's job more demanding.

As before, it seemed to me that most of Mo Tsering's efforts were invested in preventing things from going worse. Once again, she expressed the wish

Figure 22: Mo Tsering, hanging in there. Photo by Harmandeep K. Gill.

to die: "I am a problem for my daughter, for my acquaintances and myself. It's better to die, isn't it." I sensed that while she was trying to hold on to some tiny glimpses of hope, she was also trying to come to terms with her sufferings and to endure whatever was. In an effort to cheer her up, I got down on the floor to massage her and to let us momentarily return to what used to be.

Mo Tsering told the caregiver to come and study my massage technique. I laughed at her remark. The caregiver smiled and moved closer to us. I took off her leg warmers and shoes. Her left foot was swollen. The tight socks she wore to get her blood circulation going had left a detailed imprint on her legs. I squeezed out the remaining part of the pain-relief cream onto her knee and then poured some Tibetan medicinal oil. I mixed the gel and the oil and spread it around her leg and to the lower parts of her thigh.

"Watch her, how good she massages," Mo Tsering told the caregiver. It was as if I had never left, so familiar was the feeling of Mo Tsering's legs in my own muscles. I started massaging at the foot. Her legs and feet were heavy and stiff, just as I remembered. As I massaged, parts of the swelling slowly began to fade. After about a half an hour of massaging, her leg softened up some. As usual, I lowered the volume of the television in order to hear what she said. And as usual, I was unable to keep up with everything she shared. Sometimes the conversation had a steady flow about her weakening eyesight or her daughter; at other times, it trailed off to some random gossip about people I did not even know.

When I left, she held my hands and pressed them to her forehead. Tears gathered up in her eyes. "There aren't many like you, who care for us old people," she sobbed.

The guilt that had been building up in her presence was now at its peak. I did not know how to comfort her. I told her not to cry. I could not promise that I would come for another massage tomorrow, the day after, or all the days after that.

"Will you come again before leaving?" she asked.

"Of course," I reassured her. I would come as many times as I could before I left.

That stopped the tears and opened up the possibility that we would once again be in each other's presence; and for a brief period in time, we could hold on to what used to be.

Interlude

I have washed my feet," Po Damchoe Ngawang tells me as I take off his shoes and socks. He always makes sure to wash his feet before my arrival, and as a generous courtesy, he also makes sure to tell me. The first time I massaged him, in August, he felt bad that I had to massage unwashed feet. I did not mind. My other elderly friends do not wash their feet before I massage them. Neither do their feet smell.

During most of the massage, Pola kept saying that his feet must smell. I could sense a tiny bit of old sock smell, but not so much that I minded. It was nothing compared to the foot smell of another elderly man I massaged a few times. I thought I would faint from it. On top of the smell, dirt and dead skin cells had peeled off onto my hands. But I could not say anything to him. Mo Dickyi Sangmo, who is meticulous with her physical hygiene, made a disgusted face when I told her about it. The next time I massaged the old man, I carefully offered to wash his legs and feet first.

Po Damchoe's feet are, by contrast, a pleasure to massage. In fact, he has very beautiful feet. They are slim and light, with long and bony toes. Though he has a worker's hands—dark, rough, and hard—his feet are soft and fair.

I start with the left leg and place his foot on a small pillow with red and blue colors. The colors further enhance the beauty and fairness of his foot. Po Damchoe takes an occasional sip from his whiskey glass. He is in a happy mood. His younger daughter, who cannot speak, stands in the doorway and watches. She waves her bent wrist, which has been that way since childhood, in front of her nose while making a loud sound. She is joking about Pola's "smelly" feet and laughs innocently. Po Damchoe is not so amused. "I washed them," he says to her on a serious note. Even in old age, Pola's legs are quite muscular, yet soft. The soft muscles make it easy to grip his legs. As usual, my hands glide around Pola's legs and light feet. Massaging his legs takes no big effort, but massaging his lower back, which he asks me to do on some days, is a challenge. Tibet Charity did not teach me to massage a back, but not wanting to decline the request, I make use of what I know and try my best. The trouble with the back massage is that Pola usually falls asleep. If he does not fall asleep, it is still impossible to hold a conversation, as he cannot talk with his face pressed against the bed. So, I let him relax or fall asleep, and save the conversation for our tea break.

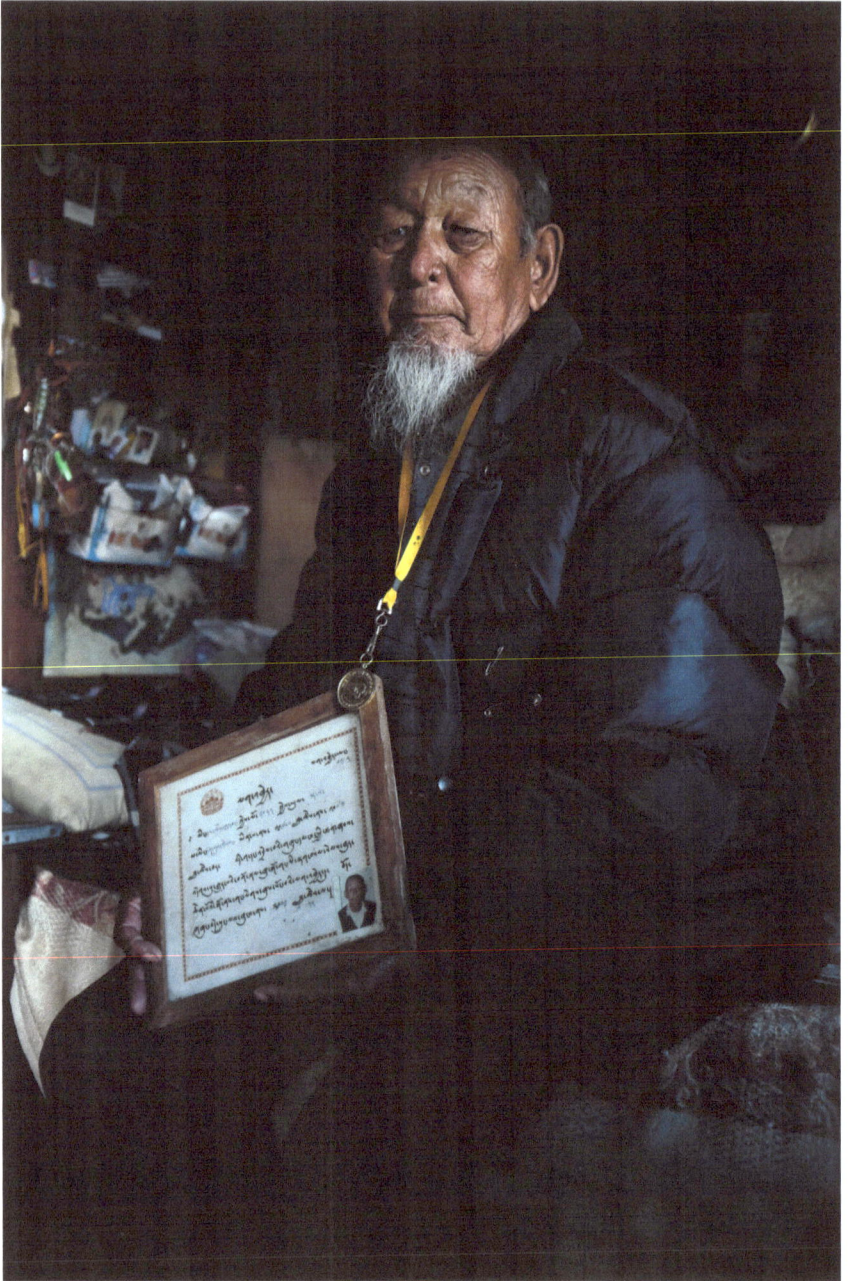

Figure 23: Po Damchoe Ngawang. Photo by Harmandeep K. Gill.

CHAPTER 4

Nostalgia

P o Damchoe Ngawang has a humble little room on the slopes of the hill facing the TCV football grounds and the school's teaching area. This area is known among local Tibetans as TCV "camp" and is the residence of the elderly Tibetans who cleared this densely forested area and then built the TCV school in McLeod Ganj.

Po Damchoe's two daughters live in the same camp area, in two different houses on either side of his room. They make food for him, and he also spends time in their homes. But most of the time, he prefers to sit in his own room, which he built with his own hands. This is where I visited him several days a week and massaged his legs or back.

In those days, the wooden room was a chaotic space. Things had gathered through the years. There were toothbrushes, empty cartons, old picture frames, posters, pens, old Indian trunks, and layers of dust. In his tiny room, one could not spot an empty corner. Amid the mess, certain possessions stood out that had unique value for Po Damchoe. There was the framed photo of two of his grandchildren, their heads leaning together as they embraced each other in a hug. On the wall behind his bed were two other cherished possessions: Beneath a photo of the Dalai Lama hung an official letter of recognition from the Central Tibetan Administration (CTA) for his service in the Tibetan guerrilla army, Chushi Gangdrug, which fought against the People's Liberation Army (PLA) and secured the safe passage of the Dalai Lama into exile in India. And, in front of the framed letter hung a golden medal that belonged with it. Po Damchoe is shown with both possessions in Figure 23.

He first fought against the PLA in Lho Gongkar, central Tibet, in 1959. Following the colonization of Tibet, the Chushi Gangdrug continued their operations from Mustang in Nepal, close to the Tibetan border, for almost fifteen years.[1] Po Damchoe participated for fourteen of those years. The resistance army was secretly trained and financially supported by the US government, specifically the Central Intelligence Agency, for much of this time.[2] Pola recounted that, in Mustang, the guerrilla army was divided into sixteen units, with one hundred men in each. Pola was part of the 10th unit, which he also referred to as the "police" group. In addition to participating in the army's operations, the members of the 10th unit were in charge of keeping order over the army—for example, by settling potential fights between the men. Chushi Gangdrug had to end its operations in Mustang in 1974 after the United States decided to withdraw its support and "the Dalai Lama convinced the soldiers to lay down their weapons."[3] Subsequently, the soldiers retreated and were sent to jail by the Nepali authorities for breaking the laws of the country.[4] Their wives and children were also imprisoned, as happened with Po Damchoe's wife and two children.[5] After their release, the family moved to Kathmandu and then to India in 1975. Although Pola expressed that "everything went to waste in the end,"[6] the Chushi Gangdrug guerrilla operations, both in Tibet and in Mustang, were still an important part of his history. He endured many difficulties, such as extreme cold and hunger, and bravely fought for his people. These experiences were shared by a few of his elderly neighbors, who also participated in the operations in Mustang. Po Damchoe said that he did not think about it much but still believed that if they had not laid down their weapons and had kept fighting, they "would have won."

Another important item he kept in his room was a photograph of his sponsor from France, assigned to him by the TCV school administration. Other elderly Tibetans in the camp area also had foreign sponsors in the past, to provide much-needed financial assistance, but many of them, like Po Damchoe, no longer needed a sponsor, because they now had children living in other countries who could send money. Pola's sponsor had been a man in his early fifties with a long, gray ponytail. In addition to his gratitude to the Dalai Lama and the TCV school administration, Pola also felt indebted to this man, even though he no longer sent Pola money.

The room and all the things it contained carried the mark of time, just like Pola. The only two things that were renewed were the annual calendar published by the CTA, featuring twelve photos of the Dalai Lama, and Pola's whiskey bottle. The calendar was placed on the wooden table next to the bed. He marked a line in the calendar with each passing day. This was how he kept track of time. On the same table stood his whiskey glass with the words

"8 P.M." painted on it. When I visited him, I found the glass either half full, less than half full, or empty. It was always covered with a lid. If Pola was cheerful, I knew he had started drinking. If he was rather solemn, not carrying even a trace of his usual cheerful self, I knew the opposite to be the case. He was happiest when he drank.

For Pola, the TCV area was embodied with a specific history, a history he shared with his neighboring elderly Tibetans. The traces of this history were visible in his stiff and bent fingers, his strong and heavy hands, and his painful knees and back. It was also visible in his addiction to alcohol. This area—and the history it embodied—was also his home. The place and he were connected, just like all the things in his room. This was the place where he shared a life with his beloved wife and raised their children: two daughters, and a son who now resides in Europe. His grandchildren go to school here. The place brought together his past, present, and future. This is also the place he is going to end his days.

This chapter is about home, in exile and in Tibet, during old age. It is about losing one's first home and rebuilding a second one in the image of the first. In an exile context, "home" escapes attempts at concrete definitions. But despite its vagueness, especially for those who were sent into exile at a young age, it is still a real place for them and the elderly generation of Tibetans. In the words of the 14th Dalai Lama, "Tibet is on this very earth," accessible by road and air, and its shape visible on world map.[7] It is also the place where all of the first generation of Tibetans-in-exile were born, raised, and left behind beloved family members. It is the place the elderly and younger exiled Tibetans are nostalgic for and dream about, yet a place most of them cannot reach under the current political circumstances. For those living in exile, home (Tibet) emerges, in the words of the exiled Palestinian poet Mahmoud Darwish, as "a map of absence."[8] It is embodied as an imagination, as a fusion of the real and possible, that is filled with nostalgia, "a pain of a wholesome kind."[9] Imaginations of home run parallel to the time-space of exile, like the promise of a possible life. In the midst of the closure imposed by old age and the prospect of death, home for my elderly friends was the unfinished time-space that called forth embodied memories, imaginations of a life and of oneself.

Guiding my explorations are also Alfred Schütz's words, that home is not simply a house or a place but all that it stands for, characterized by the highest degree of familiarity and intimacy, and thus it can also be called a space of belonging.[10] It is this "place of equanimity we work to cultivate, we wish to find," writes Sienna Craig.[11] For my elderly friends, Tibet has been at the center of their cultivation of spaces of belonging in exile.

In facing the uncertainty of old age in exile, their imaginations of home worked as another hinge that provided orientation at the precarious in-between space at the mountain pass. Furthermore, these imaginations were not only a source of intimacy and familiarity but also an encounter that up-rooted them from the world of the living. Glimpses of home also served as a reminder of the transient nature of phenomena and people, including themselves.

A Second Home in Exile

It was a bright sunny day at camp. After massaging Gen Lobsang Choedak at the TCV old-age home, I made my way up to the camp area. The walk from the home to the camp area follows a tiring uphill route. As usual, I took the shortcut through the school area, walking and climbing the stairs at a slow pace. As I reached the TCV football grounds, the camp area came into view. It was lunch break, and some children played in the big and empty football field. After crossing the field, I came to another staircase, which led to Po Damchoe's room.

For a moment, I stopped to take in the beautiful view of the camp area. The numerous prayer flags on top of the hill were fluttering in the wind. Below them, the houses of many colors rested in serenity.

Pola sat outside and soaked up the sun. He wore his thick coat and a sun hat. His hands rested on his knees. He held a rosary in his right hand as he chanted a mantra. Sometimes, he would be joined outside in the sun by his elderly neighbors. As I climbed the staircase, I would greet them one by one, as they chanted their mantras and enjoyed the sun. We would sit there in the warmth of the day and enjoy a comfortable silence while overlooking the TCV school.

Pola received me with a broad smile. We walked the few stairs up to his room for the massage. The whiskey glass was less than half empty. While I massaged him, Pola took a sip from his whiskey glass and resumed chanting *om mani padme hum*, the mantra of the Bodhisattva of Compassion.

Outside, in the background, we could hear the voices of the TCV students playing in the football field or moving between classrooms. It was pleasant to hear their voices, so full of life. Pola was fond of the students. He told me that they called him "grandfather, grandfather (*popo, popo*)," when he ran into them during his morning practice of circumambulation around the school monastery. For the elderly here, it must be a big comfort to have the TCV school so close by. One can see so much young blood running around. The TCV school is a big community in itself, consisting of students and their teachers, who, like most of the children, stay within the school compound. The school leadership and Tibetans refer to it as "the TCV family." Pola's own daughter-in-law used to be a teacher at the school.

I asked Pola how many years he had worked for the school. He thought hard but could not remember. He said that he retired around 2002: "Then I became old and they realized I no longer could work." Pola reminisced back to 1976, when they arrived here. The Dalai Lama's sister Jetsun Pema and the famous Gen Lobsang of TCV brought him here, along with about a hundred other men.[12] "When we came here, there was nothing, not the hall, not the monastery, the football ground, the classrooms in the front or these houses here. We built everything. The football ground only had a small opening to park a car," Po Damchoe said. The first Tibetans to live here, including Pola, built a few shacks, where many people stayed together. Just as Tibetans cleared the forested areas to build bigger Tibetan settlements in southern India and to harvest the land, in McLeod Ganj, Tibetans undertook similar work to build Tibetan institutions.

Now that Pola had retired, the TCV school gave him a pension of INR 1,000 every month. "That is good, isn't it. We don't have to pay any rent, no expenses for water, and food also they give," he commented. Another time, when he had been more drunk than usual, he complained it was not enough.

Before working for the TCV school, Pola built roads in northern India. He and his wife, with their two children at the time, were stationed in Patlikuhl in Kullu-Manali. In addition, he provided for his family by selling handmade chairs, tables, and beds. When he later took up work at the TCV school, his salary was raised. After a year, in 1977, he started working as a mason at the school, and his salary was raised to INR 7, which Pola recounted as a lot in those days. "The work was hard. One had to be there at 8:00 sharp, and the work finished at 5:00 in the evening. We had one hour of break at noon from 12:00 to 1:00. Attendance was taken," he told me.

The hard construction work over the years took a toll on his back and knees. As mentioned earlier, unlike my other elderly friends, Pola sometimes wanted me to massage his back instead of his legs, which he said ached more. The hard work was also one of the main reasons for his addiction to alcohol, a habit that was shared by one of his male neighbors, who also had served in the Chushi Gangdrug army and then at the TCV school as a builder.

Pola told me that if he did not drink, he was not happy. The alcohol also made the pain bearable. "I forget about my illness," he said. His daughters did not want him to drink, but Pola found it impossible to give up drinking: "I drink thinking it is a blessing of Guru Rinpoche." For him, drinking alcohol did not contradict being a good Buddhist. Apart from thinking of the whiskey as a blessing, he also chanted mantra and went for circumambulation around the TCV monastery every morning.

The main thing that seemed to bother him in those days was the gossip in the camp area. He commented a few times that some of the old folks had big mouths and spread false rumors. The lack of money also worried him sometimes. He had enough to eat, but he worried about his monthly pocket money to buy whiskey, which was held back by his daughters. Otherwise, he expressed that he was content with life. After having served the Tibetan exile community for the better part of his life, he could finally spend his days sitting around, eating, drinking, and praying for death and rebirth. Old age was an accomplishment after all the hardships he and his fellow Tibetans faced during the first period in exile, a sentiment that was also shared by many elderly Tibetans I became acquainted with at the TCV old-age home and in McLeod Ganj. Even though Po Damchoe's birthplace of Medrogongkar in central Tibet would always be his first home, he also related to the TCV area as his home. He used to say, "This is where I am going to die. I have spent all my life here."

Memories of a Working Life

For Ani Tenzin Pema, who is ninety-one years old and a resident at the TCV old-age home, the TCV school area was also embedded with a specific history, shared with her generation of fellow Tibetans who lived at the home. When Anila escaped into exile in 1959, joined by one of her uncles, she was twenty-six years old. Like most of the first generation of Tibetans-in-exile, she spent the first years working in road construction. Anila built roads in the Kalimpong area in northeast India for two years. Her daily job consisted in carrying soil on her back and lifting large rocks with another woman, called Yangchen Dolkar. After road construction, Anila began working as a caregiver for Tibetan refugee children at a private school in Kalimpong in northeast India, led by a Rinpoche. Ani Tenzin could not recall the exact number of years she worked for the school but believed that it was close to twenty. Anila took leave from the school for a few years to help her niece with her children in Bylakuppe Tibetan settlement in southern India, before moving one last time to McLeod Ganj and starting work at the TCV school.

Ani Tenzin Pema is one of many elderly at the TCV old-age home who worked as caregivers of Tibetan children at the TCV school. Most Tibetan children in their working days were born in Tibet and sent into exile with others, or brought into exile by their parents, who, after enrolling them at the TCV school, returned to Tibet (like Tsering Jamphel in the opening of Chapter 1). Thus, most of these children grew up without their families. During the holidays, children with relatives would go and stay with them. Apart from the holidays, the children stayed at the school compound, where every child was allocated to a specific household (*khyimtsang*). There, the child was looked after by the household's *amala*, or "mother" (and *pala*, or "father," if the household was looked after by a couple). Anila was the sole *khyimtsang amala* of household number five for thirteen years.

The elderly women at the TCV old-age home, including Ani Tenzin Pema, shared that in their working days (from the early 1980s to the beginning of the twenty-first century), a single adult could have responsibility for forty to fifty children in a single home. During the thirteen years Anila worked for the school, she looked after fifty children. She kept a black-and-white photograph in which many of the children she looked after were included.

She recalled the hardships of taking care of so many children: how they were disobedient and how the stiff joints of her hands and bent fingers in old age were a result of washing dishes and the children's clothes in cold water. "I was a washing machine," Anila once commented jokingly.

The older children in the household had the responsibility of helping out, something that made the job more manageable for Anila and the other caregivers. In 2016, Anila had recalled the names of all the children in the photo, but when I asked about their names in 2023, she could no longer remember. Nonetheless, she still remembered their well-routinized days:

> I used to wake up at 4:00 in the morning, make offering at the
> shrine, and then wake up the children. The senior girls would help
> make the beds, wash the dishes, and help prepare the breakfast with
> me. We made two large kettles of tea. After breakfast, they would
> help clean the home, wash the dishes, and all. Then at 7:00, the

senior children would leave for class. Then, there used to be a break, and all the children would come back home to eat snacks, sometimes *tsampa* or fruits. To make *pag* [made from *tsampa*], we would put a little oil from that big tin we would get once a week, then some sugar, some hot tea, and then knead it. It was delicious.

Anila also recalled the challenges of living with children who had hit puberty:

I would go to bed at 9:00 [at night]. I didn't stay up long. Otherwise, it would be dangerous. It wasn't right for boys and girls to get intimate. I would tell them "please turn off the lights and sleep." But nothing unfortunate happened. A boy and girl in household four got intimate and the girl got pregnant. She had to leave the school. Such things happened. Another girl at the hostel got pregnant with her sister's husband. She was sent back to her home. So, I would go to bed at 9:00. I was fortunate that nothing of that sort happened in my household.

When Ani Tenzin turned sixty-two, she was allowed to retire. She had no savings at that point, as the salary from the TCV school had been incredibly low. However, her nieces had moved abroad and were able to cover her postretirement expenses. They still send her money, as Anila's pension of INR 4,000 from the TCV school is not sufficient to make ends meet. Nonetheless, Anila, too, said that old age was the happiest period of her life:

"There is no work. Nobody is scolding me from above. For food, we get some money from the [TCV] administration. On top of that, my nieces send me money. I get by. When I have much money, I offer butter lamps here and there, like when someone is going to Dorjeedhen [Bodhgaya] or somewhere else; I send with them money for offerings. When I have less money, I keep it. It's good. I am happy."

After retiring, Anila finally got the chance to travel to holy pilgrimage sites across India and Nepal and make offerings. Then, when she could no longer move around much, Anila stayed put at the old-age home, wandering around in its premises, chatting with her fellow elderly and taking care of birds she loved to feed. Anila worried about increasing old age and whether she would "become unable to feed" herself. Fortunately, she had several relatives living close by who regularly checked on her. She was also hopeful that

Figure 24: Memories: Ani Tenzin Pema holds a photograph of household number five at the Tibetan Children's Village school. Photo by Harmandeep K. Gill.

her lifelong service to the Tibetan community might have purified her negative karma so she would not have to end her days in sickness.

For Po Damchoe Ngawang and Ani Tenzin Pema, the TCV school area
was a home-in-exile because of all that it stood for, as suggested by Schütz.[13]
It was an area embedded with collective memories that Po Damchoe shared
with his fellow elderly neighbors; and Ani Tenzin, with the fellow residents
at the old-age home. Feeling at home in old age was for Po Damchoe hinged
to his whiskey bottle (earned after all the hardships in life), the acknowledgment letter from the CTA for his service in the Chushi Gangdrug, the presence of his supportive daughters, and his fellow elderly Tibetans, with whom
he built the school area and whom he had lived next to most of his life. Home
was also found with the young children of the TCV school, those well-trodden
paths between his home and the TCV school area, and the larger McLeod
Ganj, as it also was for Ani Tenzin. Everything in this space provided a dimension to themselves and an orientation to their lives.

Regional Kinship, Material Culture, and Embodied Practices

Like Po Damchoe, Mo Dickyi Sangmo also lived in a smaller village or unit
within the larger McLeod Ganj, where she shared a collective history with
her Tibetan neighbors. In her case, another layer of connection was added:
regional kinship.

Like the rest of McLeod Ganj, Kyirong Village is located up a hill
slope. Here, elderly Tibetans do not live in rented homes like the majority
of Tibetans do in McLeod Ganj and the Dharamsala area (e.g., Mo Tsering
Wangmo). They own their houses, despite not having ownership of the land,
and many built them with their own hands. Such was the case with the
house of Mo Dickyi's eldest sister, Samdrup Drolma, which was built by Mo
Samdrup's deceased husband.

Mo Dickyi's apartment—owned by her brother, Akhu Dhondrup—was
not a "home" for her in the same way that her elder sister Ani Jamyang Choedon's apartment was to her. Anila, who lived one floor above Mo Dickyi, had
resided in the building since she moved from the Hyolmo region in Nepal to
India more than forty years ago, whereas Mo Dickyi moved in just fourteen
years ago. The life Mo Dickyi shared with her deceased husband was tied to
another apartment in a different part of McLeod Ganj. Nevertheless, her

current apartment was home in the sense that it was the space she inhabited daily, surrounded by familiar objects, and it was a space she shared with one of her siblings. Moreover, she was also surrounded by Tibetans from her birthplace of Kyirong.

Mo Dickyi's small two-room apartment was filled with objects gathered throughout her life in India. It is rare that elderly Tibetans get rid of things that are too old or stop working. Consequently, things tend to gather, as they did in Po Damchoe's room.

Among Mo Dickyi's many cherished possessions were three thick and heavy blankets made of sheep's wool[14] and a few small carpets,[15] woven in India with her sisters, according to the Kyirong traditional techniques they learned when they were young. The kitchen was equipped with pots and pans bought in India and used over decades. There was also the colorful, Chinese-style thermos with red and yellow flowers. It was broken, but she refused to throw it away, just like the worn-out floor mat in the kitchen she bought with her "deceased one" (*drongkhen*, meaning her husband) at the Indian army market in the Forsyth Ganj area in McLeod Ganj.[16] She could recall the time in her life and the place various objects were made or purchased. Her shrine room, filled with the smell of incense like a monastery, had a collection of other highly valued and sacred possessions.

One of the peculiar features of the homes of many elderly Tibetans is the old-style Indian suitcases made of iron or metal. Mo Dickyi had three of them: the smallest was dark green and was placed beneath the television, and the remaining two rested next to the television, on another table. These were the suitcases she and her "deceased one" traveled with across India for business and pilgrimage.

Next to the television stood the Tibetan Buddhist *chökhang*, the other and most significant aspect of a Tibetan home. Mo Dickyi and all of her sisters had large wooden shrines in their homes. The shrine in Mo Dickyi's home was the size of a large cabinet. This was the most sacred aspect of her home, and of Tibetan homes in general.

The shrine contained many photographs (*kupar*) of the Dalai Lama and of the main temple in Bodhgaya,[17] as well as one photograph of the 10th Panchen Lama, Choekyi Gyaltsen, and one of the 17th Karmapa, Ogyen Trinley Dorje.[18] There were also two pictures of the "Kyirong Jowo Rinpoche," which people from Kyirong brought to India and today rests inside the Dalai Lama's residence.[19] There were six statues (*kundra*) in the shrine, bought over the years in a Tibetan shop in the Tibetan colony of Majnu ka Tilla in New

Delhi: one of Guru Rinpoche; two of Chenrezig; two of Chomden-de (the Buddha)—one large and one small; and one of Jetsun Drolma (Green Tara, an important female Bodhisattva).[20] There were two thick Tibetan Buddhist texts wrapped neatly in a yellow cloth. These were *brgyad stong pa* and *gzungs 'dus.*[21] Several pictures of the Dalai Lama were also spread around in the shrine room.

Two large *thangka* hung on one of the walls. One of them was a photograph of the Dalai Lama sitting on a throne with a ceremonial hat, and the other was a painting of Chenrezig surrounded by numerous deities. The *thangka* and *kundra* in Mo Dickyi's home had, in accordance with Tibetan Buddhist tradition, been consecrated (*rabne*) by a lama. This is a ritual whereby a statue is transformed into a *kundra*, meaning a holy body in which the deity comes to reside. This is also the case with scroll paintings of Buddhist deities and other religious imagery. Both *kundra* and *thangka* are used by advanced practitioners to visualize Buddhist deities during meditative practices. This was not the case for Mo Dickyi (or my other elderly friends), but they still embodied the deities for her and are a natural part of any elderly Tibetan's home.

The things in Mo Dickyi's apartment had been gathered throughout a lifetime and were connected to specific periods in her life. Moreover, her home was a cultural space to which the self was connected and inhabited the highest degree of familiarity, especially the handwoven blankets and carpets and the Tibetan Buddhist *chökhang*, which unlike other objects was considered to be sacred.[22]

For Mo Dickyi, "home" resided not only in objects but also in her daily embodied Buddhist practice of making water-bowl offerings, butter-lamp offerings (*chöme*), and incense offerings to the Buddhist deities at the shrine. "This is the custom among Tibetans," Mo Dickyi told me when describing the importance of making daily offerings at the shrine. Even after years of use, the water bowls (*ting*) in silver shone as if bought recently.

Mo Dickyi faithfully collected the water in a clean bucket before making the offerings at around 7:00 A.M. When she cleaned the shrine at around 3:00 P.M., she took as much time as necessary to properly clean and dry the silver bowls. Anything less would count as a negative or harmful (*digpa*) act for Mo Dickyi, as one could not offer the deities (at the shrine) water from an unclean bucket or unclean bowls.

Figure 25: *Chökhang* in Mo Samdrup's home. Photo by Harmandeep K. Gill.

Making offerings at the shrine was one of the most important Buddhist
practices she did on a daily basis. Practicing such embodied traditions was a
significant part of her being at home in her surroundings and with herself.

The shrine in Mo Tsering Wangmo's home was, by contrast, empty. It held
photos of holy lamas, but because Mo Tsering was unable to make water-bowl
offerings, the water bowls had been packed away. Her caregivers made one
large butter-lamp offering on a daily basis, and it was Mo Tsering who always attended to the careful job of braiding cotton wicks for the butter lamps.
Mo Tsering told me that not being able to make water-bowl offerings at the
shrine was a loss, and something that added to her experience of the body as
alienating and to the rift between body and mind in old age.

Apart from Mo Dickyi's apartment and her embodied routines, the specific area of McLeod Ganj in which she spent her days, known as Kyirong
Village, also made her feel more at home.

In a historical overview of Kyirong, Tibet, Geoff Childs states that Kyirong became a *zong* under the political rule of *Ganden Phodrang* in the latter half of the seventeenth century.[23] From the 1630s to the 1850s, Kyirong
was also laid claim to by the kingdoms based in the Gorkha region in Nepal
and in Kathmandu, in two destructive wars. Following the Chinese colonization of Tibet and the uprising in Lhasa in 1959, Kyirong was left relatively un-
scathed because of its remote location from Lhasa. But as Kyirong soon fell
under the direct control of the Chinese government, and with the onset of
the Cultural Revolution, a large percentage of the people in Kyirong chose to
escape into Nepal, as did Mo Dickyi Sangmo and her family members in
1963.[24] Kyirong Tibetans are today spread across the globe, but they maintain as Childs states, a strong sense of regional identity, as I have experienced
firsthand with Mo Dickyi, her sisters, and other Kyirong Tibetans.[25]

Since coming into exile, Tibetans have formed communities on the basis
of place of origin, such as Ü-Tsang, Amdo, or Kham. Prior to the colonization
of Tibet, Tibetans first and foremost identified with their local region, rather
than with a larger cultural or political Tibet, which, as many scholars have
argued, gained significance only after Tibetans were exiled.[26] In exile, a new
form of pan-national Tibetan identity that strengthened the nation building–
project came into existence, and in an attempt to unify Tibetans from the
three main regions of Tibet, alternative histories were silenced and confined
to the margins by the exiled Tibetan elite.[27] But this homogenous, nationalistic identity grew stronger only gradually, over several decades, so the first
Tibetans-in-exile found (and continue to find) more intimate ties among

those from their own region, who shared their local history, customs, and dialect.

The regional Kyirong dialect is distinct, and I could get quite lost when Mo Dickyi and Ani Jamyang used local words and phrases. Despite the CTA's attempts to promote homogenous identities, regional ties continue to provide an important form of belonging for Tibetans, regardless of age.[28] For the elderly Kyirong Tibetans, identification with fellow Kyirong-wa comes before their identification with Tibetans from other regions in Ü-Tsang.

Tibetans from different regions are organized through what is known as a *kyidug*: a type of welfare committee for local districts within the three big regions of Tibet, such as Kyirong and Töpa in Ü-Tsang, or Tsawa in Kham.[29] Whereas *kyi* means "happiness," *dug* means "suffering," so people from a particular *kyidug* can be understood to be like a family that is meant to stick together in both happiness and suffering. In Dharamsala and other Tibetan settlements, one finds numerous *kyidug*, such as those associated with Kyirong, Töpa, Lhoka, Markham, and Derge.[30] The existence of a *kyidug* depends on whether there are enough people from a particular place to establish one. The Kyirong and Töpa *kyidug* share a community house, located in close proximity to Mo Dickyi's and Anila's building. It is used for functions such as weddings, wedding parties, or prayers for the Dalai Lama's birthday. The *kyidug* has an official board that takes responsibility for organizing events or, when needed, gathering donations from its members. These days Kyirong community gatherings are rare, largely because the people who initiated them upon coming into exile are now old, and most of their children have either moved to other places in India, migrated to foreign countries, or are not interested.

Mo Samdrup and Mo Dickyi recalled that from the 1970s to the early 2000s, Kyirong Tibetans regularly gathered in each other's homes for drinking, prayer sessions, or simply gossip. Akhu Dhondrup shared that it was even customary for people to help each other with building their homes:

> In the old days, when we built houses—not solid houses, but *kacha* ["mud" (Hindi)] houses—everyone would come and help. Men. Women. Everyone would help. One would serve them meals. There was no need to pay a salary. A house would be built in three or four days. Some would do the masonry work, some the wood work. And two meals, lunch and dinner, would be served to all. . . . It was a very happy time. There was no jealousy of one another. Everyone

was ready to help each other out. Now everyone has become old. Things have also changed a lot over the years. The custom of visiting each other's homes is practiced less and less.

Akhu Dhondrup's sentiments were shared by Mo Dickyi: "When we were together (in the old days), we talked a lot about the old days in Tibet. Those were happy times." Mo Dickyi and her sisters had also served in the Tibetan Women's Association for several years, organizing protests, fundraising, and volunteering for other community services together with women from Kyirong and other Tibetan regions.

Consequently, when Mo Dickyi looked out the window, she saw a miniature cultural expansion of the original Kyirong region in Tibet. The area was inhabited by significant Tibetan others, who were an expansion of her own kin. Mo Dickyi told me that she could not imagine living in another part of McLeod Ganj all by herself, despite the fact that most of the areas in McLeod Ganj are inhabited by Tibetans. When I asked her why, she said that she liked living in Kyirong Village because the people there were from her native region. The people, primarily those of her own generation, were familiar with the Kyirong dialect, the Kyirong-wa traditions, and their escape from Kyirong into Nepal, and they had had ties with one another since the start of exile.[31]

When Mo Dickyi saw a particular face out on a rooftop of Kyirong Village, or a particular house, that person and that specific house were a material link to her distant past, calling forth embodied memories. She had an extensive knowledge of the family tree of all the Kyirong-wa in town, as well as whom the children of a particular family had married and where they were staying in the present day. Moreover, she was also familiar with the various types of gossip about different families and the good and bad qualities of people. Similarly, there was also gossip about Mo Dickyi in Töpa and Kyirong Village. Having lived in town for a decade, I have not been spared either.

When Mo Dickyi spoke about a family in the village, I struggled to keep up with the intricate web of relations. She would start off by mentioning a particular elderly couple (e.g., whether one of them had passed away) then go on to speak about their children (e.g., where and whom they have married), before mentioning various in-laws and how they, in rare cases, might be related to Mo Dickyi's distant family members.

When someone passes away in Kyirong Village, the fellow Kyirong Tibetans have an obligation to contribute offerings of money and their own attendance during the forty-nine days of death rituals. Once Mo Dickyi sent me off with money offerings for the deceased Ama Lhadron, because it would be too difficult for her to walk there herself. She stood on the balcony and watched me walk into the deceased's house. From there, she could even see me step into the family's shrine room on the top floor to give the offerings. When one day Mo Dickyi will no longer be in this world, she can rest assured that her fellow Kyirong Tibetans will do the same for her in return.

As Mo Dickyi's story reveals, the home-in-exile is a space of belonging that has been created in the image of the first home in Tibet. It was cultivated through material objects, through traditional, embodied practices, and through community ties. Home was a space that embodied traces of her lived life. For Mo Dickyi, Ani Tenzin, and Po Damchoe, home was a Tibetan social, cultural, and political space to which the self was hinged.

To be home was to be surrounded by a moral community of Tibetan others, both old and young, who shared the collective memories of the colonization of Tibet and the social and political ramifications of being an exile.

Thus, it is not simply the case that Tibetans in India do not feel at home. Elderly Tibetans often refer to India as a second home after Tibet. Their movements across India and their making a livelihood there—for example, going on pilgrimage, building roads or settlements from scratch, serving in the Indian military, or making a living from the seasonal winter business—have also defined them as persons. Moreover, unlike the younger generations of Tibetans, the first generation of Tibetans-in-exile tilled the Indian soil and even built their homes on it, making them emotionally invested in the places they inhabit.[32] But ultimately, for the elderly Tibetans, home is embedded in a moral community of Tibetan others who provide kinship ties along national lines, as argued by Dawa Lokyitsang.[33]

Historical Continuations and Reimaginations

McLeod Ganj differs from other official Tibetan settlements in several ways, but Kyirong Village, the TCV camp, and the larger McLeod Ganj area can nonetheless (at least to a certain extent) be approached as "cultural villages."[34] These spaces are where Tibet is anchored in exile—socially, culturally, politically, and linguistically. As "cultural villages," these places are also regarded as appropriate places to age and die.

Namgyal Choedup writes that in Doeguling Settlement in southern India, ties with one's neighbors and the larger community present a form of social security in the absence of children.[35] Moreover, one can rest assured that the community will take care of funerary practices in the absence of children, which is a reassurance that the elderly in Kyirong Village and at the TCV camp also have. Tibetans here come together to help each other— for example, in the organization of special prayers, weddings, or death rituals.

Community networks are present in Kyirong Village but are not as strong or well organized as in the official, closed-off settlements in other places in India. The Kyirong *kyidu*g is not responsible for checking on the elderly Tibetans and offering them assistance, which is the case in some other Tibetan settlements.[36] This is primarily because most of the people in Kyirong Village are old themselves, including some of the board members.

The Tibetan settlements across India, and smaller localities within McLeod Ganj, such as the TCV school area or Kyirong Village, and regional forms of organization such as *kyidug*, secure historical continuities with a past in Tibet that has been reimagined in exile. Hence, Tibet is the point of reference in the meanings of home among the elderly and the later generations of Tibetans.[37] The Tibetan settlements echo nostalgia for the first home. Thus, as Thomas S. Eliot writes, "home is where one starts from," but it is also a place where one wishes to die.[38] Both statements certainly ring true among the elderly generation of Tibetans.

The paradoxical thing about the settlements in exile is that they are simultaneously home and not home. They echo Tibet, but Tibet remains absent, leaving exiles in a continuous in-between state. Furthermore, the fact that the land in the agricultural settlements across India and in the settlements in northern India is given to the Tibetans on lease adds to the feeling of being a foreigner in India.

Most of the Tibetan homes in Kyriong Village, in Töpa Village, and on Bhagsu Road are also categorized as illegal property, because they were built when Tibetans were not authorized to cut down trees and built houses. However, authorization was not needed, because laws to protect the forest were only introduced later. In 2013, things took a turn for the worse. The Shimla High Court made cases against all of the Tibetan homeowners, including some Indian restaurant owners, for illegally occupying government property. Their property came under threat of demolition, and all of the inhabitants were ordered to leave their homes. The homeowners' repeated appeals to the Forest Department and attempts to fight the order through a lawyer did not lead anywhere. As a last resort, they reached out to the CTA, which appealed to the central government in Delhi, and Tibetans were finally granted the right to continue living on the land, until Tibet is a free country.

To date, most of the Tibetan homes in Kyirong Village and Töpa Village have a case number painted on the main door or one of the house walls, which is synonymous with their case number in the Shimla High Court. The existing laws have not stopped Tibetans in the area from upgrading and expanding their homes, by replacing their mud houses with brick homes or by adding additional floors to their houses. Still, permission has to be sought from the right people, accompanied by the payment of a large enough bribe.

Occupying land that they do not own does make Tibetans feel like foreigners in India, despite having been born there or having made a livelihood on and from this land for decades. The current outflux of Tibetan youths also unsettles elderly Tibetans' feeling of being at home in exile. The absence of younger Tibetans is felt much more strongly in closed-off settlements in southern India. The elderly there comment that the settlements are becoming empty, and there are often no young people to harvest the huge areas of land. McLeod Ganj, too, has become increasingly unrecognizable for the elderly over the years, because of rapid development and increased tourism. The younger generation of Tibetans are not as traditionally minded as the older generations; and the younger generations who were born in exile, and those who were born in Tibet and later escaped into exile, are not "Tibetan" in the same way the older ones are. The home-in-exile is no longer what it once was. In old age, one's home seems to be constantly slipping away in memory, imagination, and the concretely real. Recollections of the past in India, and in particular in Tibet, seem to be one of the main stable factors in the everyday lives of my elderly friends. Those recollections live side by side with the present and the materially real, like a parallel possible life.

The First Home in Tibet

Since escaping into exile in 1959, Tibetans have been driven by the hope of returning to Tibet. Their struggle for Tibet's freedom is ongoing. TCV children are from the onset told that they are not at home and that one day they will return to Tibet.[39] Filmmaker Tenzing Sonam articulates in his and Ritu Sarin's documentary film, *The Sun Behind the Clouds: Tibet's Struggle for Freedom* that the hope of return provided a purpose to Tibetans' life in exile: "All of us who grew up in exile were brought up with a hope that one

day we will return to a free Tibet. That was the goal of our struggle, and justification for our lives as exiles."[40] This hope has seriously weakened over the
past decade.[41]

"Our house seems to have grown roots. The fences have grown into a jungle, now how can I tell my children where we came from?" writes poet and
activist Tenzin Tsundue on the "exile house" that was supposed to be a temporary stop.[42] Longing to reunite with one's homeland, family members, and
a life that used to be was a sentiment that was present in all of my elderly
friends and other elderly Tibetans I have become acquainted with in
Dharamsala and other settlements in India and Nepal.[43] Being uprooted from
their birthplace and forced into exile is also a traumatic event that continues
to shape the lives of most Tibetans-in-exile, even those who were born in exile. As I have experienced not only with my elderly friends but through
many years of living in the Tibetan community and interacting with both
old and young, the loss of Tibet is at the core of people's being. The presence
of the absent roams within, as described by poet Tsering Wangmo Dhompa
in speaking about her own mother:

> I realized early that despite her gregarious and inherently buoyant
> disposition, a certain sadness resided in my mother. Even I, her only
> child, whom she loved more than anything in the world, could do
> little to soothe the sorrow that had taken root within the separation
> from her parents, her two sisters and her brother. The contrast in
> the life of my mother experienced before and after leaving Tibet was
> so extreme, it must have been impossible for her to make sense of
> her life and to escape the inexhaustible longing for the past. Caring
> for me on her own, inside crowded rooms of tenement buildings in
> towns and cities, she must have felt she had dreamt of her past or
> that she was dreaming her present existence. The places and
> residences we lived in were never quite home to her and led her to
> cling, more tenaciously to the past.[44]

As Tsering Dhompa powerfully captures, separation from family members and displacement caused by the colonization of Tibet and the coming
into exile leaves ineradicable marks on selfhood, life narratives, and envisioned futures. Moreover, these marks and their accompanying griefs and
hopes are passed from one generation to the next, from parents to children,
from mothers to daughters, as writer Tsering Yangzom Lama tenderly brings

Figure 26: A home-in-exile: Mo Samdrup's bedroom. Photo by Harmandeep K. Gill.

to life in her novel *We Measure the Earth with Our Bodies*. "Do you miss that land which made your body? Do you speak of it to anyone who will listen? Or do you also find—like so many I know—that this is a loss too big to speak aloud?," expresses the character of Dolma, a second-generation exiled Tibetan when she comes face to face with the Nameless Saint, a statue from her ancestral Tibetan village that has been missing for decades.[45]

Like the Nameless Saint (who from a Tibetan's perspective is not a statue, but a living body) and Tsering Dhompa's mother, my elderly friends witnessed the invasion of Tibet. They had a firsthand experience of being torn away from their homes and families, making the treacherous journey across the Himalayas on foot, and being forced to start anew.[46] It is perhaps appropriate to say that over time the grief was, in Tsering Yangzom Lama's words, tucked within the silences of one's mind, nonetheless, still making itself apparent in the nostalgia for the absent.[47] With the prospect of death, the homesickness for Tibet was heightened for many. As the Tibetan saying goes, "When a person becomes old, they miss their home. When a bird becomes old, it misses its nest."

Even though Mo Samdrup's memory of the recent past was declining by the day, and she would repeat the same things during each visit, her memory of Kyirong was rather sharp. She could recount in detail various incidents, such as the time a monk and a nun engaged in a love affair and were exposed to public humiliation and then banished from the village. She also clearly recalled how she and the man who would become her husband escaped from Kyirong, after a family from another village had asked for her hand in marriage.[48] When I asked Mo Samdrup about her clearest recollection in life, she responded in one word, "Kyirong," without the need to think. I realized that her desire to reunite with her first home was strong, and the same was true for my other elderly friends.

In the following, I attempt to put into words the presence of this desire with Mo Dickyi Sangmo and Gen Lobsang Choedak, through recollections of their lives in Tibet. Even though the wish to return to Tibet was present in all my elderly friends, I learned that those who were aging in the absence of love from family members, as Mo Dickyi and Gen Lobsang were, had a stronger yearning for the past in Tibet than certain others, like Po Damchoe, who was surrounded by his daughters and grandchildren.

In the absence of loving companionship, Mo Dickyi's past in Tibet was like an intimate other, her very own, that provided solace in her everyday life:

I can see everything. . . . I can see the paths. *Tsampa* was so good. Milk and milk products were so good. Good butter. And the place is such a happy one. Our land was like this, full of forest [she stretched her arms across the air]. . . . Our village monastery is like this, if we live in Forsyth Ganj [where she used to live], then our village monastery is where the TCV school is. It is that much distance [between the village and monastery]. To reach the monastery, there was a steep climb upwards. In the monastery, the food was in abundance, but the monks couldn't eat eggs and meat. They could drink milk and curd. The monastery was so pure and good. Tsechokling Monastery [in Lhasa] and our monastery had connection. The monks of Tsechokling could eat and drink at our monastery. The monks of ours could eat and drink at Tsechokling.

For Mo Dickyi, the landscape, the village, and the monastery constantly flashed before her eyes. She would share about the animals or the work they undertook, which like the food was in abundance. Mo Dickyi's reminiscences of Kyirong were usually followed by a clicking of the tongue, expressing the tragic loss that followed the Chinese colonization of their homeland and their escape into exile. The elderly Tibetans describe that period as a time when "the sky and earth turned upside down." Thus, when Mo Dickyi described her homeland, it was not merely a straightforward description of the landscape or people. Her voice carried a longing and sadness for that part of her life, but her words would be more vibrant and colorful than usual. As she spoke, it was as though the words lifted her voice, transporting her right into that image in front of her eyes, as near as if she were walking through the paths in their village and up to the monastery. It was as though she could vividly recall the taste of the delicious butter and the sweet milk of Tibet, or were standing next to the *zomo* or the sheep. Left without words at these moments, she would exclaim "*Ama!*" or, with compassion, refer to the animals as *nyingje*.[49] When they escaped from Kyirong, they took the animals with them but were forced to leave them behind at the Nepalese border with a family friend. "Tears come to my eyes when I think of our animals," Mo Dickyi would say.

A few times when I asked her to imagine the hypothetical scenario of her returning to Kyirong, her face would give away to a dreamy smile, revealing the undying hope that she and other exiled Tibetans have nurtured since 1959.

When reality dawned on her, she would list all the obstacles that made it impossible, starting with her painful knees. In response, I would tell her that she could travel by airplane, and before she managed to list other obstacles, such as Tibet's still being a colonized country, I would insist: "But what if you could go?" "If I could return, I would go, of course!" she would say without hesitation.

Above all, reminiscences of the past seemed to be filled with hope and possibilities for the land she was seeing, as captured by Tsering Dhompa upon visiting Tibet: "This land makes me believe anything is possible. Here lies a gift unravelled as was meant to be: within its many folds are men, beasts, insects and grass. The green goes on and on in relentless beauty. As I look at the land, I am heartbroken thinking of the future when I will not be here and when this place, too, will be something else."[50]

Life, Mo Dickyi imagined, could thus have been otherwise, yet she was also aware of the impossibility of that other life. Mo Dickyi was at her happiest when she spoke of Kyirong. Without doubt, she was at home there and her life complete. Whereas she gave the impression of being stuck in the present—with the bad weather, the food, her body, or her room—her reminiscences of the past in Kyirong were the stark opposite: there, everything lay open, possible, "a gift unravelled as was meant to be." But eventually Mo Dickyi had to return to the present, back to the kitchen, where she sat lonely in front of the window and looked out at that which was left of the original Kyirong. While Kyirong Village was a link to the past in Tibet, it was also only a fragment left behind of the real Kyirong from another time. When the elderly Tibetans in Kyirong Village pass away, as several did in 2018, and new faces settled down in the village, it added to that vanishing part of life.

"It Is No More"

Like Mo Dickyi and Mo Samdrup, Gen Lobsang Choedak spoke fondly of his childhood days in Penpo (his birthplace) and his adult years at Ganden Monastery outside of Lhasa. Gen Lobsang did not feel quite at home in old age. While some of the other elderly related to the TCV school as their home, because they had spent most of their lives there, Genla did not speak of the TCV school in a similarly intimate tone. Neither did he share strong bonds with the other residents at the TCV old-age home. This was in part because, unlike most of them, Genla had not worked for the TCV school as a care-giver of Tibetan children. But still, Genla did know a few of them.

Genla worked for the TCV school in the school kitchen, where he made bread for the students and staff. He clearly remembered that he arrived at the school on 9 July 1982 (a few days after the Dalai Lama's birthday, on 6 July), eight years after Po Damchoe. Looking back, Genla said that his life at the school had not been easy: "It has been a happy life. Some of the happiest days were when I was in the [Indian] military. There was not much to think about. The government provided us with food, shelter, clothing, and sal-ary. There was nothing to worry about. Whatever work one was capable of doing, one could do. . . . At TCV, it was difficult. After leaving the military, work became harder. There were more worries and sufferings of the mind."

He found the workload at the TCV school to be particularly toilsome. The work in the school kitchen required him to get up as early as 2:00 A.M. At the time, they only had brick ovens, described by him as the size of his room. The oven had a small opening through which they placed wood and lit the fire. It was a demanding task to place the heavy pieces of wood through the small opening. The heat from the large oven while they made the bread was also overwhelming. After the hundreds of loaves of bread had been pre-pared and distributed among the staff and children, the heavy work for the next day began: the preparation of dough. Genla said, "In those days we did not have machines and had to do it with our own hands." He only had Sun-days off.

He worked in the kitchen for thirteen years. In early 1995, he slipped on the ice during winter and broke his left hip. Genla was hospitalized in Kangra for three months, after which he could no longer work for the school. The school administration offered him a small room outside the school com-pound. He lived there by himself with no one to provide care. Being a monk, he never married or had children.

Despite his broken left hip, Genla was nevertheless in much better physi-cal shape than my other elderly friends. He also had a sharp mind and kept well-structured days. Nonetheless, I sensed in his words a sadness about his present life. He had worked hard and served the Tibetan community for decades, but in the last phase of his life, there was no one to offer him loving support. The accident in 1995 had also unsettled his everyday life, leading to fears about the future, such as the fear of a bedridden old age.

Whereas Po Damchoe's family history was tied to TCV, Genla lacked stable significant others who could provide a sense of being at home. In contrast, his military days in India and especially his past in Tibet were filled with a sense of belonging and connection to his surroundings. Then he was also in perfect health, independent, and the world lay open to endless possibilities.

Genla repeatedly told me that he missed Tibet a lot: "I can see the face of my mother and father. I can see our place." Genla has five siblings, all younger than him. Three of the siblings lived in Tibet, while the youngest two, who had a different mother, lived in Belgium. Genla did not have any contact with them and could no longer recall the name of the two youngest siblings. Being the eldest child, his parents, who were villagers, sent him off to work for a nomad in the Penpo area when he was about twelve years old. Genla said that he recalled those days in his heart.

After those years, Genla, along with his younger brother, was ordained as a monk at Ganden Monastery. At the age of ninety-five, he recalled this as the happiest period of his life, including the times he attended *jang günchö* ("winter debate/ritual") with his fellow monks in Jang, a region to the south-west of Lhasa.

More than his homeland of Penpo, it was Lhasa that Genla missed the most. A distinct joy would fill his face when he spoke about Lhasa, and sad-ness would overcome me when he seemed to be shaking off those memories with a smile. Throwing his hand backward in the air, he would say, "It is no more. I am going to die."

Sometimes, I showed him photographs of the present-day Lhasa, of the Barkhor area surrounding the Jokhang temple, Potala Palace, or Norbulingka (the summer palace of the Dalai Lamas), in a naive effort to bring him closer to Lhasa. But Lhasa has changed drastically since he used to wander there, and unless the pictures were of significant historical and religious sites, he could not recognize them. This, too, was a form of grief.

In his mind, he navigated the streets of Lhasa from another time, just like Mo Dickyi walked through the paths of their village in Kyirong. Genla was thirty years old during the Tibetan uprising in Lhasa in 1959. At the time of his escape, the Chinese army had yet to reach Ganden Monastery: "Lhasa was lost, but the Chinese had not entered Ganden. But later they came. A lot of monks started escaping. And I, with a party of four left some time after. . . . We left Ganden and crossed the passes by walking in 1959. . . . We left Gan-den on the 14th of the 2nd month, around afternoon. We crossed the pass at night. We reached the Chushi Gangdrug army post. It [the post] was one day and one night's walk [from Ganden]." He further expressed, "It was full of sadness. We lost our country/homeland (*lungpa*), and in a foreign country/

land (*mi lungpa*), there was not much one could do. It was difficult to make a livelihood."

Genla arrived in India in Tawang, which today is in the state of Arunachal Pradesh. They stayed there for one week before they were sent to Bomdila (also in Arunachal Pradesh) and then to the state of Assam in northeastern India. He recalled that the weather there was quite warm, something that was a new and uncomfortable experience for people from "the roof of the world." He shared:

> We went to work in Assam and then to build roads in Bomdila. We didn't get any salary there. Then we returned to Missamari in Assam. All the people came there. Many bamboo huts were built there by the Indians. Many *gyashog* [group of hundred] stayed there. One hundred, two hundred, three hundred, and four hundred people were there. We had to stay there for a long time. People stayed here for about two to three months. Then, batch by batch, people were sent off to different places in northern India. We were in the last of batches. . . . Monks and nuns were sent to Buxa. Others were sent off to Gangtok, Kalimpong, and many different places. We were sent at last. We were sent to Chamba. Once again to work as road builders. We worked there for a whole summer. There were four *gyashog*. Most of the able and fit men left to join army in Dehradun. Some of us were left and most of the fit ones left to join the army. I had no company when at Chamba.

After building roads in Chamba (which today falls under the state of Himachal Pradesh) for a summer, Genla traveled to Mussoorie in the state of Uttarakhand to build roads. He heard that the salary was better there: "So, one day I packed my things and took a car to Pathankot and then took a train till Dehradun and then went to Mussoorie. After working there for a few years, I left."

Genla left Mussoorie for Chakrata in Dehradun to join the Indian military. The Tibetan men served under "Establishment 22," formed in 1962 after the Sino-Indian War. It was later known as the Special Frontier Force and had its base in Chakrata. As Carole McGranahan states, Establishment 22 was formed to regain Tibet's independence.[51] Unlike the Chushi Gangdrug operations in Mustang, where Po Damchoe fought (which were ongoing when Establishment 22 was created), the Special Frontier Force was a

joint Indian-Tibetan operation.[52] Like most Tibetan men, Genla enthusias-
tically joined hoping to fight the PLA. That did not happen, but the Tibetan
men fought in other Indian military operations, including in the Bangladeshi
war. Genla served at the Special Frontier Force headquarters in Chakrata and
was also stationed in Assam and in Ladakh. When he was allowed to retire in
1982, he had served the Indian military for eighteen years. By that time, he
had, like many Tibetans, settled into a life in exile, but the hope of return,
however dim, lingered through and through.

Old age for Genla was a sort of "falling out" of the world and an ongoing
disorientation.[53] When he escaped from Tibet in 1959, he never thought that
he would never return home or that he would spend his life searching for it.
In old age, he did not feel at home with himself. Genla said that old age had
reduced him to half of a person: "When one is young, one has the essence of
a full person." Not only were his past in Tibet and military days in India
marked by an absence, but the person he used to be was also absent, increasing in Genla's words, the "worries and sufferings of the mind."

In the context of old age, how can we understand my elderly friends' repeated reminiscences of a different way of life? Did these perhaps help them
to ground themselves while enduring the in-between-ness of the mountain
pass, fraught by uncertainty? Are the imaginations of home (Tibet) in an exile context a vessel of hope, pulling people toward a time-space where they
can begin anew?

Home: A Time-Space of Heartsickness, Hope, and Uncanniness

"We won't see our *phayül*. What can one do? . . . When I think about it, my
mind feels relaxed. . . . My mind is [also] saddened. It's our homeland. It's sacred, right." These sentiments expressed by Mo Dickyi were shared by my
other elderly friends. Their *phayül* was a space that provided comfort and
peace, as a sense of "home" does for most people, but it was simultaneously
a space associated with loss. It was sacred to them, inhabited by Buddhist deities and spirits. In exile, Tibet is the image of hope itself, while also evoking
grief and loss.

For some, like Mo Tsering Wangmo and Gen Lobsang Choedak, the
Chinese colonization separated whole families. As "the sky and earth turned
upside down," so did the moral order of their universe. As a community and

as individuals, they have striven through the Tibetan freedom struggle to reverse that order in Tibet for sixty-five years, and to preserve it in the exile communities.

Tibet—as memories, imaginations, or possibilities—has been for many exiles what Bernard Williams terms a "ground project"—defining people's activities, values, and aspirations in life.[54] For Williams, ground projects are types of commitments that are so fundamental to identity that without them, people would feel lost.[55] In the absence of children and family, the imaginations of home as a certain way of inhabiting the world grounded my elderly friends in the disorientation of old age, materialized through a changing body and the changes in the community around them. Moreover, these imaginations of Tibet were "constitutive of embodied being and understanding" of who they were and where they came from.[56]

Despite the tragedy of never reuniting with their homeland, my elderly friends found joy and comfort in their recollections of the past. Mo Dickyi said that her mind calmed down when thinking about their life in Kyirong: "I miss it. It's one's own land, you see. I miss it a lot. It's a good land, you see." Genla had a tender smile when he said that his real home was Tibet. For Mo Samdrup, Kyirong used to be the preferred topic of conversation, and all her thoughts were constantly circling around her childhood and adulthood in Kyirong. Having been confined to her home for years and being out of touch with the world outside her four walls, it was as though she lived only in the past, as though there was no present, except the future of death. Recollections of the past in Tibet, and also of certain periods in exile, here exemplified by the remembrances of Po Damchoe, Ani Tenzin, Mo Dickyi, and Gen Lobsang, opened up a space where they also felt more at home with themselves.

Andrew Irving argues that in carrying out an ethnography of the lives of others, we also need to attend to the many possible lives they could have lived.[57] For Irving, the idea of life as an unfinished, ontogenetic process implies that the events of one's life are repeatedly reimagined, relived, and retold to interpret and reshape experience.[58] This also troubles our assumed borders between the real and the imagined. Likewise, for my elderly friends, the past, in contrast to the present, was a time-space where life remained "unfinished." It was reshaped, enacted, and entailed "manifold ways of living a life rather than just one."[59]

In the context of exile and in old age, the imagined home was located in a certain landscape of the past (and even in a possible future) with a certain

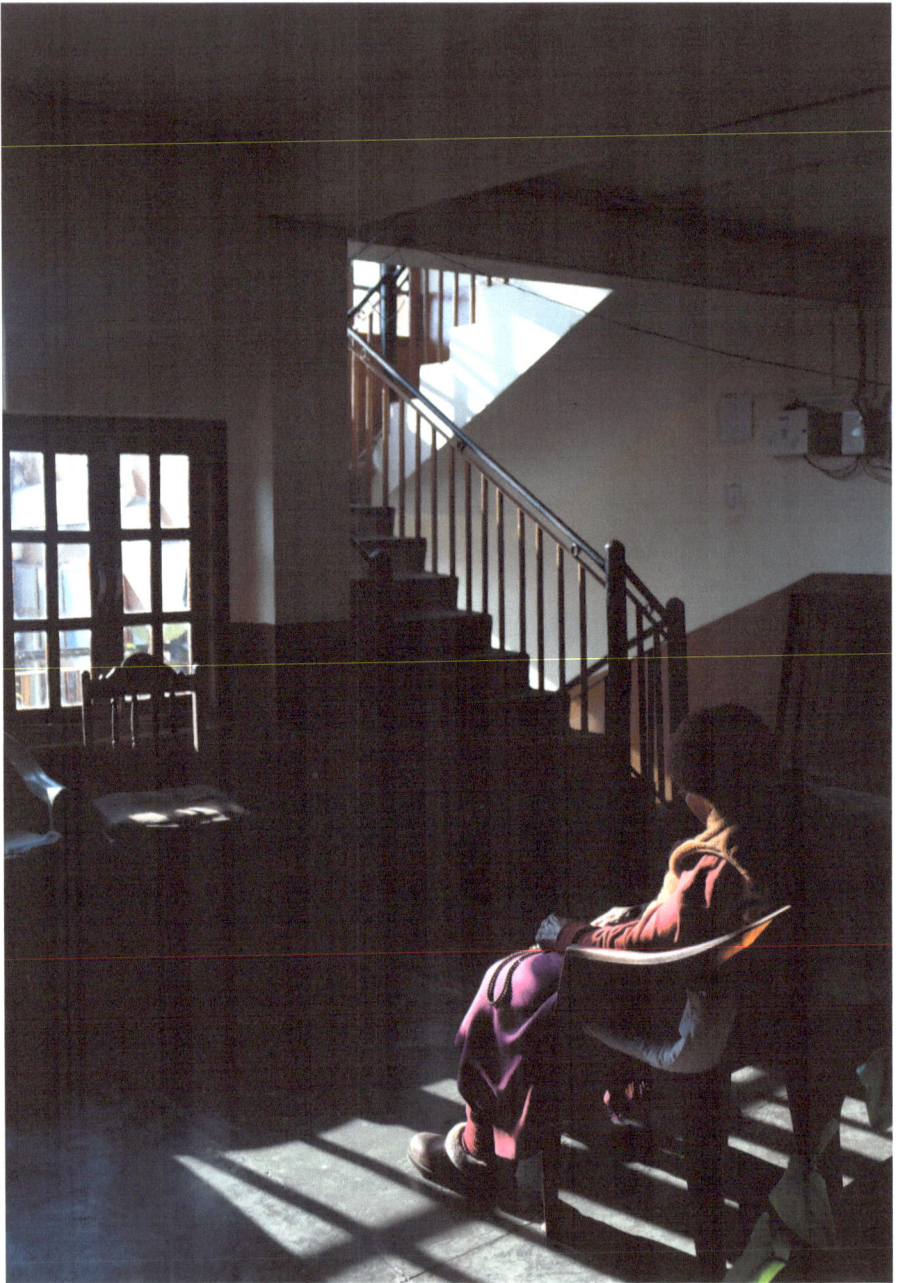

Figure 27: Ani Tenzin Pema at the Tibetan Children's Village old-age home. Photo by Harmandeep K. Gill.

moral order and was, I suggest, an important part of people's embodied being and understanding of who they were. Irving writes that people's expressions of precariousness and possibilities are embodied as questions: "Who
am I?" "What should I do?" "What's going on?" Or, simply, "Why?" In his
book on people diagnosed with HIV and AIDS in New York City, these
questions are raised in relation to the uncertainty and disruption caused
by a terminal illness. He suggests that people's taken-for-granted beliefs
and practices are brought into question and that the questions are raised not
only in search of answers but as "a pragmatic strategy for opening up a
dialogue, seeking solace, or creating stability in a context of misfortune
and uncertainty."[60]

My elderly friends found themselves facing a similar uncertainty about
the future. In the ongoing disorientation caused by old age, who was Genla
now that he did not have the essence of a full person? After all the hardships
in life, why was there no one on the other end to support and help him in old
age? Similarly, for Mo Dickyi, what happened to those strong family bonds
that were practiced in Tibet? I propose that these questions opened up a dialogue with the past in India and especially in Tibet, which provided hope in
the face of impermanence and solitude of old age. The hope I refer to was not
an optimistic hope about the concretely possible. In Jason Danely's words, it
was about reshaping loss into "moments of connection."[61] Here the world was
inhabited differently, and the elderly were more at home with themselves.
Based on her recollections, Mo Dickyi could imagine the climb up to the village monastery with heavy goods on her back. She could milk the *zomo* or
imagine seeing the thousands of sheep and goats she once witnessed in the
Changtang area when visiting relatives. Thus, home was a time-space where
life was yet not settled and inhabited many possible immediate or distant
futures, in contrast to the present, where the body was closing itself off and
the days seemed stuck in the same circle of routines and solitude, running
toward finitude. To return to Tsering Dhompa's words, the past, especially
in Tibet, "made them believe that anything is possible."

In waiting for death at the mountain pass, home was a space of hope one
could lean into and momentarily be in touch with and hold on to oneself in
a life that used to be and could have been otherwise. The everyday life of my
elderly friends was this coalescence of the concretely real, the imagined, and
the possible, embedded too with realizations of the lost and the impossible.

Furthermore, their *phayül* also gave them a kind of freedom that was
found to be absent in India. Both Gen Lobsang and Mo Dickyi emphasized

that, in contrast to their lives in India, in Tibet they did not have many worries. They lived self-sufficient lives. Reflecting on his younger days in Penpo
and at Ganden Monastery, Genla said, "It was a happy life. It's one's own land,
own house, place to stay. There was no worry. No worries about clothes, or
other things. No worry." His family was also close by, he said another time.

Ani Tenzin Pema also missed her family: "Of course, I miss my family. I
stayed home with my mother until I was twenty-six years old, helping her in
the house and the fields." The nunnery Anila was enrolled at in young age
was not wealthy, and because food was scarce there, she moved back in with
her family but did not disrobe.

Despite referring to India as their second home, my elderly friends nevertheless emphasized that this land was not truly theirs. This was repeated
to me several times by Po Damchoe: "We do not even own a handful of land."
Like Mo Dickyi and Genla, he too missed his life in Tibet. He even longed
for his days of monkhood, recalling that he had received a lot of beatings from
his scripture master because he had failed to memorize the scriptures. In
fact, he ran away several times: "I faced lots of problems living in the monastery. I never had a single *anna* in my pocket."[62] Pola certainly did not miss
the beatings, but he longed for his life as a monk at the Potala Palace in
Lhasa: "I often dream of Tibet. Dreams of being at home and at the Potala. I
stayed at Potala for six years as a monk. As a monk you have to serve at Potala
for three years, and for three years I did paid work. After that I stayed at the
Jokhang for three years. And after that, I lived at Drepung Monastery until
1959." For those aging in the absence of family, like Gen Lobsang or Mo
Dickyi, the past can be understood like an intimate other, an important
source of grounding while finding oneself in-between life and death. The
past also provided grounding and hope for Po Damchoe, who dearly missed
his beloved wife.

For Gen Lobsang and Mo Dickyi, recollections of the past opened up a
dimension of themselves and provided an orientation to their lives. As I described in Chapter 2, Mo Dickyi did not quite feel at home with herself. She
was accompanied by not only an aging body but also an altered physical appearance, which was alienating to a certain extent. Genla also expressed
that he was more like himself when he was young, when he had physical
strength and a sharp mind. He gave the impression of being left to himself,
as if forgotten by others. What I sensed particularly with Genla was a lack of
recognition for his many years of hard work for the TCV school. He said that
while people who have connections at the old-age home (people with a

certain status) were looked after until their death, others (of lower status) with no special connections to the TCV administration, by which he was in-directly referring to himself, were neglected: "Those with some reputation receive special care. But for the poor, they don't get looked after much. I wonder how it's going to be for me."

Home for my elderly friends was a time-space of the highest degree of fa-miliarity and intimacy and seemed to be located in Tibet and also certain parts of their lives in India, with a younger and different version of them-selves. The body was back then not experienced as something erratic, like it was in the present, when the condition of their knees or any other body parts could worsen any day. There was a lack of familiarity, as well as intimacy, with one's own body in old age.

In light of this, the starting point of being at home is perhaps intercon-nected with feeling at home with oneself, something that also remains hinged to the presence and loving support of significant others. Hence, home in old age emerged as a deep longing to belong, to oneself and one's surroundings.[63]

Encounters with the home in the past also added to the ongoing disori-entation in the present. There was something uncanny about the memories and imaginations of home; they called out to my elderly friends but were un-reachable. More and more Tibetans from their generation had passed away, and Tibet-in-exile was not what it once was.

As a result, memories that were anchored to specific people and a land-scape of the past were slipping away, disintegrating, in some cases because of a failing memory. The elderly were also forced to let go of the hope of returning to Tibet that had been woven into their existence in exile. That hope will not materialize in their lifetimes.

The home that my elderly friends longed for was not in the present-day Tibet. They were aware of the political realities on the Tibetan plateau. Mo Dickyi always informed me about the weekly Tibetan news she had watched on television and what the "bad Chinese" had been up to.

She did not wish to return to the present day Kyirong: "Our houses are there no more. The valley must be completely changed." Her home is a colo-nized territory. What she wished to return to, like her fellow Tibetans, was a land free from the Chinese colonization. Moreover, she yearned to reunite with the Tibet from another time, to return to a village with a certain way of life. Like Gen Lobsang, she longed for the life and the person she used to be, surrounded by significant others, and for a time with no major troubles and the freedom of her own homeland, inhabited by her forefathers and local

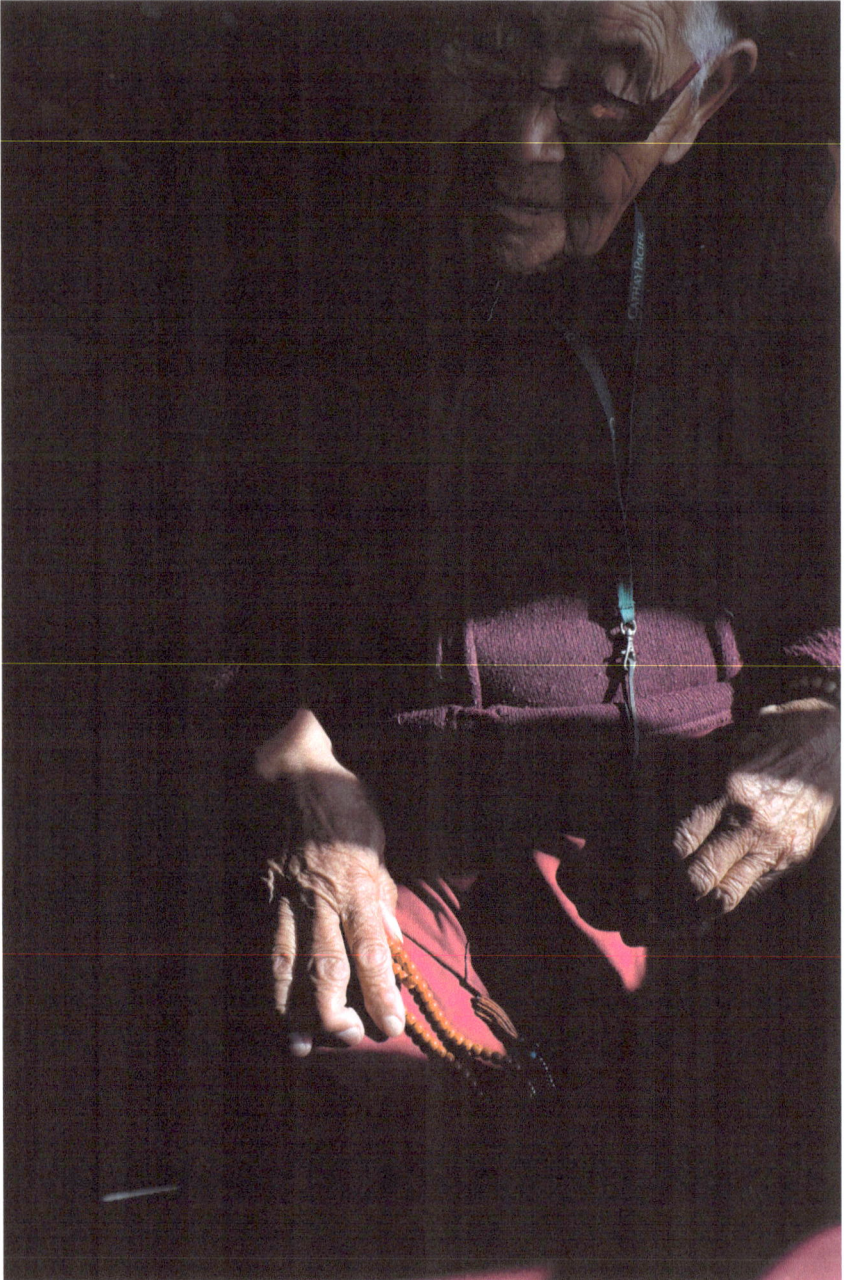

Figure 28: A close-up of Ani Tenzin Pema sitting by herself. Photo by
Harmandeep K. Gill.

deities. Mo Dickyi knew that she would never be at home in that sense. With the prospect of death, the elderly Tibetans were forced to come to terms with home (of the past in both Tibet and India) as being nothing but a distant memory. It belonged to another life and thus also uprooted them. They could not start over again.

In the final part of this chapter, I introduce another home-in-exile for my elderly friends and the other Tibetans I know in India: their spiritual leader and holiest lama, the Dalai Lama; the emanation of Tibet's patron deity, Chenrezig, also known as Avalokiteśvara, the Bodhisattva of Compassion. For Tibetans, he is a symbol of the Tibetan nation and embodies the past, present, and possible future of the Tibetan people. Whereas everything, including themselves, had an element of unrecognition, the Dalai Lama provided orientation, even being a "ground project," informing them of who they were. He is the heart of the body of exile and even the image of hope itself.

Home in the Dalai Lama

"My heart becomes empty," Mo Dickyi said to explain how she felt when the Dalai Lama traveled away from McLeod Ganj, something he used to do often because of his many commitments around the world. The COVID-19 pandemic was the first time he stayed put in McLeod Ganj for two years.

Mo Dickyi had been counting the number of days the Dalai Lama had been absent from McLeod Ganj. She kept track of the Dalai Lama's movements through the local Tibetan news channel, Tibet TV, which is run by the CTA. She watched television after completing the daily task of clearing the shrine, until she had to prepare dinner. She resumed watching television shortly after retiring to the shrine room after dinner. Apart from the Bhutanese channel, Tibet TV was her preferred channel. It gave weekly updates on the situation in Tibet, Tibetan exile related events, and the Dalai Lama's travels and activities. Gen Lobsang also preferred to watch Tibet TV on the rare days his room received a signal. If I was not up to date on the Dalai Lama's whereabouts, I could always check with Mo Dickyi, Mo Tsering, and even Gen Lobsang when he had a television signal. For Mo Dickyi, without the Dalai Lama's presence in McLeod Ganj, the town was emptier. She yearned for his presence during his absence. Despite never seeing him in person— just like she rarely saw her fellow Kyirong Tibetans when they were around in Kyirong Village—knowing that he was present at a given time lifted her spirits and made her feel more at home.

It is not an exaggeration to say that, for the elderly Tibetans-in-exile, the Dalai Lama is the center of their world. "His presence heals our bruised selves," writes Bhuchung D. Sonam.[64] The Dalai Lama was one of the main reasons Mo Tsering hesitated to move to Europe to reside with her daughter, or to live with her relatives in Gangtok in northeastern India. She told me: "I miss Jigme. But I don't want to go there [Europe]. I am old and when I die, it's good to die close to Gyalwa Rinpoche [the Dalai Lama]." Living close to the Tsuglagkhang, Mo Tsering could always hear the sirens of the security cars that drove in front of and behind the Dalai Lama's car upon his arrival and departure from town. On these occasions, she would tell anyone present to be silent. She would fold her hands together, lower her head, and recite a prayer. For Mo Tsering, my other elderly friends, and Tibetans-in-exile at-large, home is also where the Dalai Lama is. Their hearts reside with him.

Even before the Chinese invasion, when a full-blown nationalistic identity did not exist, Tibetans united in the name of faith, the highest guardians of which have been the Dalai Lamas since the reign of the 5th Dalai Lama.[65] The Chushi Gangdrug guerrilla army, which was formed in the Kham region but brought together Tibetan men from all three regions of Tibet, is a clear example of Tibetans mobilizing in the name of faith.[66]

For Tibetans, the Dalai Lama is the symbol of Tibet, connected with the land itself, and because he is in exile, the meanings of Tibet and home are also obscured. One of the most famous pieces of Tibetan art in recent times, an art installation by the prominent Tibetan artist Tenzing Rigdol titled *Our Land, Our People*, after the 14th Dalai Lama's autobiography, addressed the complex meanings of Tibet as it relates to Tibetan identity.[67] The project was also made into a documentary called *Bringing Tibet Home* (*pa sa bu thug*) by filmmaker Tenzin Tsetan Choklay.[68]

In 2011, Rigdol installed twenty thousand kilograms of soil from Tibet at the TCV school in McLeod Ganj. The project was inspired by the death of Rigdol's father, who died with an unfulfilled hope of returning to Tibet. After his father's death, Rigdol decided to bring Tibetan soil to the people in exile. The soil was transported illegally from Shigatse in central Tibet over the Nepalese border by Nepalese middlemen and later into India. The installation lasted for two days and was open to the Tibetan public. Tibetans, young and old, lined up at the school grounds to touch and walk upon the precious earth. As Sarah Magnetta writes, "It was a piece of Tibet that could be held, touched, sometimes even ingested by Tibetans in the exile community."[69] In Choklay's film, a line of elderly Tibetans can be seen touching the soil to their foreheads, saying prayers, and doing prostrations on the soil. When the installation concluded, the soil was distributed among the Tibetan audience, who had brought along plastic bags and sacks to take parts of the soil with them.

Before opening the installation to the Tibetan public, Rigdol, accompanied by his friends, took a small portion of the soil to the Dalai Lama to seek his blessings. In the film, the Dalai Lama touches the box of soil and looks at it. He then asks, "So this is from Shigatse?"[70]

Rigdol humbly nods his head.

"*Bö* (Tibet), from Shigatse, right?" the Dalai Lama asks again, pointing up with his finger.[71]

Rigdol respectfully nods.

The Dalai Lama then writes the word བོད (*Bö*) on the portion of soil with his finger. When he is done, he gives a small laugh. "Like this," he says, turning the box toward the camera while Rigdol holds onto it.[72] He wraps a ceremonial silk scarf around the necks of Rigdol and his friends, saying, "This is for you."[73] He tells Rigdol and his friends that the support of their "Chinese friends" is essential in finding a solution: "We have our right. Historically, Tibet and China were separate. As the historical saying goes, 'The Chinese are happier in China. The Tibetans in Tibet.' True in the time of our empire, but can we say that today? The world runs on power. So, we need to keep an open mind and think from a broader perspective. And when we speak of a mutually beneficial solution, many Chinese show their support. Well, you've done a good job. Thank you. Persevere and work hard."[74]

Toward the end of his autobiography, *My Land and My People*, the 14th Dalai Lama says, "My hope rests in the courage of Tibetans."[75] Rigdol's project of reuniting his fellow exiled Tibetans with their native land and forging temporary, solid connections with separated family members can be seen as keeping alive the Dalai Lama's hope for his people. Tsering Jamphel, whom we met in Chapter 1 and who has not seen his parents since he was five years old, was moved to tears by the installation, and later by seeing the film. The installation can be understood as a courageous political act of reclaiming Tibet from its colonizers. By naming the installation after the Dalai Lama's autobiography, by seeking his blessings, and by making the portion of soil with his handwritten word, བོད, a part of the installation, Rigdol also made a statement about who is the rightful and moral leader of those connected with the Tibetan soil. Through the symbol of soil and the

Figure 29: Light in darkness: the Dalai Lama's photograph in evening light. Photo by Harmandeep K. Gill.

location of the installation in the capital of Tibetans-in-exile, and home of
the Dalai Lama since 1960, Rigdol's installation can be seen to bring new
meanings to Tibet and home.

Tibet is not only bound to the geographical area of the Tibetan plateau
colonized by the People's Republic of China. Tibet continues to live in exile,
in the settlements across India, and in the hearts of Tibetans. The land is, for
Tibetans, also interlinked with the Dalai Lama, who for them is the strongest symbol of the Tibetan nation. In some ways, as Tibetan poets inside Tibet write, with the Dalai Lama's absence, their land is empty. Home is not
completely home. The prominent Tibetan writer and intellectual Tsering Woeser, who lives in Beijing, describes the state of Tibetans inside Tibet as an
internal exile: "In my internal exile, I can hear an old man around the same
age as His Holiness saying: 'We are still waiting . . . he will come back, there
will be the day when he comes back to Lhasa, I believe that'."[76] Tibetan nun,
Sangay Dolma, who set herself on fire on 25 November 2012 following the
wave of self-immolations on the Tibetan plateau that began in 2009, left
behind the following words:

> Look into the deep blue sky above
> my lama has returned
> into the tent with white rock steps
> look, my Tibetan brothers and sisters
> look at the peak of that snow mountain
> the white snow lion has returned
> look, my Tibetan brothers and sisters
> look at the fortress in the forest
> look at the beauty of the turquoise plain
> my tigress has come back.[77]

By smuggling Tibetan soil into India, Rigdol made the statement that despite
the Chinese colonization, Tibetans would continue to reclaim Tibet, guided
by their holiest lama, the 14th Dalai Lama who is referred to by the nun Sangay Dolma as the snow lion and the tigress.[78] The snow lion is the emblem of
Tibet, and two snow lions are depicted in the Tibetan national flag. Tibet,
for Tibetans, belongs with their lama and the Tibetan people. Hence, home
is where the Dalai Lama is; he provides a sense of belonging in places that
are considered far from the homeland.[79] With his installation, Rigdol, for a
brief period in time, brought Tibet home to the Dalai Lama and to the people

who are united by the land and were driven away from it. In Choklay's film, an elderly woman with folded hands expresses it thus: "I pray for all of us Tibetans in exile. May we get to return to Tibet. May there be the sun of happiness and the moon of joy. May we all get to return to our homeland. Thank you, I was able to touch this soil and put my feet on this today."[80] The hope of return continues to live on. The elderly woman will not be able to return in her lifetime, but her hope—shared by Po Damchoe Ngawang, Ani Tenzin Pema, Mo Dickyi Sangmo, Gen Lobsang Choedak, Mo Tsering Wangmo, Ani Jamyang Choedon, Mo Samdrup Drolma, and the other elderly Tibetans I know in the Dharamsala area and in other settlements—is that the Dalai Lama and the younger generations might return one day.

January 2020

The snow had settled on the vast Dhauladhar range stretching beyond McLeod Ganj. Covered in snow, the mountains looked more majestic and beyond human reach. The sun warmed the cold winter day. Resting under the warmth of the sun and the many prayer flags, the camp area looked serene.

On my way up the stairs, I first ran into Ama Nyima, who had stepped out of her home to find a place under the sun. I greeted her, and as I passed her by, I heard her say, "It's the one who massages." A few stairs up, Po Bhutruk sat, leaning on the wall behind him while he recited mantras. Further up, an elderly Pola walked up and down the same few stairs, aided by his walking stick, and recited a mantra. Toward the end of the staircase, another Pola rested under the sun. He too recited a mantra as he moved the wooden beads of his rosary. Here they all were, preparing for death and rebirth through prayers or exercise while soaking themselves in the heat of the sun and warming their cold bodies.

Po Damchoe sat on a chair at the balcony of his younger daughter's house. He watched me come up the stairs, but without recognition. I had not seen him in months, but he looked the same. When I was outside the balcony gate, a big smile spread across his face. "Come in, come in," he said. He held my hands for a long time, asking me when I had arrived and how long I would stay. I could smell that he had not given up drinking.

He inquired whether I had come directly from McLeod Ganj. As before, I had made my way up here from the TCV old-age home. I told Pola that one of the residents at the home had passed away a day earlier. Pola shook his head and followed up with news of more deaths. "Three people have died here in one month," he said, holding up three fingers.

A few days earlier, when I had gone for a walk in the forest, I had seen some Tibetan men prepare the cremation ground. I wondered if maybe it was for one of the elderly Tibetans here at camp.

"Prayers are going on at the monastery," he continued, pointing toward the TCV monastery. Po Damchoe thought for a few seconds, and then like Gen Lobsang, he said, "It is no more," shaking his hand sideways. The three deaths within a short period of time, of people who Pola had known for the most part of his life, made palpable his own ending. It was a stark reminder that he, too, would have to leave his home soon. It was not the time to hold on, but to let go.

Being at home in the world and with oneself was unsettled with the looming presence of death. As more and more people from this generation of Tibetans-in-exile passed away, the home at TCV, like Kyirong Village, was becoming emptier and unrecognizable. Many homes turned into abandoned houses. Even though imaginations of home grounded my friends, the daunting realization of death also unsettled them. One has to hand over even the most intimate parts of one's life to the workings of time and come to terms with unfulfilled longings. While every day offered my elderly friends new chances, every day was also a perpetual wait for death, and brought them one step closer to a new and alien journey, when a new time would set into motion.

Interlude

Gen Lobsang Choedak's foot is dark and heavy, like his hands, which have done so much hard work in life. The skin around his ankle is darker. In the sun, it gets burned. His calf is thin but firm. The thigh is even thinner.

I take off his sock and leg warmer, pour some medicinal oil on his leg, and start the massage. Genla closely follows my hands as they move up and down and around his knee and leg. While I massage him, he holds his thigh with both hands, as if trying to aid me by making sure the leg stands completely still. I do not know what his left leg looks like. It is the one that was fractured, and he does not want me to massage it. Genla is the only one for whom I massage only one leg.

"Genla, your ankle and foot are swollen," I tell him worriedly. The swelling is also visible in the lower part of his leg and the foot.

"Is it?" he responds, not at all worried.

After a quick look, Genla insists, like other times, that it is not swollen. Having sat in front of his foot and leg, and having massaged both for months, I can tell that Genla's observation is incorrect.

I tell Genla to be careful with his exercise routine and not to overdo it. He gives me his usual half-finished laugh. He has survived worse. Over our many massage sessions, I have observed that his foot and lower leg tend to be more swollen on days he exercises too much.

Genla told me that before I came along, a small Tibetan clinic, close to Delek Hospital, used to offer massages. Sometimes they would come to the old-age home to massage the elderly. But Genla said they charged money.

When I began massaging his leg, he actually offered me payment, despite knowing about my research. His humble suggestion had left me speechless.

When Genla feels that I have massaged long enough, he tells me to stop. He says he will manage to put on his leg warmer and sock himself, but as always, I help him anyway.

"Wash your hands well," he repeats. "Use the hot water from the bucket."

Figure 30: Gen Lobsang Choedak. Photo by Harmandeep K. Gill.

CHAPTER 5

Acceptance

t was the spring of 2018. Gen Lobsang Choedak sat down on the bed, at the usual spot. I sat down on the floor in front of him and began the massage. We could hear the chatter of the few Mola gathered in the shared sitting area of the TCV old-age home. The 2nd floor was rather lively. Here, inside Genla's room, there was silence. He was not a talker, with me or others.

I noticed the sparrows chirping outside and the sound of their wings flapping as they moved in and out through the open windows. The sky was crystal blue. Spring had slowly started making its way into the winter landscape of McLeod Ganj. Sunlight burst through the windows, warming up the old and bringing the promise of life. Life was all around, so overwhelming that one easily lost sight of decay, even at an old-age home. The elderly moved outdoors in the warmth of the sun. That was where the eldest resident of the home, the ninety-three-year-old Mo Pema Choedon, caregiver of children in the TCV school's household number nine, was usually found, sometimes sitting outside on a chair or standing by the open windows, overlooking the Kangra Valley ahead.

By the time I arrived at the TCV old-age home in 2016, Mo Pema Choedon could neither hear nor speak clearly. But the other elderly residents shared with me bits and pieces of Mo Pema's past. She was one of the very few at the home who had been with the TCV school from the very beginning. Her life in exile had been spent in service to the TCV school. Despite the frailty of old age, Mo Pema refused to become confined to her apartment. She kept pushing herself to slowly move around at the home and outside, aided by her walker. During the sunny days of spring, she seemed to embrace life, rarely missing the chance to sit outside in the sun.

Like Mo Pema, Genla embraced all the life during those lively days of spring. He read Buddhist texts outside in the sun. He used the good weather to go for longer walks. Yet every day he also prepared for death. All the life did not blind him to impermanence. Moreover, it served as a daily reminder.

While I massaged his leg, for once Genla chose to break the silence. "Mola passed away," he said to me.

The news violently shook me out of the lightness of spring. It was the first time somebody had died while I had been there. I stopped the massage and looked up at him. "Who?" I asked immediately, thinking that it might be Mo Pema.

"Mola upstairs," Genla responded pointing up. He tried to recall her name but to no avail. Half an hour later, when we had tea, it came to him, "Tsewang. Mola's name is Tsewang."

When the initial shock of the news had settled, I returned to the massage. "Did I know her, Genla? How did she look?" I asked, worrying whether it might be one of the Mola I know.

"Ahhmm . . . tall body," he said.

"And black hair?" I added.

"Yes, yes," Genla nodded.

Mo Tsewang flashed before my eyes, walking down from Dal Lake in the company of one of the nuns, giving me a fleeting smile. She was only in her early seventies. I saw her strolling around on the rooftop. It was hard to comprehend that she was gone, when her figure kept lingering around in places, in moments in time, dissolved into the present.

"How do you feel, Genla? Did her death worry you?" I asked him.

Genla gave a short laugh, as he usually did when responding to something. "Now, all people from 1959 have passed away. One by one, everybody is dying. I am also old, eighty-nine years old," he said.

That day, I did not attempt to console him by telling him that he was still fit and healthy. I am not sure that he needed it or even wanted it. On the contrary, he seemed to have accepted that death was the only inevitable end awaiting us all. Living at an old-age home, being surrounded by aging bodies, his daily preparations for death and the many deaths that were to follow in the spring made the impermanence of life strikingly present.

Gen Lobsang Choedak turned ninety-five years old in 2024. Mo Pema Choedon was only two years away from turning one hundred when she silently passed away on 15 September 2023. With Mo Pema gone, Genla is now the eldest resident at the TCV old-age home. He believes that he, too, might be gone any day now. The elderly Tibetans' reflections and preparations for the coming of death and rebirth, and how they attempted to come to terms with the uncertainty raised by both, is the subject of this chapter. What worries, fears, and hopes accompanied them in facing the inevitable?

The elderly Tibetans devote the time left to practicing *chö*, engaging in virtuous behavior in order to improve one's karma and transforming one's mind, thereby securing a good rebirth. The path to enlightenment and liberation is described as the most difficult form of striving. To be reborn as a human is something only highly devoted Tibetan Buddhist practitioners and high-ranking lamas can hope for. While they are described as having the abilities to control the process of dying (e.g., *thugdam* or *phoba)* and foresee their rebirth, this is not the case with the laypeople and monastics of a lower rank whom I worked with, and to whom the lamas direct their teachings.[1]

Death and rebirth can be approached as an "aporia" for my elderly friends, a fluid concept I find helpful even in a Tibetan Buddhist context because it refers to a state of perplexity, one in which even words fall short, especially for laypeople.[2] More precisely, as Nils Bubandt notes, "it refers to the act or difficulty of passing, the problem of dealing with something difficult, or the impenetrability of an enigma."[3]

Although my elderly friends never doubted Buddhist beliefs about the process of dying, and rebirth was taken to be an absolute certainty, both death and rebirth remained beyond their experience. Thus, I argue that doubt and aporias are not "a monopoly of the west."[4] Importantly, I recognize the "existential bewilderment" that is associated with aporia also to be at the heart of how the elderly related to death and rebirth (e.g., When will I die? How will I die? What will happen? And have I done enough to gain a good rebirth?).[5] Both death and rebirth remained to them uncertain, ambiguous, and impenetrable.

Despite the uncertainty, perplexity, and unsettling called forth by the proximity of death, the aporia nonetheless evokes practical (e.g., death rituals) and moral concerns that gave rise to sadness, fears, and hopes. Although death and rebirth as aporia withdrew from experience, that aporia also presented a horizon: an undefined and vague aspect that is unavoidable. Despite the impossibility of an aporia, "we are obliged to seek a path where there is none."[6] Aporias thus demand constant attention and work. In facing them, people need to produce solutions, however partial and inadequate those might be. Likewise, the elderly Tibetans, in accordance with the "path" provided by Tibetan Buddhism, devoted constant attention and "work" to the coming of death and rebirth through their daily Buddhist practices and in surrendering to the aporia of death and rebirth. Preparing for death and rebirth was a process fraught with afflictions and attachments, but one's time remaining also held the seeds for transforming one's karma and mind.

The Last Stop

Gen Lobsang's room was located on the 2nd floor of the TCV old-age home. It was squeezed between two other rooms. A small amount of sunlight entered through the kitchen window, but it was never enough to keep the lights off. Despite the darkness in Genla's room, it was a warm and welcoming space. Yellow, red, and dark maroon colors covered the room, just like the interior and exterior of a monastery. The first time I noticed the interior of his room, I commented, "Genla, your room is very red."

He looked around as if he were not aware of it and gave a little laugh. As a monk, these colors have dominated his life. Like the tops of doors and windows of monasteries, the entrances to the kitchen and the bathroom had small curtains hanging above them. The room was inviting. There was serenity in the way his few belongings were arranged. In his maroon robe and red jacket, Genla, for me, melted into the red monastic bubble surrounding him. The room felt like an extension of him, not only in terms of colors but also in its calm, inviting, and settled mood. Things were neatly tucked into their corners as if they were never to be used again, as though their owner would be leaving them any day.

His few pieces of clothing were hung by the door on clothes hangers. His few robes and woolen shawls were neatly folded and placed on the top of a big iron trunk settled on a wooden table next to the television. Below the table were his four pairs of shoes: two pairs of summer shoes and two pairs of winter boots. He also had two pairs of slippers to wear indoors. The shoes were all gifts from his niece. She was the only relative he had in India, but he rarely saw her because she kept moving between places, something Genla was not very happy about.[7] "She does not benefit me much," he said. Six pairs of shoes for an elderly monk seemed to be a lot to me, as if she were bringing a pair each visit, not only as a respectful and caring gesture but also to make up for her absence. Genla made sure to use all the pairs of shoes. I saw him wear various pairs during different parts of the year.

Other objects rested still, such as some perfectly folded blankets on the bed that he never slept in and the television that rarely received signal. At the center of the room was a beautiful, humble shrine. It was filled with photos of the Dalai Lama and decorated with one set of red and yellow plastic roses. At the front of the shrine stood a butter-lamp offering and a row of water-bowl offerings. On the wall next to the shrine were four more images. Two of them were *thangka*: one of Chenrezig, the Bodhisattva of Compassion, and one of Sangye Menla, the Medicine Buddha. The other two were photographs: one of the Dalai Lama and one of the Dalai Lama's teachers, the third Trijang Rinpoche, Lobsang Yeshe Tenzin Gyatso.

Unlike the homes of my other elderly friends, Genla's room was not overflowing with things gathered over a lifetime. No object stood in the way of another. Apart from the shrine, his two Indian vintage trunks pulled my attention. These heavy trunks symbolized two significant periods in his life in India. The smaller one—placed on a table in front of the shrine and with the word *base* written on its side in a military green color—was a material trace of his time in the Indian military.

After eighteen years of military service, he packed his belongings in the small trunk and moved to the TCV school in McLeod Ganj to work in the school kitchen. In 1995, when he was allowed to retire, Genla packed his few pieces of clothing, blankets, and utensils and moved to his new residence, which was also hidden from the sun. When the school administration offered him residence at the TCV old-age home in 2016, Genla packed his belongings for the last time into those two iron trunks and moved to his last stop on his journey.

When I asked Genla whether his room in the old-age home felt like his home, he responded, "This is where I am going to die." Genla's words made clear that the old-age home was a temporary stop at the end of his life. It was not the place to settle in but rather the place from where he would set off for his rebirth. He had reached the mountain pass.

The Pressing Presence of Death

The presence of death became stark after Mo Tsewang's death that spring in 2018, when several deaths followed one after another. To use Genla's words, people were literally dying "one by one." Butter-lamp offerings burned continuously for months, and the sight of new, strange faces who had come to make offerings for the deceased became a part of life. Genla anticipated that soon he would be next.

The son of an elderly woman at the old-age home once commented that the elderly were always counting who would be the next to go. When the next death occurred only two weeks later, no one, certainly not Genla, had anticipated that Mo Tsewang would be followed in death by her husband, who was only in his early seventies. Genla told me that he died after a long-term illness, which was even more surprising because when I had met him two weeks earlier, while making offerings for Mo Tsewang, he had looked healthy and upright.

Twenty days later, his death was followed by the death of the oldest resident of the home, a ninety-five-year-old Pola who passed away after long-term illness. But his death did not come as a surprise to Genla or anyone else.

With each passing death, I sensed in Genla an increased anticipation about the unknown. Whenever I asked him what thoughts occupied his days, he only had one answer for me: death. "I am very old, isn't it. I won't stay for long now," he would say with an accepting smile.

When I told Mo Tsering Wangmo that Genla was always thinking about death, she firmly gave me a thumbs-up. "That is very good," she praised him, and then again emphasized, "very good." For elderly Tibetans, numerous meditations on death on a daily basis are common sense. Anything else would entail complete ignorance of the mind.

The day after the ninety-five-year-old Pola passed away, Genla said to me, "Now two more people are sick here. Po Ugyen, who is eighty-nine years old, he is quite sick. And Mo Yangchen."

"What happened to her?" I asked.

"She has jaundice. Her face is all pale. She can't talk or open her eyes."

I had known Mo Yangchen since 2016. Like Ani Tenzin Pema and Mo Pema Choedon, she had worked as a caregiver of Tibetan children at the TCV school. I decided to visit Mo Yangchen on my next visit. When I arrived at the home two days later, visitors were moving in and out of Mo Yangchen's and her husband's residence. By now, I knew what that signified. Ani Tenzin Pema, who was on her way to Mo Yangchen's room holding a *khata*, whispered to me that Mo Yangchen had passed away the previous day.

Whereas I lived as if time were a luxury, postponing my visit to Mo Yangchen, Genla and the others could never take time for granted. Whereas I, in my youth, was blinded to my own end, the end was all they saw. And while the loss of another elder was something I still found hard to

Figure 31: The Tibetan Children's Village old-age home. Photo by Harmandeep K. Gill.

comprehend, for Genla and other elderly at the home, loss (and death) had become a part of life. They donated money for butter-lamp offerings (*chöme jeldeb*) and then returned to their everyday lives, albeit with a heightened awareness of death's looming presence and a concern about who would be the next to go. These thoughts were accompanied by the hope that they themselves would die a sudden death, meaning disappearing quickly, without falling into long-term illness.

Worries over a Bedridden Death

Mo Yangchen was bedridden for three months before passing away from jaundice. Her husband, sons, and a young Indian caregiver took good care of her. On her passing, her husband, Po Ngodrup, a former teacher at the TCV school, said, "There was no *arraa . . . ooroo*. Without pain, she left quietly. That is very good."

Mo Yangchen's quiet passing without pain was a comfort for Po Ngodrup. Pola himself hoped for a sudden and peaceful death, a sentiment shared by all of the elderly Tibetans I have come to know. The possibility of dying a bedridden death and in suffering, especially in the absence of family members, was feared.

Gen Lobsang did not trust that his niece would come to his rescue in case of a severe illness. Although the staff at the old-age home provided care, such as serving food and cleaning the body when an elderly person was bedridden, Genla did not have high hopes for how he would be supported. He said, "Sometimes my mind feels relaxed. That is how the mind is. Sometimes I have suffering in my mind. Sometimes the mind cannot be happy. Being old and wondering how it will go, it worries me sometimes. Here [at the old-age home] they won't do much for you. They will not provide support. That's my biggest worry. Many people have died here. Their corpse is taken care of. But that's about it." Genla worried that he would "suffer in the absence of no helper" if the worst-case scenario became a reality. This had been the case with one of Genla's peers, Po Ugyen, who lived on the 3rd floor, exactly above Genla's room. The eighty-nine-year-old man had been bedridden for a long time. The staff visited him a few times a day to make a butter-lamp offering, feed him, and clean him. The rest of the day, he lay alone in his bed, under the weight of several layers of blankets. His only son resided in the United States and could not aid Po Ugyen during his period of sickness.

Once, when I visited Po Ugyen, he did not notice me until I stood by his bedside. His things had been randomly stuffed into corners and in the shelves of the large wooden cabinet and left to decay. Most of the kitchen had been emptied by the TCV staff. Only a gas stove and some ingredients to make chai stood on the empty kitchen counter. It was as though I had walked into an abandoned home. Pola lay under several blankets, but I could not feel his presence. Moving closer to him, I saw that he lay there with eyes wide open, staring toward the ceiling. I asked whether I could make him more tea, but I was not sure he could hear me. As I was about to move away from his bedside, he slowly moved his face toward me and nodded his head, perhaps saying yes to the tea or acknowledging my visit. Witnessing his condition, I could understand Genla's worries. The following week, Po Ugyen was moved to the TCV hospital, where he passed away after a few months. His death was the type of death no one wanted to befall them.

Confined to her home, Mo Tsering Wangmo feared that this was how she might end her days. Upon hearing about my other elderly friends, she always commented that her condition was the worst of all. Despite hoping that the condition of her legs might improve, she was aware that it was unlikely. Her greatest fear was of becoming completely bedridden and being at the mercy of a caregiver. Once, when I told her about deaths at the TCV old-age home or in other parts of town, Mo Tsering said, "Everyone is dying, except me." Death in her case would be a liberation from the sufferings of the present and the fear of a grim future, and she prayed for it to come. As I sensed from her and Gen Lobsang's words, if the future might lead to a bedridden death, they were ready to die now, while they were still able to look after themselves.

A bedridden death was dreaded not only by my elderly friends but also by other Tibetan Buddhists in the Himalayas. The poor peasant, Tashi Dondrup, from Geoff Childs's *Tibetan Diary*, faced a lonesome old age and expressed the same worries as Genla.[8] Furthermore, Tashi Dondrup shared that he would "stop eating and just fade away" if the dreaded future should become a reality.[9] The Tibetan Buddhist Hyolmos in Robert Desjarlais's *Subject to Death: Life and Loss in a Buddhist World* express similar concerns.[10] To die in sickness and pain is regarded as a bad form of death.

Dying a lonesome death was another concern expressed by some of the elderly Tibetans. When I interviewed Po Ngodrup and Mo Yangchen during my preliminary fieldwork at the TCV old-age home in 2016, they had been going through a difficult time with Mo Yangchen's sons from her previous marriage. During one conversation, Mo Yangchen said to me: "Pala, mine, and our children's lives are separate, completely separate," a statement she gestured by separating her joined hands. Soon after, Po Ngodrup fell ill. Once again, Mo Yangchen's sons, who lived close by, had not lent a particularly helpful hand.

During one incident when Po Ngodrup was taken to the hospital, one of the sons had asked whether he had enough money. The general manager of the old-age home who informed me about the incident commented, "Who asks their parents to pay when they are ill?" Po Ngodrup had treated his step-sons as if they were his own children. He had offered them a lot of financial help in the past and had never asked for anything in return. The son's statement had hurt him deeply. During an interview with Po Ngodrup in 2016, when I asked him how he felt about old people dying in the absence of their children, his eyes filled up with tears. He tried his hardest to push down the lump in his throat: "It is bad. If one dies in a sad state because one couldn't meet one's children, it is not a good way of dying. And going to 'the interme-diate stage' [bar] there is danger. It is saddening to die without [the presence of] one's children." After a brief pause, he added, "When they themselves get old and have no one to put even a drop of water in their mouth, then they will understand."

When Mo Yangchen passed away in 2018, Pola told me that the sons had offered considerable help. I also saw them in Po Ngodrup's apartment the day I went to make offerings for Mo Yangchen, and around at the home during the period of the forty-nine days of death rituals. In the aftermath, Pola said that the sons had been good and helpful to him. But with Mo Yangchen gone, and his own children from his first marriage living in a Tibetan settlement in central India, he expected to die a lonesome death: "These days, old ones stay behind and the young ones go abroad. The old ones live alone, not know-ing whether they will die tomorrow or the day after. If they die in the middle of night, no one will know. There is no one who can give one some water. . . . I think the elderly worry that they might not meet their children upon dying."

Worries over a bedridden future and dying a lonesome death can be un-derstood in relation to the future of rebirth. One's state of mind before death and specifically at the moment of death is believed to have powerful rever-berations for one's next rebirth. Margaret Gouin notes, "One's last thought exercises a powerful influence on one's subsequent rebirth: dying with a calm mind full of virtuous thoughts will lead to a good rebirth."[11] Dying in the ab-sence of family, and in a state of physical suffering, increases the chances of dying with negative thoughts and strong attachments to loved ones. This can lead to a bad rebirth or, worse, never leaving the *bardo*, the intermediate stage between death and birth.

The negative effect of dying in a sad or restless state of mind was clearly articulated by Po Ngodrup when he said that going to "the intermediate space"—meaning the intermediate period after death—can involve "danger." As Desjarlais describes at length, the purpose of the forty-nine days of death rituals is to cease the deceased's attachments to the world of the living and help them pass onto the next life: "They must render the deceased no longer a living, fully human, flesh-and-body person."[12] Thus, the practice of death rituals is important for ensuring the well-being of both the deceased and the living. In this period, it is common practice to not utter the name of the deceased. One is also supposed to burn their things so that the deceased can swiftly pass on to their next rebirth, but times have changed and not everyone burns all of the deceased's possessions these days. If the deceased fails to pass on from the *bardo* due to strong attachments to family members— for example, in incidents of lonely deaths—the deceased can, in theory, remain as a ghost in the afterlife.

In 2016, neither Po Ngodrup nor Mo Yangchen worried that death rituals would not be carried out for them. They had set aside money, just like Genla. If the children failed to show up, the staff of the TCV old-age home would take care of the rituals on their behalf. After Mo Yangchen's passing, Po Ngodrup was not concerned. His relationship to his stepsons seemed to be better. He trusted that they or his own children would take care of the death rituals. Finally, he had the old-age home as a reassurance.

The worries and sadness over a bedridden and lonely death can, on the one hand, be made sense of in relation to religious beliefs—that is, the consequences it has for the subsequent rebirth. But on the other hand, these worries were equally about a basic human need for attaining a worthy and dignifying closure in the absence of family. I clearly remember one episode when Gen Lobsang advised me to get married: "If you don't get married, your life will go to waste." I was surprised that these words came from a monk. In response, I said that I would spend my life in solitude just like Genla. He smiled at me and said, "When you get sick and old, no one will look after you." The sadness over aging alone and facing a lonesome death, especially in a state of illness, was more than clear in Genla's words.

Genla did not expect to be remembered by others, not even by his own relatives. These days, community ties in McLeod Ganj are not strong, and many solitary old people feel forgotten even before death. That was what

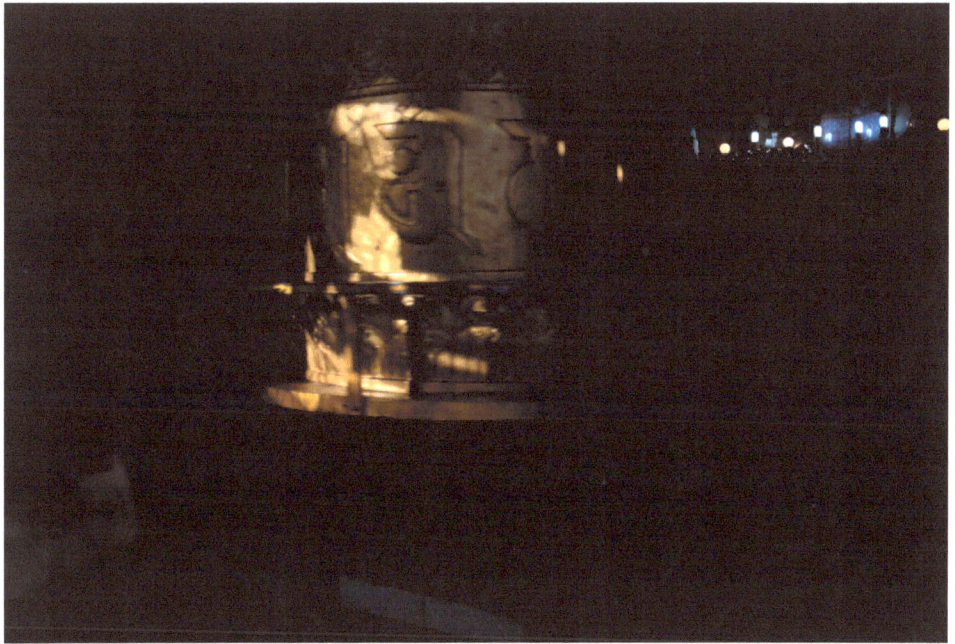

Figure 32: A big prayer wheel (*mani khorlo*) spinning, symbolizing the cyclic existence of death and rebirth. Photo by Harmandeep K. Gill.

I sensed so strongly with Gen Lobsang and Mo Dickyi; it was as though they had become absent for others even while alive. To me, Gen Lobsang's, Mo Tsering Wangmo's, and Po Ngodrup's concerns also entail a kind of self-care in the absence of family. Slipping away peacefully was the only optimistic hope they cultivated for themselves on a daily basis, and that for them was a dignifying closure. All of their daily Tibetan Buddhist practices were directed toward this end. The other fear raised by death was the fear of death itself.

Dying Unsettles

It was a warm summer day in late May 2018. Mo Dickyi had agreed to sit outside on the balcony. The heat had settled down, and a soft and soothing breeze caressed our naked arms, necks, and faces. As we sipped our tea, Mo Dickyi's eyes were fixed on the house of the newly deceased Ama Lhadron. She pointed out the house to me and told me what she knew about Ama Lhadron's family. When she was done, Mola kept staring at the house, seemingly lost in her thoughts. "Now, the name of Ama Lhadron is no more," she said with a pensive expression. She returned to silence. I imagined that, in her silence, she might be counting the number of people from Kyirong who had passed away this year. And now another name was gone.

Ama Lhadron was hospitalized in Chandigarh before she passed away in her home in Kyirong Village.[13] That fact stuck in Mo Dickyi's mind, and she established a solid connection between the hospitalization and death. She repeated many times: "Ama Lhadron passed away after she went to the hospital in Chandigarh."

When Mo Dickyi fell seriously ill with an aching pain in her chest and stomach in April and May 2018, the doctor advised her to seek treatment at a bigger hospital in Chandigarh. With Ama Lhadron's death still fresh in her mind, Mo Dickyi believed that the hospital visit would also bring her an early death.

Mo Dickyi had been ill since I met with her in February 2018. A cough that at first seemed innocent turned severe in March, and soon she began suffering from an aching pain in the chest. In the beginning of April, she was hospitalized at Delek Hospital in McLeod Ganj for one week, for what turned out to be pneumonia. But that did not bring an end to the cough or the chest pain. Both continued after she was discharged. After more checkups and computed tomography (CT) scans of her lungs, she was advised to go to a lung specialist in Chandigarh for a biopsy and further treatment.

I was with Mo Dickyi the day the Tibetan doctor gave her the news. The doctor could not detect any illness, but on the basis of the CT scans, he referred to her condition as severe and said that it seemed as if she had a "bad disease," words that would be understandable to Mo Dickyi.

Mola's immediate response to his words was a clear *no*: "How can I go to Chandigarh? It's too far away," she said. Mo Dickyi had no one to accompany her. All of her siblings were old, and she had almost no contact with her son, Tashi, at the time. In the end, I was the only one who could help her, so I offered to go with her.

Mo Dickyi was hesitant from the beginning. Her reasons were many: she was more than eighty years old and saw no point in wasting money on checkups. Moreover, she dreaded the heat in the lowlands and believed that all the hassle would bring her an early death, just like it had Ama Lhadron. I gave her a few days to think about it. Mo Dickyi did not change her mind. In fact, she became more and more certain that the hospital visit—even for the simple procedure of a biopsy—would bring her an early death.

Ani Jamyang Choedon also saw no point in going to Chandigarh. "It's a waste of money. And it's not good to take a piece of flesh like that from the lungs," she said, using words that were mimicked by Mo Dickyi.

Even though Mo Dickyi did not want to risk an early death, she defended her decision to not go to Chandigarh: "If I die, I die. Everybody has to die one day. No one can stay behind."

This calm and accepting attitude toward death changed near the end of April 2018, when the pain worsened. Painkillers that had been prescribed by the Tibetan doctor failed to provide relief. Mo Dickyi believed that her time had come. "Now I will die soon," she said in a worried tone every time I visited her. On other occasions, she also added, "I am afraid."

One day, when Mo Dickyi believed that the Lord of Death was close by, she summoned the courage to leave her home and walk to the house of her elderly sister, Samdrup Drolma, located only about two hundred meters away. When I asked Mo Dickyi why she decided to visit her sister all of a sudden, she replied, "I had so much pain. I thought I was going to die." She wanted to see her Acha—whom she had not seen for two years at that point—one last time before vanishing away.

But restless as Mo Dickyi was, she did not even stay for half an hour, and she soon rushed back to lie down on her bed. Although Mo Dickyi earlier said, "If I die, I die," and on other occasions even declared that there was no point in fearing death, her response was rather different when she thought that death had come knocking on her door. In the summer of 2019, she fell ill again. Once again, the doctor advised her to go to Chandigarh, and once again, Mo Dickyi was hesitant to go. Not being able to make up her mind, she sent her son, Tashi—who at the time was there to assist her—to a local lama for divination (*mo*). The lama predicted that she would heal on her own, and Mo Dickyi decided not to go.[14]

Death awakened an existential fear in Mo Dickyi and made her cling harder to life. It was not easy to accept that her name would disappear, just like Ama Lhadron's and those of the other Kyirong Tibetans who had passed away over the years. In Desjarlais's words, dying tore at herself: "Dying pulls indefinitely. It draws us away from any easy models of life and death and situates us in moments of pain and nonclosure and a terrible, unending openness," even for devoted Tibetan Buddhists who take rebirth to be a certainty.[15] Despite the detailed descriptions of the process of dying and the process of rebirth in the text *Bardo Thodol*, in practice, death and rebirth were not only beyond the lived experience of my elderly friends, they were also unsettling to them.[16]

For Gen Lobsang, the old-age home was itself a mountain pass, where he witnessed people disappearing and leaving for the new journey. Death had been upstairs in Po Ugyen's room and downstairs in Mo Yangchen's and Mo Tsewang's rooms. One might expect that, given the lingering presence of death, and with a rigorous Buddhist practice, Genla would not fear death. That was not the case. When I asked Genla whether he was afraid of dying, he replied, "I have worries. And fear too arises [thinking about death]. No one wants to die, but one will die. There is no escape from it."

In the teaching *Advice from an Experienced Old Man*, by Gungtang Rinpoche (1762–1823), an old man expresses a similar sentiment to a young man: "Everyone wants immortality and the methods to attain it. But to be born and not to die is impossible. Even thousands of Fully Enlightened Beings, including Shakyamuni Buddha, have passed away."[17]

Mo Dickyi and Gen Lobsang feared death. They also shared their immediate attempts, like the old man in Gungtang Rinpoche's teaching, of coming to terms with death: "No one wants to die, but one will die." In another conversation, Mo Dickyi said, "I am afraid, but what to do? Everyone has to die. That's how it is." Death evoked fear, but the fear of death also necessitated the contemplation of impermanence, of working on the mind and coming to terms with finitude. The only certainty in facing the aporia of death was that there is no escape from it. Impermanence is the way of life. Po Ngodrup said, "Even the Buddha who liberated himself passed away. It's impermanence. So we are nothing [in comparison with the enlightened Buddha]." As articulated by Po Ngodrup and repeated to me by other elderly Tibetans, if even someone like Buddha Śākyamuni or another enlightened being passes away, then no one can remain immune to the fate of death. It befalls everyone: rich and poor, enlightened and ignorant.

Considering these reflections on death, I suggest that facing death not only unsettled my elderly friends, giving rise to worries and fear, but in facing it, they also realized that they had no choice but to surrender to forces beyond them. In fact, death was already dwelling in their bodies.

Meditating on Impermanence

For Gen Lobsang, his aging body was the clearest manifestation of death's looming presence. It was there in the weakening strength of his legs, arms, digestion, and eyesight. He said: "When one is young, one can do anything. One is fit, has physical strength. Mental strength. Now, in old age, the mind is not very lucid. And physically without strength, it is difficult." For Genla, so much of who he used to be was already gone, and more was disappearing day by day. As Menriwa Lobsang Namgyal articulates (see Chapter 2), in old age the Lord of Death was just behind him.[18] According to a Tibetan Buddhist perspective, which informs Lobsang Namgyal's and Gen Lobsang's understanding of the relation between life and death, death is present in life from the moment of birth, but as Lobsang Namgyal writes, we only become aware of it once physical decline sets in. In old age, the process of dying speeds up. The Lord of Death takes hold of the body, to the point that death can no longer be ignored.

In *Advice from an Experienced Old Man*, Gungtang Rinpoche also describes in various ways how the presence of the Lord of Death is felt in the decaying body. The following are some excerpts from the teaching: "The lines on my forehead are not the creases on a pudgy infant drinking milk from his mother. It is the count by messengers of the Lord of Death of how many years I have already lived. . . . When I dribble and snot comes from my nose, it is not a pearl adornment on my face. It is a sign of the thawing of the ice of youthful vigor by the sunshine of old age. . . . When my hands shake, it is not that I am waving my hands out of greed to get something. It is a sign of the fear of everything being taken away from me by the Lord of Death."[19]

Like the old man, for Gen Lobsang, physical decline was the unsettling manifestation of death. Mo Samdrup Drolma took her almost complete loss of hearing and a disastrous memory of the recent past as a sign that she was near death. The loss of these faculties had isolated her in a way that even several years of home confinement had not. Genla and Mo Samdrup spoke of old age and their current state as if old age and death were not two separate phases. Instead, as the old man speaks in Gungtang Rinpoche's teaching, death had already manifested itself in their bodies. Further on in the teaching of Gungtang Rinpoche, the old man advises the young man, "Since the suffering of death is inevitable, we must do something about it. We cannot just sit and be depressed." His advice to the young man is to meditate on impermanence and "dedicate his life—body, speech, and mind—to Dharma practice."[20]

Apart from the certainty of death, rebirth was another certainty for the elderly. However, unlike death, the future of rebirth could be shaped to a certain extent through daily Buddhist practices, large offerings to holy lamas and monasteries, and the performance of death rituals. Thus, one's time left should not be wasted in depression or denial. It is a precious resource that should be spent in preparing for death and rebirth by improving one's karma and transforming the mind.

Preparing for Death and Rebirth

Gen Lobsang rarely joined the many afternoon gatherings in the shared sitting area on the 2nd floor. Whatever free time he had, he spent in solitude. Genla was not only quieter than others by nature, but as I understand it, he deliberately steered away from the distraction of long conversations. As Genla said to me, all of his thoughts were directed toward death and, accordingly, his everyday life was dedicated, from morning until evening, to Tibetan Buddhist practices.

A general idea repeated by the elderly Tibetans is that each repetition of the same practice, and even a single recitation of the words of the Buddha, will bring merit. As I have witnessed, many of the elderly keep turning the beads of their *mala* even when engaging in conversation, gossip, or watching television. The words of a mantra, usually that of Avalokiteśvara, can be

Figure 33: Mo Samdrup, between worlds. Photo by Harmandeep K. Gill.

seen behind moving lips. Po Ngodrup said the following about the importance of practicing *chö*: "It brings peace of mind. People have attachments.
They desire to be better than others. If one practices Buddhism, it will bring
peace of mind, happiness, and one's mind will become relaxed. And then,
for us Buddhists, there is also a next life. Unlike other religions, like Chris-
tianity, in Buddhism your body transforms after death. That's why it is very
important to practice Buddhism." Another elderly monk acquaintance, Gen
Jampa, said the following about the practice of Tibetan Buddhism: "*Chö*
means to train your mind. It involves clearing the ignorance which our mind
is filled with. As Gyalwa Rinpoche [the Dalai Lama] says, *chö* is the transformation of the mind." Po Ngodrup and Gen Jampa (and other elderly Tibetans) emphasized the transformative dimension of practicing Tibetan
Buddhism, which helps one to clear attachments and ignorance and to achieve
a peaceful state of mind. Moreover, continuous practice also influences one's
karmic destiny in the next life, as clearly stated by Po Ngodrup.

For my elderly friends, the practice of *chö* in old age involved reading
Tibetan Buddhist texts, chanting mantras, practicing circumambulation
around monasteries and other holy sites, doing prostrations, making daily
offerings at the home shrine, and occasionally making bigger offerings (to
monasteries, for example). The practice of reading Buddhist texts, reciting
prayers, and chanting mantras is commonly referred to as *khatön* (prayers).
What kind of practices the elderly carried out on a daily basis depended on
whether they were literate or illiterate, monastics or laypeople, and it also depended on their physical condition.

For my illiterate friends, such as Mo Dickyi Sangmo, Mo Tsering Wangmo,
and Mo Sangye, their daily practice consisted in the daily recitations of mantras and making water-bowl and butter-lamp offerings at their home shrines.[21]
It also involved occasional monetary offerings to the Tsuglagkhang and attendance at teachings by Tibetan Buddhists teachers. Because of their physical condition, they were not able to go for circumambulation or do prostrations.
When they were younger, all of them, including Mo Samdrup, undertook
plenty of *Nyungne* practice, a fasting ritual for Avalokiteśvara that lasts for
two days and is believed to be highly effective for purifying negative karma
and developing compassion. It is practiced together with others and is led by
a high-ranking monastic practitioner. For the duration of the ritual, one is
not allowed to speak. In McLeod Ganj, many people take part in the practice
at the Nyungne Temple.[22] Moreover, Mo Samdrup and Mo Tsering had also
completed *Ngöndro*, also known as "preliminary practices," several times.

Mo Samdrup began practicing *Ngöndro* at a young age, when she and her family still lived in Kyirong. *Ngöndro* is believed to be powerful for purifying one's karma and transforming the mind, and it consists of five to nine practices that should be performed one hundred thousand times each.[23]

Ani Jamyang Choedon, too, had done several rounds of *Ngöndro* and a lot of *Nyungne* throughout her life. Gen Lobsang Choedak had practiced neither. He said he never had the time during his military days or afterward at the TCV school. In old age, both of them spent all of their days immersed in Tibetan Buddhist practices. As monastics, a rigorous daily practice was essential to the fulfilment of their monastic vows. While my other friends, such as Mo Samdrup, who learned to read while in Tibet, finished reading Buddhist texts during the morning hours and returned to the chanting of mantras during different parts of the day, for Genla and Anila, these two practices extended from morning until evening.[24] On a regular basis, both of them were immersed in their prayers when I showed up at their door. I tried to keep my visits short and leave as soon as possible after the massage and the cup of chai or Tibetan butter tea (*bö cha*) they offered me. They were not very fond of chatting during their practice, as it was a distraction.

Regarding her daily practice, Ani Jamyang said, "I have to keep reading until death. This is like my work. I have taken vows (*dompa*)." The daily practices and preparations for death and rebirth can be understood as a type of work, especially in the case of Ani Jamyang and Gen Lobsang, and a continuous striving for transformations that does not cease until the moment of death.

The small daily breaks both of them enjoyed in their busy schedule were for breakfast, lunch, and dinner. At other times, they went to town for shopping or to buy Tibetan medicine. They also took a break from their daily practices when participating in *sobyong* (a ritual for mending vows and purifying breaches) at the Tsuglagkhang, or when attending the Dalai Lama's teachings, which take place several times a year but came to a halt during the COVID-19 pandemic from 2020 to 2022. Attending the Dalai Lama's teachings was also an important part of their religious practice, but when *sobyong* and the Dalai Lama's teachings resumed in the spring of 2022, Ani Jamyang and Gen Lobsang found themselves too frail to attend.[25]

Their rigorous daily practice in old age was not an easy undertaking. Anila spent her days sitting in a cross-legged position on the bed. This was a difficult task for an old body. It gave rise to pain in her neck, back, and knees.

Daily cooking tasks were a much-appreciated break in her schedule. They offered the chance to stretch her body or enjoy a short walk on her balcony. During the summer, especially before the monsoon when the weather is warmer, Anila was more prone to falling asleep. Once I found her asleep, still sitting cross-legged, as she held onto her rosary. If she had to skip her practice for some reason, it gave rise to a certain uneasiness. Because of old age, Ani Jamyang also had to reduce the number of Buddhist texts and prayers she read on a daily basis, telling me, "I do not have the strength in my body."

Because of a fractured hip, Gen Lobsang, was not very comfortable sitting in a cross-legged position. He usually sat on his bed with his legs down and the Tibetan Buddhist texts placed on the table in front of him. In addition to making daily offerings at the home shrine, reading religious texts, and chanting mantras, Genla did a daily practice of prostrations. For him, the practice of prostrations was not only a practice of *chö* but a form of exercise. The practice of circumambulation around the Tsuglagkhang and around the Boudhanath Stupa in Kathmandu was described similarly by the elderly people who carried it out on a daily basis, or several times a week. Some also said that circumambulation offered the opportunity to meet other people. Thus, these two forms of practice not only involved karmic transformations but also had a practical side that involved socializing with others and maintaining one's physical health, both of which were regarded as essential for securing what the elderly understood as a good death.

For Genla, too, working for a peaceful death involved keeping himself healthy and fit. Besides reading Buddhist texts, chanting mantras, and attending prayer sessions at the TCV old-age home or teachings at the Tsuglagkhang, exercise was an important part of his day. Despite being the oldest of my elderly friends, Genla was the fittest.

In 2018, his morning water-bowl and butter-lamp offerings were followed by thirty prostrations. In the evenings, he used to do another round of thirty prostrations. When I visited him in January 2020, he had increased the amount to fifty-five, both morning and evenings. After a cup of tea, he headed out for his daily morning walk, aided by his walking stick. On rare occasions, he would take the tiring steep climb to the TCV monastery, located at the highest point inside the TCV school area. But on a regular basis, he walked up to Dal Lake, either following the car road or the more peaceful path through the TCV school area. Reaching Dal Lake, he usually walked once around the lake. His left hip had healed significantly since its fracturing in 1995, although his left leg was now slightly longer than the right. When he

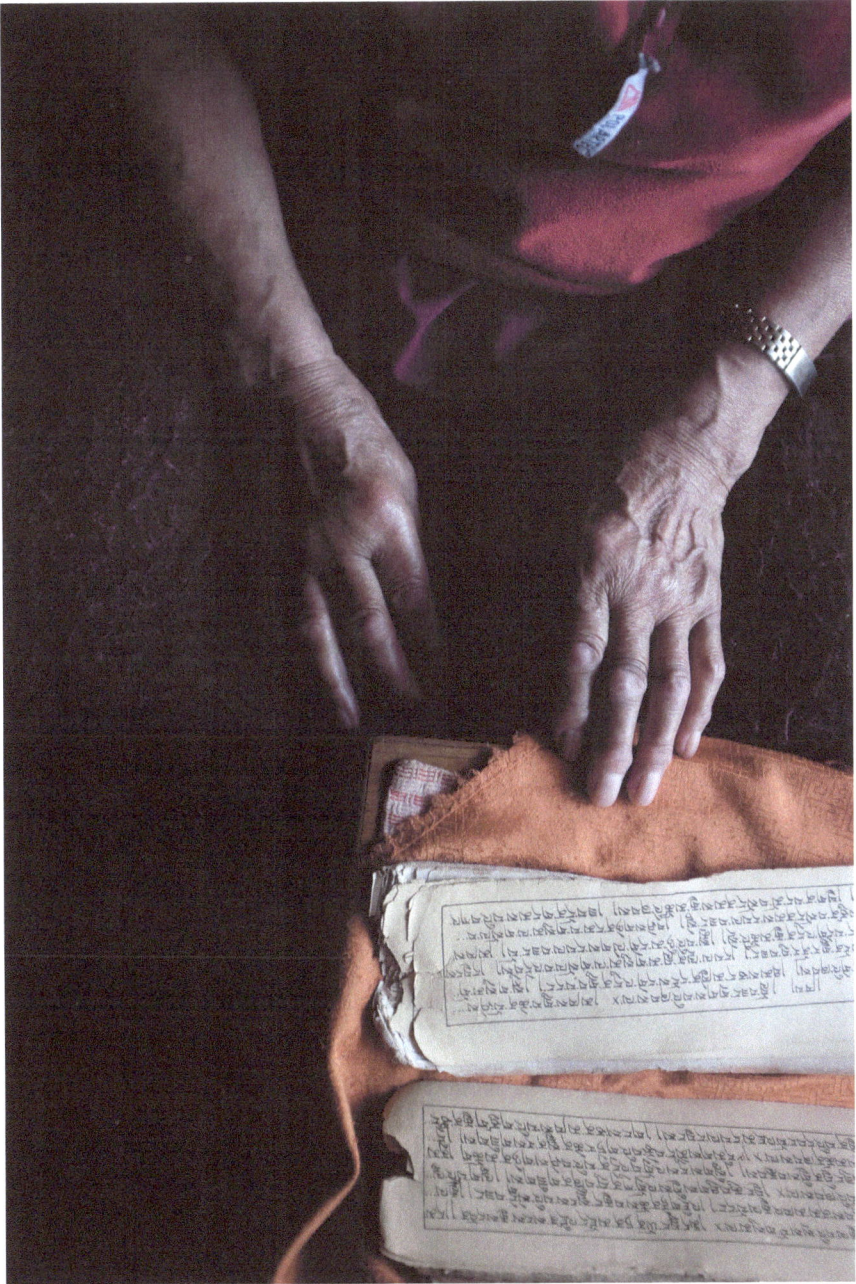

Figure 34: Ani Jamyang reading *pecha*. Photo by Harmandeep K. Gill.

stood up, his knee could not be properly stretched. Apart from the moderate climb and the descent upon return, the condition of his left leg and old age also slowed him down. The entire walk (of approximately two kilometers) took him between one and a half and two hours. In January 2022, Genla reduced his daily walks to a few times a week, partly due to the COVID-19 pandemic. To compensate for his lack of movement, Genla increased the daily amount of prostrations to 250. His solitary walks came to an end in November 2022, when one of the elderly residents from the home suffered a bad fall while out walking. The incidence forced the staff to forbid the residents from going for walks alone, taking away the main contact Gen Lobsang had with the world, outside the TCV old-age home. But from the spring of 2023, he was allowed to resume his daily walks, which these days (summer 2024), owing to his increasing frailty, only happen about three times a week, but he carries out 108 prostrations daily.

Offerings for Rebirth

Despite Gen Lobsang's worries and fears about death, he had nonetheless prepared himself in the best way possible. He had devoted himself to Buddhist practice and exercise, and he had made two big offerings to the Tsuglagkhang. Making offerings to ensure a good rebirth is a common practice among Tibetans. The first time Genla offered to the Dalai Lama was in 1995, after fracturing his left hip—"for it to heal," he said with a half-finished laugh. At the time, he offered about INR 500 and three sets of water bowls in silver. Genla made the largest offering to the Dalai Lama in the 10th month (Tibetan calendar) in 2017, about a year after moving into the TCV old-age home, believing that death was now close by. He offered INR 200,000 at the time. An offering of this amount is, for many Tibetans living in India, made by family members of the deceased during or after the completion of the death rituals, but Gen Lobsang had made it on his own.

These days, he lives on the pension from the TCV school. He has also set aside INR 200,000, as his monthly TCV salary of INR 4,000 is not enough to get by on, despite living rent-free at the old-age home and having three meals a day covered by the home for only INR 620 a month. The meager pension he receives from the Indian government for his military service is also of some help.[26] In addition to the two offerings to the Dalai Lama in old age, he had also made a smaller offering in the mid-1960s, with money he had brought from Tibet. Gen Lobsang could not recall the amount but remembered that it was not a lot. In addition to the money, he also offered two sets of water bowls.

Namgyal Choedup, in his work among elderly Tibetans in Doeguling Settlement in southern India, refers to this traditional practice of offering money and other possessions (e.g. jewelry) to holy lamas as *ngoten*, meaning a dedication and aspiration offering for a good rebirth.[27] Genla remarked that it was important to make the offerings while one is still alive. Likewise, Mo Tsering Wangmo had offered between INR 200,000 and INR 300,000 to the Dalai Lama. Over the years, she had also made monetary offerings to the three big Gelug Monasteries of Ganden, Sera, and Drepung; to the Gyume Tantric Monastery in Hunsur in southern India; and to Gyuto Monastery in Dharamsala.

When I visited the Tibetan settlements in Bylakuppe and Mundgod in southern India in October 2018, Mo Tsering asked me to carry four kilograms of roasted barley to two of the monks at Gyume Tantric Monastery in Hunsur, less than an hour's drive from Bylakuppe. During her former travels to southern India, she had spent extended stays at Gyume Monastery and had become close friends with some of the monks. The roasted barley was an offering that would bring merit not only to her but also to me for taking it to them, Mola pointed out. In 2018 and 2019, she offered INR 300 to the Tsuglagkhang every month (INR 10 a day) for butter-lamp offerings. She also prayed for the sufferings of all sentient beings (*semchen thamche*) to befall her. For Mo Tsering, this was one practice for clearing negative karma and gaining merit. The bigger offerings after her death would be taken care of by her daughter.

By contrast, Genla felt that he could not trust someone else to make these bigger offerings on his behalf, so he undertook them himself. He could not take it for granted that his niece would be present in McLeod Ganj upon his death.[28] Out of the remaining INR 200,000, Genla had put aside INR 100,000 with his niece for her and the TCV old-age home to take care of his corpse and attend to the connected rituals: "When one passes away, money is needed to take care of the corpse. For that I have put aside some money." Money would be needed to buy wood for the cremation, make butter-lamp offerings, and make offerings to monks who perform the rituals and prayers, and as I witnessed, it was also a custom to offer chai and Tibetan butter tea to the fellow elderly and others who made donations for the butter-lamp offerings.

The offerings that Genla had taken care of before his death were, in the case of Mo Yangchen, Mo Tsewang, and her husband, performed by family members. In the case of Mo Tsewang and her husband, two of their children living in the United States and one in McLeod Ganj took responsibility for the death rituals and made offerings to monasteries. Po Ngodrup shared that Mo Yangchen's sons offered INR 100,000 to different monasteries: "The astrologer performed calculations and told us the proper rituals (*shabten*) for a good rebirth. But he can't see what she would be reborn as."

An astrologer is contacted as soon as possible after a death, and death rituals are always made in accordance with the advice from the astrologer from Mentseekhang. The timing of cremation and the types of rituals that should be practiced before the cremation and afterward are based on the person's birth-year horoscope (*lotag*) and the timing of death.[29] During an interview with one of the Mentseekhang administration officers, I learned that the astrologer advises family members on who can touch the corpse, as well as on how to keep the corpse—such as in which direction the corpse should be taken away from home. He added that a person is generally cremated one to two days after death. This was also my experience in the TCV old-age home. After cremation, prayers are performed once a week and end on the 49th day.[30]

Early in 2018, I attended the 49th day of death rituals for an elderly acquaintance, Mo Nyima Choekyi, who used to live in McLeod Ganj and had struggled with alcohol addiction for a long time. I got to know her for a brief period through volunteer work with Tibet Charity. Her death rituals were carried out at the home of her daughter, who lived an hour's drive away from Dharamsala, where Mo Nyima moved in after becoming seriously ill and bedridden in February 2018. She passed away there on 16 February, the first day of the Tibetan New Year. Her daughter invited me to attend the prayers on the final day, when family members and friends of the deceased would also be treated to delicious food.

In the shrine room, where the monks had offered the last of prayers, bags of *tsog* offerings were stacked on top of each other (divided into 130 bags) in one corner. This is a feast offering consisting of snacks, including small beverages that have been blessed during the rituals. It is a common practice to distribute the *tsog* offerings among the friends and acquaintances of the deceased twice during the forty-nine days of death rituals— once in the middle and once on the final day, if one can afford it.[31] Outside the shrine room, one hundred eight butter-lamp offerings burned peacefully, facing the bright noon light from the window. In the room where Mo Nyima Choekyi passed away, five butter lamps were offered, placed below a photograph of the Dalai Lama and two small *thangka* of Chenrezig.

Mo Nyima's grandchildren, her daughter's neighbors, a friend of mine, and I were present on the day. The mood was not at all solemn. Mo Nyima's daughter, Tsomo, was glad that the rituals had concluded. They had demanded much effort (e.g., one hundred eight butter-lamp offerings on a daily basis and the big offerings of *tsog* twice) and money. Acha Tsomo's two siblings in the United States covered most of the expenses. They also sent money for the offerings to monasteries. Acha Tsomo said that without the financial help of her siblings, she would not have the means to take care of the rituals. Moreover, she emphasized that because they did not come to India to offer any practical help, sending money was the least they could do. We enjoyed delicious food, and I had pleasant conversations with Acha Tsomo, her children, and the monks. When we finished eating, Acha Tsomo commented, "We did this, but who will do this for us? Children are going abroad. They won't care about it. And in foreign countries [*chigel*] they can't do all these prayers." Acha Tsomo echoed a worry that was shared by many elderly Tibetans.

In Po Ugyen's case, his son was unable to come to India to attend to the death rituals. The staff at the TCV old-age home called the astrologer, as they always do, but afterward, they handed responsibility (for duties such as taking care of the corpse) to Po Ugyen's distant relatives in Dharamsala. After the cremation, the relatives handed over responsibility to a monastery, with the offerings of money sent by Po Ugyen's son. Those who doubt whether close or distant family members will take care of the death rituals can rest assured that the home will at least take care of the corpse, and possibly also the subsequent rituals, as long as the deceased has left behind enough money.

In the case of another elderly man whom I came to know through Tibet Charity and who died a bedridden and lonely death, funerary services (primarily taking care of the corpse) were handled by his elderly Tibetan neighbors and the Tibetan settlement office in McLeod Ganj. In Doeguling Settlement, the regional chapters of two of the biggest Tibetan NGOs in exile—Tibetan Women's Association and Tibetan Youth Congress—take care of the funerary practices for those who have no one or do not have family living nearby.[32] This is not the case in McLeod Ganj. When alive, the old man relied on Tibet Charity's sponsor system, which provides basic aid to poor elderly Tibetans. Occasionally, a relative living in Lhasa sent him money. He lived in a poor one-room accommodation in Amdo Village, located off Bhagsu

Road. An old wooden shelf functioned as his shrine. Above the shelf, a big photograph of the Dalai Lama and small posters of Avalokiteśvara were taped to the wall. A dirty, worn-out shawl with multiple holes was used as a curtain and covered only parts of the window. It was in front of this window that he passed away. The nurses described him as a humble-hearted and very kind man, something that was apparent upon meeting him. He had a boundless gratitude for the free medicine and the small monetary donations Tibet Charity secured for him. Despite being sick, he smiled and appeared calm and at peace. When he was in good health, Pola used to volunteer at the Tsuglagkhang, sweeping floors and doing other types of cleaning work. Had his volunteer work at one of the holiest temples in exile and his gentle nature perhaps earned him enough merit to gain a good rebirth?

According to elderly Tibetans, actions in this life decide one's rebirth. In 2016, Po Ngodrup referred to death rituals as a tradition or custom (lugsöl) only: "We have been doing this in Tibet for a very long time." He added that it might bring "a little" benefit to the deceased, but not much. "What benefits is keeping a good mind while alive." For Po Ngodrup, if one failed to practice compassion toward others while alive, offerings and rituals alone could not ensure a good death or rebirth. In 2020, when I again asked him about the benefit of death rituals, he said, "What help would shabten do? One has to be genuine. . . . I am sick, I did shabten of [INR] 100,000. What could that help? Won't help much. Be good. If you get sick, go and see a doctor and take medicine. That's the right thing to do. When some people get sick, they perform divination, do shabten. That won't help. 'I am cursed by lha [deities], lhu [nagas], dre [ghosts].' It is all fake. I don't believe such things. Other people may."[33] He said that, most importantly, "Every day after getting up, one has to think about impermanence. Today you go to bed, and whether you will get up the next morning, you cannot say one hundred percent. So one has to remind oneself of impermanence, keep a kind mind, motivation, and not harm others. If one can't benefit others, then try at least not to cause harm. That is very important. Getting up in the morning, one has to think good."

The Dalai Lama's numerous teachings constantly highlight the importance of cultivating the right motivation and practicing virtuous behavior while alive. In the absence of children, the Dalai Lama's advice is a source of consolation for many lonely elders and helps them to die in a peaceful state of mind.

The elderly trust that the purification of negative karma in this life will help them on the journey after death and in attaining a good rebirth. Gen

Lobsang felt he had done his best to practice diligently and to be kind to others. He had made all the necessary offerings prior to his death, which provided some reassurance, but uncertainty always lingered. Gen Lobsang also added, "But it's difficult to know whether I will be reborn as human or not."

The belief that it is incredibly hard to attain a human birth adds to the vague and unsettling aspect of rebirth, just like death. Mo Dickyi echoed a similar uncertainty to Genla's: "I worry. Where or what I will be reborn as, wild animal or cattle? It's hard to say what I will be reborn as. If you have done good, you will be born as something good. If you haven't done good, you will reborn as something bad. Some people steal and think of bad things, I have never stolen. I don't have greed over others' possessions, honestly. . . . If you have greed over others' things, then bad things will happen to you. I don't. Even if it's only a cup of tea, I offer it to others. Some aren't like that. To my acquaintances and others, I say, 'Have a cup of tea.'"

Like others, Mo Dickyi trusted that she had held the right motivation and done good to others in this life. All she could do was hope that it would bear fruit and result in a good rebirth.

Ready to Die

The 3rd of November 2022 was an auspicious day for Ani Jamyang Choedon. Anila recalled the events of the day in great detail. She got up at 5:00 A.M. It was still dark when she made one cup of chai for herself and one cup for Tenzin, her relative who looked after her eldest sister, Samdrup Drolma. After drinking the tea, they slowly walked down the stairs to Tipa Road, where a taxi awaited them. From there, they set off for the Dalai Lama's residence. Ani Jamyang had been granted an audience with the Dalai Lama. Akhu Dhondrup, her younger brother, signed her up for an audience not long ago. It is important for elderly Tibetans to have received blessings from the Dalai Lama throughout their lives, especially in old age. Ani Jamyang Choedon had seen the Dalai Lama in her dreams several times in life. She could recall in detail three of the dreams when the Dalai Lama had also blessed her on the head. [34]

Anila was one of few people who had been granted an audience on 3 November. She recalled that there were a few people from Nepal and Western countries waiting in line. When it was Anila's turn, she lowered her head and held the Dalai Lama's hands. As the Dalai Lama put his hands on Anila's head and blessed her, she prayed, "May you live long, may you live long, may you live long." Then she made him an offering of INR 100,000 tied with a rubber band and wrapped neatly inside a yellow *khata*. This was the biggest offering Ani Jamyang made to the Dalai Lama, with the generous help of one of her younger sisters who lived in Europe and had sent the money. The money had been with Anila for some time. She had believed, "One day, I will offer this to *Sangye* [the Buddha]."

After the audience, the security guards helped Anila into a wheelchair and dropped her off at the gate of the Dalai Lama's residence, where Tenzin was waiting for her. From there, they slowly walked to the Tsuglagkhang and did three rounds of circumambulation inside the temple, before offering money for one hundred butter-lamp offerings.

The audience and blessing from the Dalai Lama in old age was a life-transformative event for Ani Jamyang.[35] This was her second audience with the Dalai Lama, but it had been more extraordinary for Anila than the first one, which took place in Bodhgaya in India more than fifty years ago. When Anila told me about the audience in late December 2022, she said that tears come to her eyes whenever she thought about it. And as she spoke about the auspicious day, especially the moment when the Dalai Lama blessed her, tears indeed gathered in her eyes. She folded her hands multiple times during our conversation, while uttering a prayer to express her gratitude for getting so close to the Dalai Lama and getting the chance to make an offering before her death. "I never thought that I would get this lucky. . . . I must have prayed for it in my past life," she kept repeating. Ani Jamyang believed the event was a result of the merit she had accumulated through her lifelong devotion to Tibetan Buddhist practice. She recalled the religious commitments she had sincerely observed since becoming ordained as a nun at the age of eighteen, including playing religious instruments, working as the discipline head, and sweeping floors at her nunnery.

Anila believed the precious blessings from the Dalai Lama to be a result of the hardships she had endured in life, especially during the years in the Helambu region of Nepal after she and thirteen other nuns from their nunnery in Kyirong escaped to the region. Their escape took place before the People's Liberation Army had reached Kyirong.

Helambu is inhabited by the Hyolmos, who trace their ancestry to Kyirong. It is also a sacred area for Tibetan Buddhists, believed to have been blessed by Guru Rinpoche and other Buddhist masters, including Jetsun Milarepa, who was a famous Tibetan Yogi and spiritual poet. He underwent great hardships in life, including solitary meditation in multiple caves before reaching enlightenment.

The Hyolmos were generous to the nuns. They gave them a piece of land, and from time to time, offered them food. The nuns built basic accommodation for themselves and a prayer hall. It was while Anila was in the Helambu region, when food was scarce and she and her fellow nuns did plenty of *Nyungne* practice, that she had a dream about meeting the Dalai Lama in Tibet. She remembered that she dreamt it around dawn:

> In front of the cave, there was a throne of the height of Kyabgön Rinpoche [the Dalai Lama]. There was a nun, a chanting master. She was walking swiftly before me. By the time I got close to the throne, she had received her blessing and had already left. Then I slowly approached Kyabgön Rinpoche's throne. In a plate placed on the table next to the throne, there was an offering of coins, white coins and black coins. Kundun [the Dalai Lama] told me to make an offering in it. And I happened to have a coin in my pocket. So, I made an offering in the plate. It was a kind of plate we used in Tibet. Then I received *chawang* [a hand blessing on the head]. I dreamt it very vividly. I have dreamt of Kyabgön Rinpoche many times. But this dream, it was as if it happened in real life.

For three of the years Ani Jamyang spent in the Helambu region, she worked in the construction of a monastery of the Drukpa Kagyu order, which is a sublineage of the Kagyu lineage of Tibetan Buddhism, in which Jetsun Milarepa is one of the lineage's great masters. Anila recalled the experience of extreme cold and hunger. They lived solely on porridge and nettle soup. "There was no sight of Tibetan butter tea or chai," she said. When there was no food, which often happened to be the case, they went to bed hungry. Ani Jamyang recalled that she did such arduous physical labor—carrying wood planks, rocks, and sand on her back—that she lost all of her hair.

When the construction concluded, Anila returned to the accommodation she shared with the other nuns in the lower part of the valley. Some of the nuns had, at the time, left for Kathmandu. After her return, Anila fell seriously ill. She recalled how none of the other nuns checked on her, not even offering her a cup of water, except for a local Hyolmo nun who lived close by. Word was sent to Anila's family, who at the time were settling into their new lives in exile in India. To this day, she recalled how her eldest sister, Samdrup

Drolma, had traveled to the Helambu region to get her: "My sister looked at me and cried. She said, 'You look as if you are near death.' She told me that I couldn't stay there and offered me to go with her [to India]." Despite being sick and frail, Anila declined her sister's offer. But if she remained, there would be no one to feed and take care of her. She finally made the decision to join Samdrup Drolma one morning when she was so frail that she could hardly breathe. From Helambu, they set off for Kathmandu. Men were hired to carry Ani Jamyang on their backs. In old age, Anila felt bad for the trouble she had caused her family, especially Samdrup Drolma: "*Nyingje*, I troubled her a lot. And now, in her old age, I cannot even assist her." After reaching Kathmandu, Anila was hospitalized for about half a month. When she had recovered, the sisters set off for India by bus. Anila was about forty years old at the time.

Ani Jamyang's time in Nepal was, for her, the hardest period of her life. But she believed that those years of struggle had purified her negative karma. She even likened her struggles to those of Jetsun Milarepa: "I think I have done my little bit of what Jetsun Mila did." Anila believed there was a karmic connection between these hardships and the auspicious audience with the Dalai Lama in November 2022. After the audience, Anila even commented that this (old age) was the happiest period of her life.

Anila had always told me that she had no regrets in life. She had committed to her monastic vows to the best of her ability. After having received the Dalai Lama's blessing in 2022, she said that she was now ready to die: "What more does one need in life. I have lived long. So, by the grace of Kyabgön Yeshe Norbu [the Dalai Lama], I am ready to die any time. What I could have offered, I have offered."

As Ani Jamyang's story exemplifies, the potential for transformations is present until the moment of death: in the elderly's repetitions of Buddhist practices, in the practice of virtuous behavior, and even in the blessings received from holy lamas. In Anila's case, the audience with the Dalai Lama—most likely to be her last one—not only ignited her spirit and gave her hope for the future, it also reshaped her experience, bringing an increased appreciation for the hardships she had endured. Yet, in spite of this, Anila recognized that death and rebirth remained indeterminate.

Anila said that she hoped to be reborn as a human in the next life, so she could continue her Tibetan Buddhist practice and carry on down the path to liberation. But in the next sentence, she raised a doubt: "It's hard to be born into human form. Whatever, I always pray to be born close to Gyalwa Yeshe Norbu [the Dalai Lama]." This was a hope that was shared by all of my elderly friends. They hoped not only to be reborn as a human but also as a Tibetan Buddhist, and ideally, somewhere close to the Dalai Lama. But all of them recognized that their efforts ran up against forces beyond their control.[36] Yet the aporia of death and rebirth continued to demand their daily attention and work, and the hope of dying peacefully and attaining a good rebirth persisted and motivated them.

The Invisible Path

Death and rebirth triggered many questions, uncertainties, and hopes for my elderly friends. Regardless of their numerous reflections, Tibetan Buddhist practices, and various offerings, both death and rebirth remained unsettling events, confronting them with what Alfred Gell refers to as the "objective" qualities of time—in other words, impermanence.[37] "When death strikes our loved ones, most of us stand defenseless and have to face the irreversibility of time," writes Rane Willerslev, Dorthe R. Christensen, and Lotte Meinert.[38] They recognize, as did my elderly friends, that one cannot undo the flow of time. But still, we need to cope with the objective, or abstract, qualities of time somehow, as they suggest, by "taming" time through concrete religious or cultural technologies. This is one way people try to clear a path in the midst of uncertainty from that which is given to them.[39]

The elderly Tibetans' daily work and attention to the coming of death and rebirth represented practical, mental, and emotional efforts to clear a path with the help of religious and cultural resources. Importantly, as emphasized by the elderly, their daily practices had a transformative dimension. These transformations involved staying healthy and fit, the purification of negative karma, letting go of negative emotions and attachments, cultivating the right motivation toward others (such as compassion), and accepting impermanence.

Thus, the time that was left was a precious resource, and by "taming" it, one could also cultivate something new. It was a process of constant becoming, which in one sense meant the purification of negative karma and in another sense meant ceasing attachments and coming to terms with the inevitability of death. The former would improve one's karmic destiny, and the latter would bring a peaceful mind. Each repetition of the same practice with the right attitude, including blessings by holy lamas, carried the potential for these transformations.

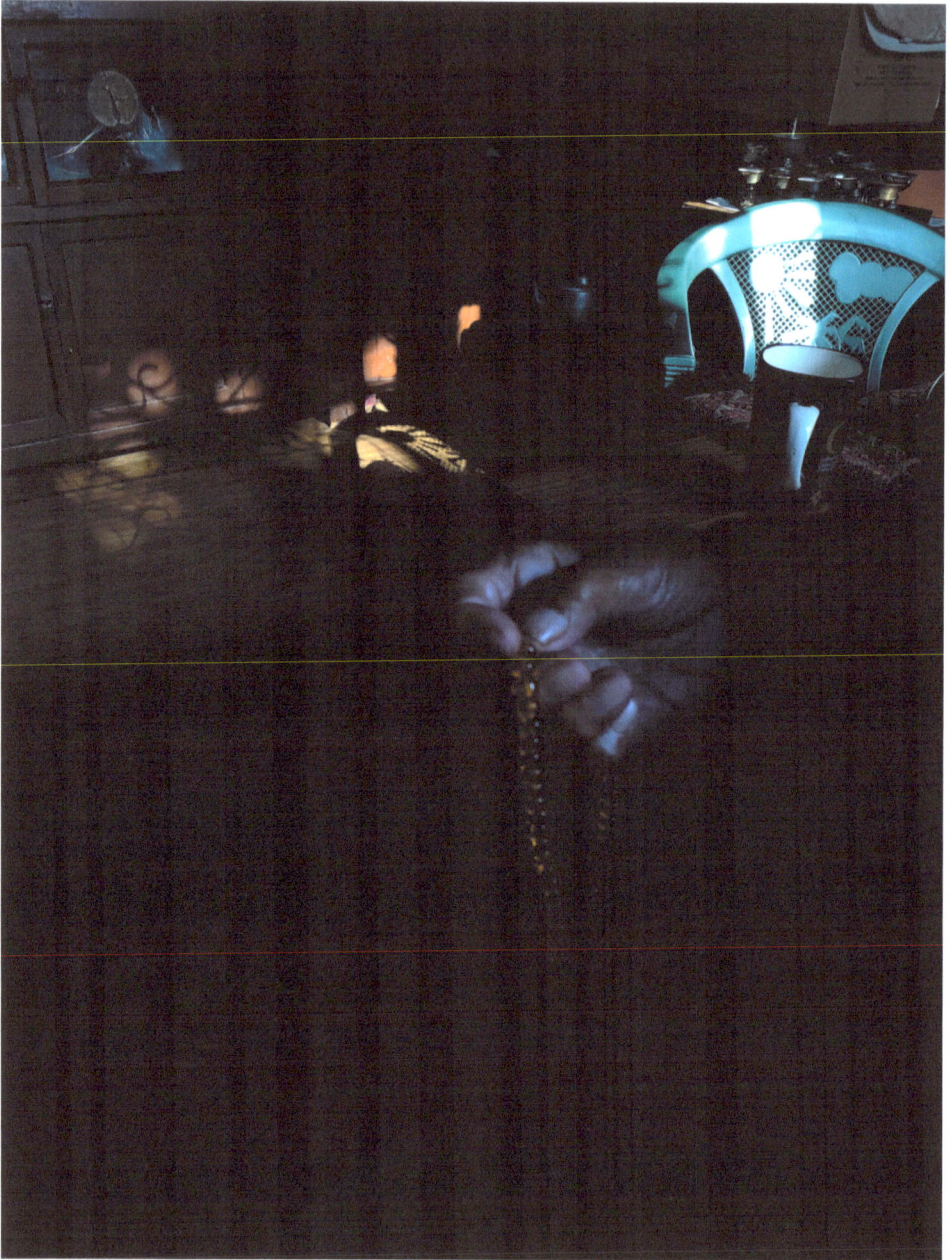

Figure 35: Clearing the path: Mo Samdrup reciting *mani* in the last rays of sunlight. Photo by Harmandeep K. Gill.

Even though time could to a certain extent be "tamed" by making the best use of it, one also had to come to terms with the fact that time and death remained unpredictable. Any day could be one's last. One could go to sleep today and not wake up tomorrow, as so wonderfully captured in a famous poem by the Buddhist philosopher Nāgārjuna:

> Life flickers in the flurries of a thousand ills,
> More fragile than a bubble in a stream.
> In sleep, each breath departs and is again drawn in;
> How wondrous that we wake up living still![40]

The crucial thing one needs to come to terms with in a Tibetan Buddhist context is the impermanence of life. We are limited creatures, and death and rebirth cannot be brought within the realm of the layperson's experience or control. One must surrender to impermanence and accept the uncertainty it evokes. However, despite the elderly Tibetans' acceptance of forces beyond them, doubts, worries, and fears continued to arise.

The path that was being fashioned, cleared, or followed through daily Buddhist practices remained invisible to the naked eye. But through continued practice and the belief that one had done what one could do sincerely, hope was also woven into this invisible path, I suggest.

Anand Pandian writes that we often tend to think of hope as the desire of something specific, cultivated by the optimistic, the devoted or ambitious.[41] Furthermore, it can be dismissed as "flimsy, fickle and naïve. . . . Think of it as a current sweeping from an unknown source to an unforeseeable destination."[42] Such a hope was present in the lives of my elderly friends, as evoked, for example, by Ani Jamyang Choedon after her audience with the Dalai Lama. Such a hope was present not only in relation to death and rebirth but also in relation to their recollections and imaginations of the past, or possible futures.

Hope in their everyday lives could have an optimistic nature, but in relation to death and rebirth, it remained vague and unsettled. I understand hope to be more like Pandian describes it: as a current from an unknown source and an unforeseeable destination that seems to be pulling at one. For my friends, hope was that invisible path being cleared down the mountain pass. The pull of hope was present in their daily ritualized practices: in the weaving and creation of something new from what was given to them, such as physical condition, religious practice, and the singularities of their lives (e.g., life history, family relations, and material conditions). The pull of hope was also evoked in the belief that they had done their best. The challenge was to not let oneself get carried away by the strong emotional sensibilities that were awakened by that pull of hope, or by the worries and fears awakened by the future, but as I have shown in the various chapters, it could be incredibly difficult to practice this in real life, as these were a part of people's embodied being.

Acceptance

On 24 March 2023, Gen Lobsang received his final audience with the Dalai Lama. I signed him up for an audience on 10 March, after he asked me to do so. Dawn was breaking when the taxi arrived at the gate of the Tsuglagkhang at 6:00 A.M. on the 24th. Genla and I slowly made our way inside, where more people were waiting, also for an audience. Genla was carrying in his bag another offering of INR 100,000, which would be his final offering to the Dalai Lama. At 8:00 A.M., they were all invited inside. Meanwhile, I waited in the courtyard of the Tsuglagkhang. At 8:30, I saw Genla walking toward me, wearing a *khata* around his neck. His face mask was still on. When I asked, he told me that it all went well. He was able to place his offering in the Dalai Lama's hands. In the evening, I got ahold of the photographs of Gen Lobsang's audience with the Dalai Lama; Genla is standing face to face with the Dalai Lama with folded hands, his head bowed and his face covered with a mask. The Dalai Lama touches Genla's hands, while saying something to him, and then blesses him on the head. Genla got the images framed into one frame that hangs above the entrance to the kitchen. Genla commented that he thinks that no one else at the TCV old-age home has been so lucky as to receive three audiences with the Dalai Lama. From his bed, where he spends his days reading *pecha*, reciting *mani*, eating food, or just sitting in silence, Genla looks directly at the images of their holiest lama blessing him for the last time in this life.

Perhaps Gen Lobsang Choedak is one of my elderly friends who can teach us about what it would mean to accept and let go, while also giving every day his best effort. His spirits would rise when we for example spoke about Tibet, but in each conversation, he would add an acceptance of the loss and the transient nature of human life. The sadness in him was not overt, nonetheless, it slipped into certain statements. I also felt it in his silent character, in his letting go of even speech itself, and in how he responded to almost every question with a humble smile or began a laugh that could not properly reach out. Hopes pulled at him, but his silence and humble smile hinted at an acceptance of things as they were: of dying a lonesome death, letting go, and surrendering to the uncertain journey down the mountain pass.

April 2022

On 25 April 2022, around 4:30 A.M., Mo Dickyi shouted the names of her relative, Tenzin, and her son, Tashi, who had been jointly taking care of her. She was in extreme physical pain. "I am going to die," she said in distress. They massaged her feet and back. Mo Dickyi calmed down. Tashi thought everything was all right, as this was not the first time Mo Dickyi had experienced grave pain, and suggested that they go back to sleep. Around 6:00 A.M., Tashi woke up and thought of Mo Dickyi immediately. He rushed back to her room and found that Mo Dickyi Sangmo was gone.

Mo Dickyi repeatedly said that it was better to die than to suffer the way she was suffering. After being bedridden for almost two months and in great pain, her body gave in. From around the Tibetan New Year onward, Mo Dickyi's family members and I began witnessing her weakening condition. No longer able to feed herself, walk, or go to the toilet on her own, on the first day of the Tibetan New Year, she moved in with her sister, Mo Samdrup Drolma, who was cared for by their relative, Tenzin. During her final days, her weight dropped to thirty-five kilograms. As she herself would say: There was nothing left but bones.

At 4:30 A.M. on 25 April 2022, I was on a flight from New Delhi to Copenhagen, traveling for a conference. Before leaving, I had given Mo Dickyi a tight hug, telling her that I would see her after ten days. Being unable to speak, she had carefully nodded. I feared that Mo Dickyi might pass away in my absence and repeatedly told Tenzin to call me if anything happened while I was traveling to New Delhi or while I was waiting there for my flight to Copenhagen. I would immediately return. The first message I sent after landing in Copenhagen was to Tenzin. He replied, "Mo Dickyi passed away early morning today." The news paralyzed me.

Mo Dickyi was taken very good care of by family members, including her son, who, after learning about her condition, arrived on 1 April. But I am not sure whether Tashi's presence comforted her. Perhaps because she was too

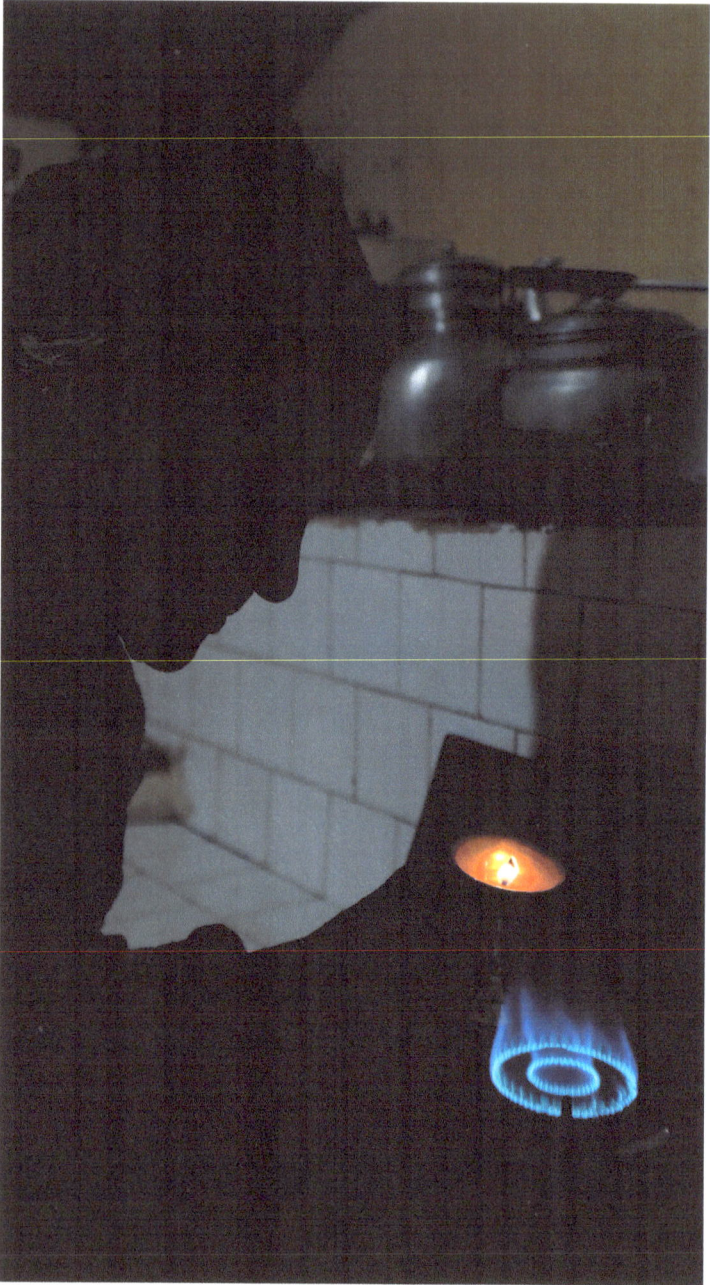

Figure 36: *Chöme* in Mo Dickyi's hand. Photo by Harmandeep K. Gill.

frail and sick? Tashi, too, behaved like a stranger. Yet, when I returned to McLeod Ganj, it was actually in him that I felt her presence the strongest. Every time I looked at his face, she was right there.

Mo Dickyi died barely one meter away from Samdrup Drolma, who did not sense her passing until she was told of it by Tashi and Tenzin. Returning to McLeod Ganj after ten days, I sat on the bed where she took her last breaths, letting my hands rest on the new mattress, which was bought by Tenzin and me on 22 April to make her more comfortable.

Her death rituals were handled in the best way possible. Monks and family members jointly did proper prayers. Monetary offerings were made to monasteries for her good rebirth. While she lingered in *bardo*, butter lamps were offered for forty-nine days in Mo Samdrup Drolma's home. Tenzin cleaned, refilled, and lit the lamps each morning, while I took responsibility for these tasks in the evening. During this period of time, Tashi offered food and prayers to her spirit three times a day.

Mo Dickyi's fellow Kyirong-wa and family said that she passed away on a good day. It was sunny and warm. And it was during the time of year when Tibetans were not away for the seasonal winter business. The days when people were locked in their homes due to the COVID-19 pandemic were also gone. Thus, most people from Kyirong Village came to make offerings and do prayers for Mo Dickyi. Importantly, it was perceived that she died a good death in the presence and care of family. Everyone, including family, friends, and acquaintances, was present in her death. It was believed that all of this would aid her in gaining a good rebirth.

Because of her auspicious death, the Kyirong-wa now said that Mo Dickyi must have been a good person. Despite her temper, she must have had a good heart, they said.

Postlude

My elderly friends looked down from the mountain pass, to the unknown journey they would inevitably one day make. As they waited, their gaze also turned backward, to the views they had left behind. Their eyes chose to rest on specific parts of their journey thus far, such as the paths of a village in Kyirong, scenes at Ganden Monastery, the streets of Lhasa, a dream dreamt while living in the Hyolmo region of Nepal, battles fought against the People's Liberation Army between the high passes of Mustang, or their early days of exile in a country that they thought would be only a temporary stop. As they waited to cross the mountain pass, life was for them finished. In the absence of a future in this life and, for some, the absence of loving companionship, their thoughts were split between dying and togetherness with others in the past. Distant and intangible hopes echoed from two different directions: from down the unknown mountain pass and from the journey already traveled.

Mo Dickyi Sangmo was not the only one to cross over to the journey of a new rebirth in 2022. Mo Tsering Wangmo passed away on 3 March, the first day of *losar*, in the presence of her relatives in northeastern India. Before I left McLeod Ganj on 28 July 2023, Mo Samdrup's speech had become severely limited, as had her ability to move around, understand others, and make herself understood. When I said goodbye to her before my departure, I suspected I would not see her again. As I held her hands in mine, I silently thanked her for everything, multiple times. I also apologized for any mistakes I might have made. It is difficult to walk away when one suspects a goodbye to be final. On 22 November 2023, around 6:30 A.M., Mo Samdrup Drolma crossed the mountain pass in her sleep.

At the time of this writing (July 2024), the remaining others are still at the mountain pass. Gen Lobsang Choedak is in good health but insists that not much remains of him now, and he says this always with an accepting smile. Po Damchoe and Ani Jamyang endure painful knees, just like the others, but their appetite is consistent. When I returned in December 2023,

Anila told me that since the passing of her sister, Mo Samdrup, she had not been happy, especially because she had not seen her elderly sister for a long time before she died. Anila remembered Mo Samdrup's kind heart and cried, repeatedly referring to her as *nyingje*. Ani Jamyang and the others echo Mo Samdrup's words: "I have no thoughts. Whenever the day of death comes, I will have to go."

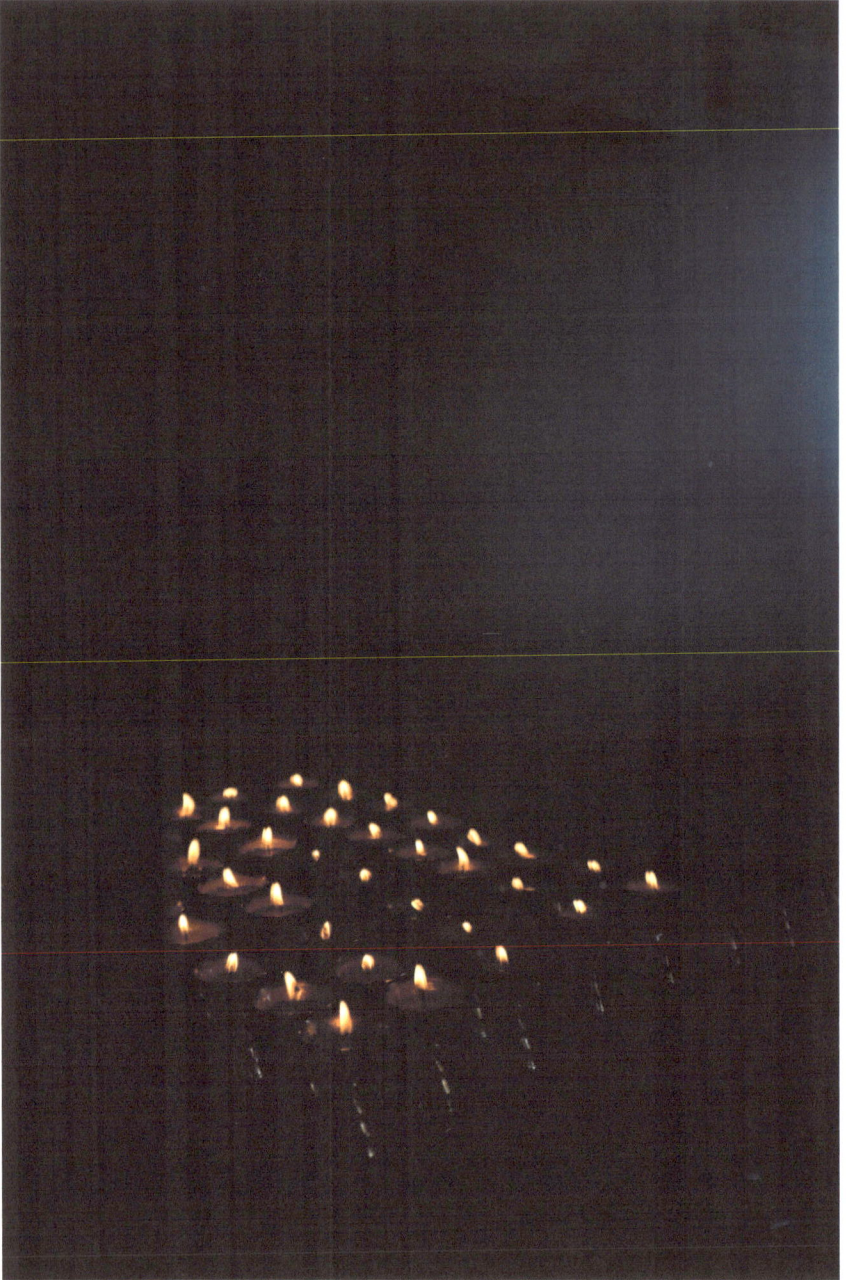

Figure 37: *Om mani padme hum*. Prayers and offerings for those who are gone.
Photo by Harmandeep K. Gill.

CONCLUSION

Endings and Continuations

Is this all you?
Mysterious and lucid
present and absent at once.

—Mahmoud Darwish (2009)

The alarm rings, for the second time. It is 6:40 A.M. I find myself in Oxford, but I am back to my usual wanderings to other places and times, moving between my time in McLeod Ganj, somewhere else in the world, and into the future. On a daily basis, I move through a number of rooms in my mind: rooms located in the future, and rooms in the past; some real, and some imagined. The rooms I move through daily are the homes of my elderly friends. In the process of writing this book, it has often felt like I only live there, in the past with them, my own present becoming somewhat absent to me. When I sent video messages to all of them a long time ago, I was not lying when I said, "I always think of you."

On some days, my attention is directed toward them from morning until evening. I attempt to visualize and feel their presence; I listen to their words and silences. I see Mo Dickyi Sangmo looking out the window, even though she is no more. I imagine the empty road below her house. I see us clearing the water-bowl offerings together or cleaning her kitchen for *losar*. I even listen for her rare laughter. Since her passing, such impressions are also accompanied by the sight of her lying in bed, crumpled in pain during her final days. I hear myself telling her repeatedly, "I will see you in ten days." I wonder what images might have flashed before her eyes when she realized that she was slipping away, when she distressfully said, "I am going to die," as if her son and Tenzin would be able to hold her back in life. Did she see herself as a small girl in Kyirong? Did she see the fields of their village? The face of her son as a child? The faces of her parents and siblings? Was I in her mind's eye too?

I used to visualize Ani Jamyang Choedon coming down Tipa Road to buy groceries. She would not notice me until I stood right in front of her. But these days, I keep seeing a younger version of her, doing heavy labor in the Helambu region, or lying sick in a hospital bed in Kathmandu. My mind is also dominated by the sight of her inside her small apartment, where she became confined after falling down the stairs below her home, once in 2022 and then in 2023, first twisting her right ankle and then breaking her right wrist. I see the portable toilet chair placed not too far from her bed, with a bucket underneath. This image is accompanied by flashbacks of myself rushing back and forth between my own room and Anila's residence, emptying and cleaning the toilet bucket over the course of one month in 2022. Anila has also become forgetful. The timeline of her life keeps shifting and moving into an incomprehensible order, leaving me confused.

Mo Tsering Wangmo is sitting on a chair or on a bed somewhere in northeastern India, where she moved in with her relatives in late December 2019. But we meet in her room in McLeod Ganj. The remote control is in her left hand. She switches between channels while uttering something about whatever she sees on the television. I hear her voice over the phone, affectionately ordering me to hurry, calling me by the Tibetan name given to me by a friend, "Dadon, come fast! The food is getting cold." Her other words echo in my ears too: "Did you call your mother? No one loves like a mother." Pasang-la, Bhuti-la, and other caregivers move through the room. It could be Pasang-la who is cooking in the kitchen, but Bhuti-la could be the one eating with us, even though I know that she, too, is no longer in this world. She passed away suddenly in August 2019. I used to have her messages on my WeChat; her voice sounded joyous over getting a job where she would once again take care of Tibetan children. How strange to hear her voice and the voices of Mo Dickyi, Mo Tsering, and Mo Samdrup in the videos saved on my iPhone; they seem so real, as if they are still in this world, living in McLeod Ganj.

Many times, I go to the TCV old-age home in my mind. I still see Mo Pema Choedon sitting all alone in the shared sitting area on the 1st floor, even though she, too, is no more. She cannot hear much, or talk. As I am about to pass her, I bow my head and hold up my right hand as a gesture of greeting. She shakes her head slightly. Gen Lobsang Choedak is upstairs in his room on the 2nd floor. The walking stick is leaning on the wall, confirming to me that he is inside. In Genla's company, there is mostly silence. When I am done massaging his leg, I sit on the bed next to his. He looks around in the room and scratches his head. The chai he used to make for me was far too sweet to my taste, but I would drink it anyway. It took over six months before I cultivated the courage to ask him to add less sugar, being overtly conscious of not making demands of a gesture that was delivered with so much kindness and care.

From Genla's room, I usually walk up to the TCV camp area. As I pass the TCV school ground, some naughty young Tibetan boys and girls test their Hindi on me. They giggle and whisper when I respond to them in Tibetan. When I start walking up the stairs to TCV camp, it is suddenly winter. I can see Po Damchoe sitting outside in the sun and mumbling a mantra. He reaches for my hand to greet me. I sit down next to him and take a deep breath as we take in the view in front of us. One of my beloved dogs, Tyler, who accompanied me every day during my fieldwork, faithfully sits at my side and also takes a nap in the glorious winter sun.

My elderly friends rest in my eyes. These images of them are accompanied by numerous other flashbacks, some real and some imagined. I keep wandering through their homes, the streets of McLeod Ganj, and paths in the forest, longing for that time and place whenever I am away, even in my dreams.

Sometimes, I find it hard to distinguish between my elderly friends and me: the absences in me and the absences in Mo Dickyi, the restlessness in me and the restlessness in Mo Tsering, the silence in me and the silence in Gen Lobsang, or the loneliness in me and the loneliness in all of them.

What Remains at the Mountain Pass?

Tenzin's three pet cats were roaming around on Mo Samdrup Drolma's balcony. One of the stray dogs, Nagri, whom Tenzin used to feed, tried to enter through the main gate to sit inside the property, or maybe she was looking for water. Mo Samdrup used to keep a strict eye on the dogs and cats. She was not fond of animals, especially cats. When the cats happened to come near her, she would hit them with her stick and curse them in her heavy, stern voice. The cats seemed unbothered by her words, so she kept at it, switching between calling them names—"(the) one that should be eaten" (*sha zagyu*, an expression of exasperation)[1] or "on my father's corpse" (*ape ro*)—and making an irritated sound: "Shaaazaaa." The stray dogs were not spared either, but unlike the cats, they seemed frightened of Mo Samdrup.

Mo Samdrup's face has been covered in wrinkles since I first met her. Over the years, they have only deepened. A small seizure in the summer of 2020 left her with a partial disability. She could no longer use the toilet and had to start wearing diapers. Fleece pants and sweaters replaced her *chupa* and *onju*. Language began failing her too. However, Mo Samdrup made an amazing recovery, even regaining her ability to move around the house, thanks to the precious care of Tenzin, not to mention her own determined spirit. She regained her ability to make full sentences, although her language became increasingly simplified. She no longer spoke about Kyirong as she did up until 2020. Sometimes, I wondered whether she could see those mental images of her *phayül*, despite not having the language to express them anymore, or whether they too were disintegrating and becoming fuzzy, just like her memory of the recent past. Yet, despite her limited words, Mo Samdrup's voice remained strong. I was amazed by the strength she was able to muster to shout at the animals at the top of her lungs, willing to do her utmost to keep them off her property. Remembering the tenacity of her will, I am struck by the unchanging nature of our habits, by their stubbornness.

During such episodes, when she shouted at the dogs, cats, or monkeys, I would see glimpses of Mo Samdrup. The woman she used to be was still in there, intact in her habits, or in her use of local words, phrases, and even curse words from Kyirong. When she was ready to go back inside the house, there was no chance she would leave behind the small handwoven carpets for chairs. Despite the slowness of her body and lack of strength in her arms, she would patiently collect the carpets and carry them back inside, only to come out to sit at the balcony again in half an hour or so, once again carrying the carpets back outside. Similarly, her lifelong habit of using electricity sparsely remained intact. If the kitchen lights happened to be turned on during the day, she would tell Tenzin to turn them off. Her hospitality remained gracious, evident in the way she would insist that any visitor should drink tea and eat something. In old age, because of her poor memory of the recent past, she tended to insist even more, forgetting that the person had declined her offer multiple times. Mo Samdrup also never forgot that the water-bowl offerings had to be cleared from the shrine after 12:00 noon.

So many of Mo Samdrup's lifelong habits remained at the age of ninety-three. For the Tibetan New Year celebrations in 2021, when she had recovered sufficiently and become more like her former self, she cooked a *losar* delicacy from Kyirong, filled with tons of butter. She had managed to eat an entire bowl of it, whereas I could hardly get down five spoonfuls. Even though her habits remained intact, resting in her body, they were, nonetheless, not as precise as before—for example, she might clear the shrine before noon, instead of at 3:00 or 4:00 P.M., like she always did when I first met her in 2015. By 2020, she also kept forgetting that one of the dogs she cursed at was Tenzin's pet and had lived with them for over three years. She called Tenzin different names too—Tashi, Tsering, Lobsang—changing from day to day, or from one part of the day to the next.

Mo Samdrup Drolma's singular ways could be seen in the performance of the simple household tasks she was capable of completing. Similarly, the habits of my other friends, nurtured over their long lives, remained steady. Mo Tsering Wangmo kept insisting that the caregivers do things in a certain way—for example, clean the house a certain way or store the food in a particular manner. This usually resulted in dissatisfaction on both sides. Ani Tenzin Pema had grown more frail since I first met her in 2016. She was no longer able to walk to McLeod Ganj from the TCV old-age home. Yet, her spirit was always joyous. Five minutes of chatter with Ani Tenzin could still turn into an hour-long conversation, as she switched from topic to topic, usually without waiting for a response from the listener. Her devotion to birds, too, remained unfaltering. They would fly into the home for Anila's daily gracious gifts of rice and bread. Po Damchoe's desire for alcohol had not diminished, although he could not drink as much as before. His voice stayed at the same decibel level, never sounding too sad, happy, or disappointed. His patience with everything and everyone was also as steady as before.

While my elderly friends grew frail and even fell sick during the years we spent together, their voices, just like their habits, remained distinctive. Like the voices of her three sisters, Mo Samdrup's voice was terrifying when she was angry. All of the sisters had strong and stern voices. Ani Tenzin Pema's and Gen Lobsang Choedak's voices were by comparison sweet, gentle, and open to persuasion. When Mo Dickyi was bedridden, she was even capable of shouting at Mo Samdrup, because her elderly sister would not stop making incoherent comments in an effort to communicate with Mo Dickyi. Sometimes it was not possible to make sense of Mo Samdrup's utterances; and being in grave physical pain, Mo Dickyi simply wanted to be left in silence. Even though Mo Dickyi Sangmo, Mo Tsering Wangmo, and others are gone, their voices continue to echo in my ears. I still hear Mo Dickyi's rare laughter or the husky and heavy voice of Mo Yangchen from the TCV old-age home, and how she, in her broken and limited Hindi, used to call me *bhen-ji* ("sister"). I also clearly recall Mo Yangchen's direct-ness, which combined with her heavy voice often scared me, even though I knew that she had the purest heart. Nor will I forget the singing voice of Mo Penpa, which tried the patience of Ani Tenzin Pema, for singing at an old-age home was not appropriate, according to her and some of the others. The voice of Gen Lobsang, in contrast to those of my female friends, became in-creasingly silent. His words were always limited, although on some rare days he could keep a conversation going on his own.

The voices of my elderly friends might not continue to echo clearly in my ears ten or twenty years from now, but I will still be able to recognize their voices, if I ever heard them again.

As my elderly friends waited to cross the mountain pass, their bodies began to fall apart. The life force (*sog*) that had ignited their existence into being was fading. Hands and feet turned cold. Food became difficult to chew. Digestion slowed down. Bones dried up, as they themselves would say. Memories began failing. Looks faltered. And their faces began to re-semble one another. They even became unrecognizable to themselves, as Mo Dickyi's reaction suggested when she looked at photos of her younger self, or when Gen Lobsang said that in old age, he did not have the essence of a full person. Layers of dust and spider webs settled on the tops of shelves, win-dows, and picture frames in the homes of those who no longer had the strength to keep them clean. Relationships that once had held the world to-gether were thinning out, or were entirely absent. Connections to others and one's surroundings, built up over a lifetime, began to unravel. These ruptures left them between life and death, leading to a fragmented sense of self.[2] But as remarked by Mariana Ortega, such ruptures can also bring reflec-tive orientation toward life and its activities.[3] Despite the uncanniness evoked by physical decline, solitude, and a future of death, it also made my elderly friends more aware of what truly mattered to them.

Even as they faced death, their singular ways of being, including their likes and dislikes, remained embedded in their habits and voices until the very end. Days before Mo Dickyi passed away, I bought her the first man-goes of the 2022 season. She was not able to eat much at that point, but she would never say no to meat dumplings, and certainly not to mangoes, one of her favorite fruits. After her passing, it was a comfort to know that she got to relish the flavor of fresh mangoes one last time. Although Genla felt that he was disappearing in the face of death, certain parts of him, so distinctive to who he was and how others knew him, persisted, such as his humble nature and quiet smile. While my elderly friends' memories of the recent past declined, images from their childhood and adulthood in Tibet only seemed to become more vivid. Genla said, with a tender smile, that he could still visualize the landscape and scenarios of his childhood in Penpo.

Moreover, even in the face of death, my friends reached out and practiced care for themselves and others. Their care was apparent in their embodied daily habits: in Ani Tenzin's concern for birds; in Mo Dickyi's weekly washing of her hair when the weather was no longer cold or in her refusal to get rid of broken items used over the years; in Gen Lobsang's daily exercise routines or his annual preparations of *khapse* for the Tibetan New Year—even though he did not get many visitors during the new year holidays. It was also visible in Ani Jamyang's attentive cooking which always resulted in delicious dishes or in her continuous religious practice, despite the hardships of sitting cross-legged from morning until evening; in Mo Tsering's concern for the Bhutanese singers, and other strangers; in Po Damchoe's insistence on spending his days and nights in the small room he built with his own hands; and in Mo Samdrup's generosity toward people, or in the way she took care of her belongings and her home built by her beloved husband. All of them (except Mo Samdrup Drolma, because of her poor memory) also continued to offer prayers for the long life of the Dalai Lama.

Thus, despite being suspended between life and death, and being so close to leaving for their next rebirth, my elderly friends did not give up on themselves and the world of the living. Traces of those who were gone—Mo Dickyi, Mo Tsering, and Mo Samdrup—also continue to linger among the living, even in my own hands.

"I Know, I Don't Know You. But I Know This."

I conclude this book with some unfinished remarks on what it might mean to let someone enter one's skin and to allow oneself to be touched by that person—its possibilities and limitations alike. I do not view such limitations in a negative light. Rather, I see them as paving the way for a type of knowing that cultivates patience for the intangible and the unresolved, while still allowing one, in the writer Jhumpa Lahiri's words, "to strike at the heart of things."[4] In fleshing out my thoughts, I begin with some reflections offered by the writer Toni Morrison in the documentary about her life, *The Pieces I Am*:

> I was in a place once, in Vienna. They had an art festival there. And I was asked to go into this room and move in front of a mirror. In a room that was totally dark. And I was instructed to lift my hand and put it on the mirror. And just stand there [*Morrison raises her hand and holds it in the air with the palm facing the camera*]. And then I saw, off in the distance, a figure, that came closer and closer and closer. And she put up her hand. And our hands touched. Neither one of us said a word. Just interest, curiosity, and human connection. That experience says more and much about what I think I am doing when I write: I know I am not you. I know, I don't know you. But I know this [*hands touching*].[5]

For me, Morrison's words echo my experiences of how getting to know the elderly Tibetans happened during fieldwork and continued in the process of writing. It has been a process through which my elderly friends and I grew closer and closer, a process that from my side has been one of interest, curiosity, and human connection. The intimacy my friends and I forged was not simply the result of my touching and massaging their legs. That certainly opened up our access to one another, but more than anything, I believe it was the act of seeing and listening, through words, in silence and other gestures, that approached and caressed, allowing us to be touched by each other's presence, sufferings, and joys.

Just as their legs and feet required different kinds of touch, meaning adjusting the movement of my hands and points of pressure in accordance with their needs, I had to adjust my ability to listen, respond, and empathize with them as persons. Whereas Mo Tsering Wangmo clearly vocalized how she wanted to be cared for and insisted on my ethical responsibilities to her, Gen Lobsang never tried to tighten the bond between us. As a result, I often felt confused about what I could do for him, apart from the massages. Thus, I did my best to put my heart into the massages, despite often being tired. Through his silence and limited words, I came to know Genla as someone who had learned to expect very little of others. The silence in Mo Dickyi

Sangmo, unlike Genla's silence, did not soothe. It was sad, annoyed, and heavy, and I witnessed her descending further into it. Yet, from somewhere deep inside, she called out to me, to be with her, even in her somber moods. Though my heart has always stretched a bit extra for Gen Lobsang, it was Mo Dickyi I felt the closest to.

Of course, there were times when massaging, listening, and responding compassionately was difficult to practice, both during fieldwork and while writing, because I was either tired or had problems of my own. I did not share my deepest pains with my elderly friends, but I do believe they were touched, now and then, by my presence and my efforts to show them care. This was apparent to me in their efforts at caring for me, such as Gen Lobsang's and Ani Jamyang's inquiries about whether I had eaten; Mo Tsering's insistence on feeding me, medicating me, or telling me to rest; Mo Dickyi's wishing that I stay longer with her; Gen Lobsang's big, precious hugs; Po Damchoe's so lovingly and proudly introducing me to everyone in the room during a lunch for the TCV camp elders; and, finally, in all of their repetitions that they prayed for me. It humbled me to know that they prayed for me, but it also made me ashamed of myself, as I knew I would never be able to repay them for all they had done for me.

Touch—physical and affective—the "this" Morrison refers to, connected my elderly friends and myself, helping me gain an experience near understanding of aging and dying in a Tibetan Buddhist world in exile, one that sits in my body through memories and sensations. Yet, my closeness to my friends also made them blurrier over time, because the closer I got to them, the more confusing they became. At times, they seemed to be joyful and at peace; at other times, they seemed worried and sad. Sometimes, the day was an exercise in negotiating between what is, was, and could have been, while at other times, it was about being at peace with whatever was but still doing what was possible in order to prevent things from getting worse. The days seemed stuck in the same circles of repetitions, while still providing a possibility to move forward. Every day could be the last but was also another day to live.

Thus, our closeness also brought the recognition that my understanding of their lives remains incomplete. While being touched by the other opened me up for a haptic vision and *care*-ful understanding of their lived experiences, it also crystallized my limitations. In the end, as I hope the reader has sensed, I do not know the main reason behind Mo Dickyi's melancholic mood or the chief reason Mo Tsering treated her caregivers the way she did. There are also other aspects of my elderly friends that remain beyond my experience: the tremendous difficulty of being confined to one's home for years, what it must be like to face a lonesome death, and what it means to long for something in the face of death while having to come to terms with its impossibility. In many ways, Mo Dickyi Sangmo, Mo Tsering Wangmo, Gen Lobsang Choedak, Ani Jamyang Choedon, Po Damchoe Ngawang, and others remain a mystery to me. The most important things were those that rested in the gaps between us and were not always spoken of aloud. Out of respect for my friends, I have let them rest, in the architect Juhani Pallasmaa's words, in "dim light and shadow," while attempting to listen and write, "through the gaps in knowing, in what can be known, to some form of answer," as encouraged by Sienna Craig.[6]

Reflecting on my friendship with the elderly Tibetans and others, I have at least begun to learn that being touched by "this," as that which exists between people, is perhaps all one can ever really hope for. One might never fully know the content and shape of that which one is touched by, or what truths people's "beautiful lies"—to borrow an expression from Dante—conceal, truths that lurk behind the eyes or are hidden under a quiet smile, in the silence between words, or in the contradictions people embody.[7] What really matters, I believe, is to recognize how the unspoken lingers in other bodies, shaping their interactions with others, to respond appropriately to those beautiful, fragile lies most of us carry and the vulnerabilities hidden underneath them. These are the moments one would see and listen as if one were touching, opening up for an infinite understanding of the other.

Figure 38: View from a mountain pass. Photo by Harmandeep K. Gill.

GLOSSARY

Tibetan Terms

Phonetic Transliteration	*Wylie Transliteration*	*English Translation*
Acha	a cag	elderly sister
Akhu	a khu	uncle
Amala	a ma lags	mother
Ani	a ne	nun
Ape ro	a pa'i ro	on my father's corpse
Bardo	bar do	the intermediate stage between death and birth
Bumo	bu mo	girl
Bö	bod	Tibet
Bö cha	bod ja	Tibetan (butter) tea
Bö cholka sum	bod chol kha gsum	the three regions of Tibet
Chagtsel	phyag 'tsal	prostration
Champo	'cham po	friendly, close
Chawang	phyag dbang	hand blessing (on the head)
Chigel	phyi rgyal	foreign country
Chinlab	byin brlabs	blessing
Chö	chos	teachings of the Buddha
Chöd	mchod	offering
Chökhang	mchod khang	Tibetan Buddhist shrine
Chöme	mchod me	butter-lamp offerings
Chöme jeldeb	mchod me zhal 'debs	donation for butter-lamp offerings
Chöpa ngenpa	spyod pa ngan pa	evil behavior
Chupa	phyu pa	Tibetan traditional dress

Dagme	bdag med	ownerless/no-self
Densa sum	gdan sa gsum	the three seats/monasteries
Digpa	sdig pa	harmful/negative/evil action
Dompa	sdom pa	vows
Dre	'dre	ghost
Dri	'bri	Yak's female counterpart
Drokpo	grogs po	male friend
Drongkhen	grongs mkhan	the deceased
Drongseb	grong gseb	village
Dü chungpa	dud chung pa	small householder
Dungel	sdug bsngal	suffering
Gabur	ga bur	camphor, a medicinal herb
Ganden Phodrang	dga' ldan pho brang	the Tibetan government in Lhasa
Gegen	dge rgan	teacher
Genkhog	rgan 'khogs	old people/old person
Genla	rgan lags	teacher
Gensokhang	rgan gso khang	old-age home
Gewa	dge ba	religious merit
Günchö	dgun chos	winter debate/ritual
Gu yangpo	gu yangs po	vast/open-minded
Gusu dogpo	gu sug dog po	narrow/narrow-minded
Gyashog	brgya tshogs	group of hundred (households)
Jütog kubkya	jus gtogs rkub kyag	the gossip chair
Kangel	dka' ngal	difficulty/pain
Kangyur	bka' 'gyur	"the translated words (of the Buddha)"
Kartag sum	bka' btags gsum	three characteristics of existence in Buddhism
Khapse	kha zas	sweet and salty fried Tibetan snack
Khata	kha btags	silk scarf
Khatön	kha bton/don	prayer
Khelpa	khral pa	taxpayer
Khyimtsang	khyim tshang	household
Kora	skor ra/ba	circumambulation
Kundra	sku 'dra	honorific term for statue
Kupar	sku par	honorific term for photograph
Kyidug	skyid sdug	welfare committee

Le	las	karma, Buddhist law of existence
Leka chekhen	las ka byed mkhan	worker
Lha	lha	gods/deities
Lhu	klu	nagas/spirits
Lingkor	gling skor	circumambulation of a monastery/temple
Losar	lo sar	Tibetan New Year
Lotag	lo rtags	Tibetan birth-year horoscope
Lugsöl	lugs srol	tradition/custom
Lungpa	lung pa	homeland/country
Lungta	rlung rta	"wind horse"/prayer flag
Mani	ma ni	Tibetan Buddhist mantra
Mani khorlo	ma ni 'khor lo	prayer wheel
Mentseekhang	sman rtsis khang	Tibetan Medical and Astrological Institute
Mi lungpa	mi'i lung pa	foreign country
Mitagpa nyi	mi rtag pa nyid	impermanence
Mo	mo	divination
Momo	rmo rmo	grandmother
Momo	mog mog	dumplings
Nekor	gnas bskor	pilgrimage
Ngagpa	sngags pa	a nonmonastic, tantric practitioner
Ngoten	bsngo rten	dedication and aspiration offering
Ngöndro	sngon 'gro	preliminary practices
Nyamshib	nyams zhib	research
Nyingje	snying rje	compassion
Nyungne	snyung gnas/ smyung gnas	fasting ritual
Onju	'og 'jug	blouse
Pa	pha	father
pa sa bu thug	pha sa bu thug	"son meets fatherland"
Pag	pag	barley dough
Pecha	dpe cha	(Tibetan) Buddhist text
Phayül	pha yul	fatherland/native land
Phoba	'pho ba	transference of consciousness at death
Phodrang nyingpa	pho brang rnying pa	the old palace
Pola	po lags	grandfather

Popo	po po	grandfather
Pünkya	spun kyag	relative
Rabne	rab gnas	religious consecration
Rangzen	rang btsan	independence
Rawang	rang dbang	freedom
Rogpa chekhen	rogs pa byed mkhan	helper
Samlo	bsam blo	thought
Sar jorpa	gsar 'byor pa	new arrival/"newcomer"
Sem	sems	mind
Semchen thamche	sems can thams cad	all sentient beings
Shabten	zhabs brtan	rituals performed to remove obstacles
Sha zagyu	sha za rgyu	"the one that should be eaten"
Shibjug	zhib 'jug	research
Shinje	gshin rje	Lord of Death
Sipe khorlo	srid pa'i 'khor lo	wheel of existence/samsara
Sobyong	gso sbyong	ritual for mending vows/purifying breaches
Sog	srog	life/life force
Tendrel	rten 'brel	Dependent Arising
Thabzing	thab 'dzing	struggle sessions
Thangka	thang ka	scroll paintings
Thugdam	thugs dam	meditative state (at death)
Ting	ting	(water) bowls
Tongpa nyi	stong pa nyid	emptiness
Tsampa	rtsam pa	barley flour
Tsar	tsar	finished
Tserab letsi	tshe rabs las rtsis	natal horoscope
Tsog	tshogs	feast offering
Tsorwa	tshor ba	feeling
Tsuglagkhang	gtsug lag khang	temple/Dalai Lama temple in exile
Umeylam	dbu ma'i lam	the Middle-Way Approach
Yönchab	yon chab	water-bowl offerings
Zhotön	zho ston	Tibetan festival/opera festival
Zomo	mdzo mo	crossbreed of a cow and a yak
Zong	rdzong	district-level administrative unit
Yak	gyag	yak

Tibetan Sayings

Phonetic Transliteration	Wylie Transliteration	English Translation
La gor thön gi dug.	la mgor thon gyis 'dug.	(I am) about to reach the mountain pass.
Nga la goi nyima re.	nga la mgo'i nyi ma red.	I am the setting sun.
Nga tsho la gor thön tsar re.	nga tsho la mgor thon tshar red.	We've already reached the mountain pass.
Ngönma gang che tande lu la tos. jema gar dro tande sem la tos.	sngon ma gang byas da lta'i lus la ltos. rjes ma gar 'gro da lta'i sems la ltos.	To know what you did before, take a look at your body. To know where you will go, take a look at your mind.
Chigpo kye pa re. chigpo do go re. chigpo shi go re.	gcig por skyes pa red. gcig por sdod dgos red. gcig por shi dgos red.	One is born alone. One must live alone. One must die alone.
Zamling sangma 'ulta' cha dug.	dzam gling tshang ma 'ulta' chags 'dug ['ulta', hindi].	The world has turned upside down.
Nying tongpa cha dug.	snying stong pa chags 'dug.	My heart feels/has become empty.
Mi ge na yul dren. cha ge na tshang dren.	mi rgas na yul dren. bya rgas na tshang dren.	When a person becomes old, they miss their home. When a bird becomes old, it misses its nest.
Nam sa go ting logpa.	gnam sa mgo rting slog pa.	The sky and earth turned upside down.

NOTES

Note on Transliteration, Names, Photographs, the Use of *Tibet*, and Tibetans

1. Barnett 2014.
2. Goldstein 1989, 1997, 1998.
3. This strategy was implemented in the Chinese government's "White Paper" (International Campaign for Tibet 2023), released on 10 November 2023.
4. Snellgrove and Richardson 2003. David Snellgrove and Hugh Richardson argue that cultural or ethnographic Tibet extends beyond the boundaries of political Tibet, also including other regions in the Himalayas such as Ladakh and Bhutan. Melvyn Goldstein (1997, 1998) argues that ethnic Tibetan populations are also found in Nepal, Bhutan, and in northern and northeastern India, such as Ladakh, northern Uttar Pradesh, Sikkim, and Arunachal Pradesh.
5. The simplified division between "ethnographic" and "political" Tibet, initially known as "inner" and "outer" Tibet, was made by the British colonial administration for the sake of advancing their own imperial interests. It did, however, not correspond with Tibetan geopolitical realities at the time, see for example McGranahan 2010, 42–44.
6. Tsering 1997.
7. On political protest in Tibet, see for example, Barnett 2012; Schwartz 1994; Shakya 2012.
8. Shakya 1993.
9. Tibetans are one of the officially recognized "ethnic minorities" (*minzu*, Mandarin) in the PRC.
10. In fleshing out these conceptions of Tibet, I have also relied on the following: Dreyfus 1994; McGranahan 2010; Norbu 1987; Richardson 1984; Samuel 1993.

Introduction

1. Anzaldúa 1987, 3. See Ortega 2016 for an application of Anzaldúa's concept of "borderland."
2. Crapanzano 2004, 57. On the in-between, see also Stoller 2008.
3. Ibn al-'Arabi, cited in Chittick 1989, 117–118.
4. Sperling 1979, 434.
5. Sperling 1979, 434, 441.
6. Sperling 1979, 442.
7. Ekvall 1980; Goldstein and Beall 1997.
8. Goldstein and Beall 1997.
9. See also Childs 2001, 2004; Childs, Goldstein, and Wangdui 2011; Choedup 2018.
10. Goldstein and Beall 1997, 158.
11. Goldstein and Beall 1997, 161.

12. Goldstein and Beall 1997, 173.

13. Choedup 2018; Gill 2022; Tseten 2020; Wangmo and Teaster 2009; Wangmo 2010.

14. Childs and Choedup 2019; Craig 2020a; Desjarlais 2016; Gagné 2018.

15. Cole and Durham 2007; Dossa and Coe 2017; Hromadzic and Palmberger 2018.

16. Amrith, Sakti, and Sampaio 2023; Danely 2014; Dossa and Coe 2017; Lamb 2009.

17. Childs et al. 2021; Ekvall 1989; Gill 2023a; Goldstein and Beall 1997; Shneiderman 2006.

18. Goldstein and Beall 1997.

19. Since the 1980s, much scholarship has framed old age as successful and healthy aging. Sarah Lamb (2014, 43) notes that this view gained wide acceptance after the publication of "Human Aging: Usual and Successful," by the physician John Rowe and the psychologist Robert Kahn, in 1987. Furthermore, the medicalization of old age has marked the geriatric and gerontological conceptions of old age with distinctions between "normal" and "pathological" aging, or "function" and "dysfunction" (Cohen 1994, 1998; Katz 2006; Katz and Marshall 2004). Critical approaches in anthropology and gerontology (e.g., Lamb 2014; Liang and Luo 2012; Moody 2009; Weil 2005) emphasize the need to come to terms with human decline.

20. Childs et al. 2021; Gill 2023a.

21. The meaning of *Kangyur* is "the translated words (of the Buddha)." The Kangyur is the collection of texts regarded as "Buddha-word," which are not only records of the Buddha's own words but also explanations and teachings by others ("Facts and Figures" 2010).

22. Bernert 2019, lines 1–1.11.

23. Bernert 2019, lines 1.4–1.7.

24. Bernert 2019, lines 1.4–1.7.

25. Thera 2013.

26. See Duckworth 2019, who expands upon how emptiness is understood in the two main philosophical schools of Tibetan Buddhism: the Madhyamaka school (the "Middle Way") and the Yogācāra school (the "Mind-Only").

27. Thera 2013.

28. Patrul Rinpoche 1999, 78–85.

29. Powers 1995, 63.

30. Cohen 2003, 126.

31. In his biography on Jamgon Kongtrul, Alexander Gardner remarks how biographies of Tibetans in English and other European languages continue to treat their subjects more as archetypes and less as real people (2019, x).

32. See Atwill 2018; Childs 2004; Craig 2020a, 2020b; Fjeld 2008; Gellner 2007; Gill and Hofer 2023; Gyal 2021; Holmberg 2007; Lewis 2014; Makley 2007; March 2022; McGranahan 2010; Nulo 2014; Rajan 2018; Ramble, Schwieger, and Travers 2013; Robin 2015; Shneiderman 2006; Valentin and Pradhan 2023.

33. Butler 2012, 10. See also Butler 2015.

34. On how old people in other cultural contexts transform the loss of old age: Baars 2017; Danely 2014; Grøn and Mattingly 2017; Lamb 2000, 2014; Mattingly and Grøn 2022; Schlütter and Jensen 2023.

35. Stoller 2008, 4.

36. On dealing with impermanence and change: Danely 2014; Geismar, Otto, and Warner 2022.

37. Stoller 2008, 4, 6.

38. Singh 2018, 60.

39. Dhompa 2023.

40. Abu-Lughod 1986, 1991; Behar 1996; Biehl 2005; Crapanzano 1980, 2004; Das 2006, 2014, 2020; Desjarlais 1997, 2003; Jackson 2005, 2013, 2017; Mattingly 2014, 2019; Narayan 1989, 2012; Stoller 1989, 1997; Wikan 2012.

41. Guenther 2011, 201.

42. Sonam in Tsagong 2023.

43. Abu-Lughod 1991, 150. On critique by other postcolonial scholars: Asad 1995; Bhabha 1983, 1994; Gandhi 2006; Said 1978, 1993.

44. Abu-Lughod 1991, 152. See also Fabian 2014.

45. Hall 1997. For critiques of racialized stereotypes and uncritical celebrations of other-ness: Bhabha 1983; Fanon 2021; Hall 1981, 2021; hooks 1990; Said 1978, 1993.

46. Behar 2022, 26.

47. Das 2014, 200.

48. Abu-Lughod 1991, 157–158.

49. Jackson 2013, xii.

50. Jackson 2013, xii.

51. Dalai Lama in Iyer 2008, 9.

52. Abu-Lughod 1991.

53. Mattingly 2019; Narayan in McGranahan 2020, 89.

54. Das 2014, 200. This has been effectively evoked by multiple scholars who write in experi-ence near or experimental styles. Apart from the ones already mentioned, see also Bourgois and Schonberg 2009; Craig 2023; Garcia 2010; Hurston 1935, 2018; Mead 1928; Narayan 2007; Pan-dian 2015; Scheper-Hughes 1993, 2001; Suhr 2019.

55. See also Desjarlais 1997, specifically for a discussion of the term "experience."

56. As for example encouraged by Behar 1996 and Jackson 2013.

57. I am also inspired by philosopher Emmanuel Levinas who sees singularity as arising in the self's response to the other (Chapter 3), and Sara Ahmed's "modes of encounter," that names "the meetings and encounters that produce or flesh out others, and hence *differentiates others from other others.*" (2000, 144).

58. McGranahan 2018a, 1. On the ethnographer's commitments to the communities they work with and beyond, see also Behar 1996; D'Amico-Samuels 1991; Eriksen 2005; Gammeltoft 2006; Harrison 1991; McGranahan 2022; Meinert and Whyte 2023; Scheper-Hughes 1993.

59. Such as Adams 1996, 1998; Chettri 2017; Childs 2004; Choedak 2023; Craig 2020a; Dasel 2016; Dhompa 2014; Dickie 2023; Diehl 2002; Dolma and Denno 2013; Fjeld 2005; Gardner 2019; Gayley 2017; Gellner 2013; Gutschow 2004; Gyal and Dondrup 1983; Gyatso 2016; Harris 2012; Havnevik 1989; Hofer 2018; Jabb 2015; Jinba 2023; Kaysang 2016; Klieger 1992; Lama 2022; Loden 2022; Makley 2007; McGranahan 2010; Norbu 2007; Nulo 2014; Shneiderman 2006; Sonam 2012, 2015; Tseden 2011, 2015, 2019; Tsering 2012; Tseten 2020; Woeser 2020.

60. Sonam in Tsagong 2023.

61. Ahmed 2000, 144.

62. Anzaldúa 1987; Ortega 2016. Likewise, anthropologists (Ewing 1990, 1991; Lamb 1997; McHugh 1989; Ortner 1995) have argued that relationality does not preclude the notion or expe-rience of individuality. See Lamb 1997 for a critique of the rigid academic dichotomies between "Eastern" and "Western" notions of selfhood as relational/fluid versus autonomous/self-contained, respectively.

63. Ortega 2016, 64. Anzaldúa (1987) employs both *plurality* and *multiplicity.* Ortega chooses to stick with *multiplicity* because *plurality*, through its suggestion of multiple selves, does not capture how the self is also singular (2014, 64–65).

64. Anzaldúa 1987.

65. On opacity: Glissant 1997; Meinert 2022.

66. Glissant 1997, 193.

67. Without a touch of compassion, I believe that the undesirable in someone can be pinned down as an inherent, unchanging essence that is subject to negative judgments.

68. Dharmakīrti in Kellner 2010.

69. Merleau-Ponty 1964a, 160.

70. For imagistic-oriented approaches to anthropology that are inspired by the domain of art: Mattingly and Grøn 2022; Odgaard 2022; Stevenson 2014.

71. Maurette 2018, 8. Pablo Maurette notes that the term "haptic" was introduced by historian Aloïs Riegl toward the beginning of the 20th century (2018, 7). Berkeley 1709 and Von Herder 2009 [1778] gave inspiration to the coining of the term.

72. Maurette 2018, 8.

73. Dharmakīrti in Kellner 2010, 203–231.

74. Cézanne in Merleau-Ponty 1964b, 17.

75. Merleau-Ponty 1964a.

76. This is a privilege that comes with doing ethnography, but it can be difficult to practice outside the role as an ethnographer, scholar, or writer.

77. Davé 2021, 146; Merleau-Ponty 1964a; Tagore 1933, 2010. On Tagore's reflections on what the artist and poet seeks, see also Sarkar 2021.

78. Didi-Huberman 2005, xvi.

79. Maurette 2018, 8.

80. Davé 2021, 148.

81. See Haraway 1988 for the taken-for-granted distinctions between subject and object.

82. On the relationship between images and imagination: Bachelard 2014; Campt 2023.

83. Anzaldúa 1987.

84. hooks 2019, 2.

85. My stays were as follows: March 2019 (3 weeks), July to August 2019 (4 weeks), September 2019 (4 weeks), January 2020 (3 weeks), January to mid-May 2021, November 2021 to July 2022, December 2022 to August 2023, and December 2023 to August 2024. I also made a brief return in October–November 2017 (4 weeks).

86. Brand in Miller 2021, xv.

Interlude

1. *Phayül* usually refers to the region one descends from.

Chapter 1

1. Sonam 2022, 11.

2. Goldstein 1989; Kapstein 2009; McGranahan 2006; Shakya 1999.

3. Kapstein 2009, 287.

4. Dalai Lama 2016.

5. On the Chushi Gangdrug, see McGranahan 2010; Norbu 1986.

6. Gill 2023b. For elderly Tibetans' memories of the Chinese invasion and of exile, see the Tibet Oral History Project (https://exhibits.stanford.edu/tohp), created by Marcella Adamski, and the Tibet Memory Project (https://tibetmemoryproject.wordpress.com), created and carried out by Tsering Topgyal and Tsering Choephel.

7. Avedon 2015, 93–115.

8. Avedon 2015, 115.

9. Brox 2012, 453.

10. Brox 2012, 454. The full text of the revised Charter of Tibetans-in-exile (1991) is available at https://tibet.net/wp-content/uploads/2011/06/Charter1.pdf.

11. Grunfeld 1987.

12. Grunfeld 1987, 202–203.

13. Bureau of His Holiness the Dalai Lama [BHHDL] 1969, 1–2.

14. Avedon 2015, 117.

15. BHHDL 1969, 129.

16. BHHDL 1969, 135.

17. BHHDL 1969, 130.

18. Avedon 2015, 118; BHHDL 1969, 3. For scholarship that has explored the linkages between displacement, Tibetan nationalism, and refugee identity in exile: Anand 2000; Bhoil and Galvan-Alvarez 2018; Diehl 2002; Hess 2009; Houston and Wright 2003; Lokyitsang 2022; McConnell 2013; McGranahan 2018b; Swank 2014; Yeh 2007.

19. As of January 2024, according to Central Tibetan Relief Committee data at https://centraltibetanreliefcommittee.net/settlements/tibetan-settlements-in-india/south-india/.

20. BHHDL 1969.

21. In Tibet, these three monasteries of the Gelug lineage (to which the Dalai Lamas of Tibet belong) enjoyed special relations with the Dalai Lama's government in Lhasa (McGranahan 2010, 41).

22. As of January 2024, according to Central Tibetan Relief Committee data at https://centraltibetanreliefcommittee.net/settlements/tibetan-settlements-in-india/south-india/doeguling-mundgod/#population/.

Two other Tibetan settlements are found in southern India: Rabgyeling in Hunsur (population, 1,941) and Dhondenling in Kollegal (population, 3,065).

23. BHHDL 1969.

24. Dalai Lama 2016, 203.

25. Information Office of His Holiness the Dalai Lama 1981, 21.

26. Choedup 2017; Nowak 1984; Shakya 1993.

27. BHHDL 1969.

28. The TCV old-age home in McLeod Ganj opened in 2000, with a single building that housed thirty-three people. In 2013, another building was constructed. Although fifty elderly Tibetans had accommodation here, during parts of the year, some left for other places in India or the world to be with their children. There is also a small TCV old-age home in Patlikuhal, in the state of Himachal Pradesh, an area where the first generation of exiled Tibetans (e.g., Po Damchoe Ngawang) built roads. However, only three or four people live here.

29. It was increased to 5000 INR in 2024.

30. The original Mentseekhang is in Lhasa and was founded in 1916. Although the medicine itself is free of charge, the elderly have to pay consultation fees as well as a 12-percent Goods and Services Tax on the purchased medicine.

31. Tibetan Youth Congress was founded in 1970 in McLeod Ganj, and the Tibetan Women's Association in 1984, also in McLeod Ganj.

32. See https://tibet.net/support-tibet/pay-green-book/.

33. On the dilemmas between citizenship and Tibetan identity: Brox 2012; Lama 2023; McGranahan 2018b.

34. The majority of Tibetans do not qualify for Indian citizenship. For those who qualify for it, the process of obtaining a passport is hazardous and unaffordable, which holds people back from applying. More on who is qualified for Indian citizenship by birth, descent, registration and naturalization, can be read here: https://indiancitizenshiponline.nic.in/Documents/User Guide/Citizenship_Act_1955_16042019.pdf/. Obtaining Indian citizenship also leads to a loss of rights with the CTA. Those who apply for citizenship argue that it does not weaken their Tibetan identity or commitment to the Tibetan cause. They add that if Tibetans in the United States, Europe, and Australia can be citizens of their host countries, why should not the same principle apply for Tibetans in India, who often live more precarious lives?

35. In India, 94,203; in Nepal, 13,514; and in rest of the world, 18,999. See https://tibet.net /about-cta/tibet-in-exile/.

36. Choedup 2018.

37. Choedup 2018, 82.

38. Choedup 2018, 76.

39. In Dharamsala, Norbulingka was established to preserve Tibetan art and crafts.

40. Nechung (Dorje Drakden) is the state oracle of Tibet. The Dalai Lama and the CTA consult the oracle for various matters.

41. Christopher 2020.

42. Goodman 1986, 316.

43. The romanticizing myth of Tibet as Shangri-la was introduced by James Hilton in his novel, *Lost Horizon* (1933). The orientalizing images of Tibet and Tibetans have been contested and unsettled by numerous scholars (Brauen, Koller, and Vock 2004; Dodin and Räther 2001; Drefyus 1995; Klieger 1992; Lopez 1998; Martin 2017; Norbu 1986, 2007; Shakya 1991). Dipyesh Anand (2007) argues that exiled Tibetan elites have actively participated in the construction of the fantasy of Tibet as a Shangri-la (see also Lopez 1998). And even though it has attracted the attention of the West, this myth is the reason the Tibetan political struggle is treated "as a question of sentimentality versus political expediency," argues Tsering Shakya (1991, 23).

44. After Tibet was opened up in 1979, the first fact-finding delegation of the Tibetan government-in-exile was sent to Tibet and China. For an overview of Sino-Tibetan dialogue: https://tibet.net/important-issues/sino-tibetan-dialogue/an-overview-of-sino-tibetan-dialogue/.

45. According to the state laws of Himachal Pradesh, most of the construction qualifies as illegal, because outsiders, namely those who are not natives of Himachal Pradesh, are not allowed to own property there. However, investors buy their way in by offering bribes to the right people.

46. The worrisome development in McLeod Ganj sped up when the Indian government declared Dharamsala as one of its "Smart Cities" in 2015, allocating the local government a total of INR 186,00,00,000 (One Hundred Eight Six Crore). The money has been used to improve old roads and build new ones, and to construct a ropeway that runs between Dharamsala and McLeod Ganj. Although the development of McLeod Ganj, including the increase in tourism, has created economic avenues for many local Indians and Tibetans, it also comes at an immense price, causing locals to worry about and fear for their homes, the future of their families, and the place that is their home-in-the-world.

47. Stephen Christopher (2020) analyzes these tensions in depth and argues that the "Tibetan ethno-commodification" of Dharamsala leads to an exclusion of the Gaddi community.

48. A local Gaddi youth was stabbed to death by a Tibetan man in April 1994. Keila Diehl notes that this incidence unleashed years of anger and hostility toward Tibetans among the Gaddis and other local Indians (2002, 40).

49. Kajal 2021.

50. Kerouac 1958.

51. The official settlements are divided into various camps. The two Tibetan settlements in Bylakuppe have twenty-three camps in total, and Mundgod has eleven.

52. Choudhary 2019.

53. *Zhotön* is classical secular Tibetan theater with music and dance.

54. The organizer of the Miss Tibet pageant, Lobsang Wangyal, left India in 2022, bringing an end to the pageant era in exile in India.

55. The Dalai Lama's departures and arrivals are special occasions for the Tibetan residents of McLeod Ganj. The news of the timing of the Dalai Lama's departure and arrival spreads fast. People line up along the road stretching from the lower parts of Gangkyi to the entrance gate of his residence.

Chapter 2

1. Adams 1998; Craig 2012; Dorjee 2005; Hofer 2014; Ozawa-de-Silva and Ozawa-de-Silva 2011; Samuel 2014.

2. Adams 1998, 89. Adams explains that this is linked to Tibetan notions of embryology and karma. A human being is seen to come into existence as a result of *sog* (the life force). It is *sog* that connects the mind (*sem*) to the physical body, thus bringing a life into existence. The quality of the *sog* is determined by karma, both of the one whose life is being created and those others who constitute this life (1998, 89). For an in depth exploration of *sog* and how it supports the lifespan, see Gerke 2012.

3. Merleau-Ponty 2013.

4. Guenther 2013; Leder 1991; Namgyal 1986.

5. Leder 1991.

6. See also Gungtang Rinpoche 1975; Gyalpo 1963.

7. Ngorchen Konchog Lhundrub 1991.

8. Ngorchen Konchog Lhundrub 1991, 41–42.

9. Ngorchen Konchog Lhundrub 1991, 41.

10. Ngorchen Konchog Lhundrub 1991, 41.

11. Gungtang Rinpoche 1975; Patrul Rinpoche 1999.

12. Gungtang Rinpoche 1975.

13. Samuel 2014.

14. Namgyal 1986. For a brief biography of Lobsang Namgyal, see Khrinley 2002, 1644.

15. Tibetan name: *Shinje.*

16. Samuel 2014, 33.

17. Guenther 2013, 29.

18. Guenther 2013, 29.

19. Leder 1991.

20. Leder 1991, 1.

21. Leder 1991, 75.

22. Leder 1991, 76.

23. Leder 1991, 79.

24. Leder 1991, 81.

25. Leder 1991, 81.

26. On first-person narratives of how pain, illness, and disability alters one's relation to others and sense of self: Crosby 2016; Murphy 2001; Singh 2018.

27. Leder 1991, 92.

28. Leder 1991, 82.

29. Leder 1991, 91.

30. Leder 1991, 91.

31. Crosby 2016; Scarry 1985.

32. Leder speaks of "threatening the self." I choose to speak of "unsettling," as old age is not understood as a threat among the elderly Tibetans. They accept it, but as I learned during field-work, the onset of old age does unsettle their lifeworlds.

33. Guenther 2013, xiii.

34. Adams 1998, 89.

35. Guenther 2013, xi.

36. Guenther 2013, xii.

37. Guenther 2013, 155.

38. Guenther 2012, 5.

39. Guenther 2013, xxi.

40. Guenther 2013, 125–157.

41. On the therapeutic importance of social support: Cacioppo and Patrick 2009; Chen, Talwar, and Ji 2015; Corwin 2012; Taylor 2008.

42. Guenther 2013, xiii–xv.

43. Guenther 2012, 5.

44. See Childs and Choedup 2023, 94.

45. Tibetans buy sweaters, hats, gloves, jackets and other winter wear from Indian retailers in Ludhiana in the state of Punjab and sell them in cities across India.

46. Going for pilgrimage to holy sites is an important Tibetan Buddhist practice.

47. It is not common among the elderly Tibetans to wash their bodies and hair on a weekly basis.

Chapter 3

1. Tibetans from the Kham region are known as *Khampa*.

2. E.g., Guenther 2011; Taylor 2005.

3. When the Communist Party took over Tibetan regions, they introduced what were called *thabzing*, or "struggle sessions." These were public humiliations and torture of aristocrats and monastics, or anyone categorized as a "class enemy," meaning an enemy of the state and its people.

4. Kalachakra is a highly advanced level of initiation given by the Dalai Lama. But for Mo Tsering Wangmo and other laypeople, the Kalachakra is a periodic religious festival, during which the Dalai Lama also gives teachings. It lasts for about a month and attracts Tibetans (including from inside Tibet) and non-Tibetan converts to Buddhism.

5. Mo Tsering Wangmo found caregivers through her network of friends, distant relatives, and acquaintances.

6. As someone from the Tibetan capital, Mo Tsering spoke very politely. Tibetans from Kham, by contrast, are often known for their lack of an honorific tongue, like the caregiver, and they tend to be straightforward in their communication, in a way that would be considered rude by a Lhasa-wa.

7. Beauvoir 1972.

8. Wangmo and Teaster 2009; Wangmo 2010.

9. Childs 2001, 2004.

10. Childs 2001, 57.

11. Childs, Goldstein, and Wangdui 2011.

12. Childs, Goldstein, and Wangdui 2011.

13. Childs, Goldstein, and Wangdui 2011, 6.

14. Childs, Goldstein, and Wangdui 2011, 6.

15. See also Childs and Choedup 2019.

16. In Childs, Goldstein, and Wangdui 2011, 6.

17. Buch 2013, 638.

18. Buch 2013, 639.

19. On this point, see Buch 2013, 2014; Taylor 2008; Thornton 2015.

20. As mentioned in Chapter 1, the TCV school only provides free accommodation to the first generation of Tibetans-in-exile, who worked at the school for very low salaries. Although Mo Tsering felt that the school administration had treated the teacher unjustly, according to the policies of the TCV school, the later generation of staff are not guaranteed residence at the old-age home, and those few who are admitted have to pay rent.

21. Thornton 2015, 66.

22. Annaud 1997; a film that has contributed to the ongoing romanticization of Tibetans.

23. This incident took place when she had returned to New Delhi at the end of seasonal winter business. There are stories of other Tibetans who were robbed of all of their seasonal income, and according to a rumor, even killed for it.

24. Irving 2017, 50.

25. Literature from gerontology has noted the importance of computers in reducing isolation and increasing social connection for the elderly: Cotton et al. 2014; Dickinson and Hill 2007; Mitzner et al. 2019.

26. Kleinman 2012, 1551.

27. Buch 2014, 604.

28. See Buch 2013, 2014; Kleinman 2012, 2020; Kong 2008.

29. Kleinman 2012, 1551.

30. Thornton 2015, 67.

31. Taylor 2008.

32. Taylor 2008, 313.

33. Taylor 2008, 318.

34. Taylor 2008, 326.

35. Løgstrup 1997, 18–46.

36. Levinas 1996. See also Benson and O'Neill 2007; Guenther 2011.

37. Morgan 2013, 10, 19–21.

38. Morgan 2013, 54–65.

39. Pahuus 2018, 32.

40. Pahuus 2018, 31.

41. Løgstrup 1997, 14.

42. Løgstrup 1997, 16.

43. Løgstrup 1997, 10.

44. Morgan 2013, 9–10.

45. Morgan 2013, 9.

46. Guenther 2011.

47. Morgan 2013, 66.

48. Taylor 2005. See Danely 2022 for an ethnography on unpaid family caregiving, where he explores not only how caregiving is made meaningful but also the pain and grief that accompanies it.

49. Løgstrup 1997, 16.

50. On the role of touch in other contexts: Blake 2011; Davé 2021; Peloquin 1989.

51. Buch 2014.

52. Tsing 2013, 22.

53. Kleinman and Geest 2009, 169.

54. Taylor 2005.

55. Taylor 2005, 218.

56. Taylor 2005, 219–220.

57. Taylor 2005, 234.

58. Taylor 2005, 225. On the physical and emotional fatigue caused by caregiving work, see Danely 2017, 2022.

59. Taylor notes that in Levinas's earlier works, *Time and the Other and Existence and Existents*, the alterity of the other is described as "the feminine" and as "having alterity as its essence," whereas in his later work, *Totality and Infinity*, the other is referred to as a generic, simple human, but the feminine still continues to play an important role (Taylor 2005, 220).

60. Feminist thinkers argue that the notion of care needs to be balanced out with a notion of justice and charity (Taylor 2005). Otherwise, the infinite responsibility toward others can overburden and cause guilt.

61. Buch 2014.

62. Bergen-Aurand 2002.

Chapter 4

1. McGranahan 2010, 137.

2. McGranahan 2010, 103.

3. McGranahan 2010, 2.

4. McGranahan 2010, 159.

5. Some men had relationships with the local Lo women in Mustang. Some of them married those women and had children (McGranahan 2010, 138). Po Damchoe was one of them.

6. Pola emphasized that this was especially due to some internal conflicts in the army. See McGranahan 2010.

7. Dalai Lama 2016, 205.

8. Darwish 2005.

9. Darwish 2010, 85.

10. Schütz 1945, 370.

11. Craig 2020b.

12. Gen Lobsang is not the same person as Gen Lobsang Choedak, who is a central character in this book. Gen Lobsang was the person in charge of the TCV school branch in Ladakh "from 1 July 1975 (when it was founded), and until 16 November 1990," he told me precisely. Until his death in 2019, he was a resident at the TCV old-age home, where he lived together with his younger sister and her husband. I came to know him toward the end of my fieldwork and interviewed him after several people at the home recommended that I do so.

13. Schütz 1945.

14. In colloquial Tibetan, Mo Dickyi and others referred to the blankets as *tsugdru* (my own transliteration from pronunciation). They are incredibly warm, and all people in Kyirong and other regions in Tibet used (and continue to use) them during the harsh winters.

15. Mo Dickyi, in colloquial Tibetan, called the carpets *tsugden*.

16. Even ten years after the death of her husband, Mo Dickyi refrained from using his name. According to Tibetan Buddhist belief, one should not utter the name of the deceased following his or her death (especially during the forty-nine days of death rituals). That being said, my other elderly friends do say the names of their deceased ones after the forty-nine days of rituals have concluded.

17. This is where Buddha Śakyamuni attained enlightenment under the Bodhi tree. It is located in the state of Bihar in India and is one of the most important pilgrimage sites for Buddhists from all over the world.

18. Panchen Lama is the second highest lama of the Gelug lineage after the Dalai Lama. Karmapa is the head of the Karma Kagyu lineage, which is a sublineage of the Kagyu lineage. He escaped into exile in the year 2000, and his monastery, Gyuto Monastery, is located nearby the Norbulingka Institute in the larger Dharamsala area. Among Tibetans-in-exile, he is the most revered lama after the Dalai Lama.

19. The Jowo is the most sacred image of the Buddha to Tibetans. It "embodies the living presence of the historical Buddha Śakyamuni in Tibet" (Warner 2011, 1). The Jowo rests inside the Jokhang temple in Lhasa, Tibet, which is regarded as the most sacred temple in Tibet. There

were other *kundra* (images of the Buddha in Tibet called *Jowo*). Devotees worship the Kyirong Jowo as a manifestation of Tibet's patron deity, Avalokiteśvara (cf. Ehrhard 2004).

20. Padmasambhava, usually known among Tibetans as Guru Rinpoche, played an important role in establishing the first Tibetan monastery, Samye, in the eighth century CE.

21. *Brgyad stong pa*, meaning "the eight thousand," is short for *Aṣṭasāhasrikā Prajñāpāramitā Sūtra*, or "Perfection of Wisdom in Eight Thousand Lines," an important sutra for Tibetans. *Gzungs 'dus* is the collection of *dhāraṇīs* (incantations). Mo Dickyi was illiterate and could not read these texts.

22. On the linkages between material culture and memory: Appadurai 1988; Navaro 2009; Parrott 2010.

23. Childs 2008.

24. Childs 2008, 53–54.

25. Childs 2008, 55.

26. See Barnett 2014; Choedup 2023; McGranahan 2010; Norbu 1992; Shakya 1993.

27. See Choedup 2023; Dhompa forthcoming; Frechette 2002; Karmay 1998; Norbu 2016.

28. Regional ties are often seen to pose an obstacle for Tibetan unity, which is regarded as essential for strengthening the Tibetan political struggle. The Dalai Lama, parliamentarians, and activists often emphasize the need for unity across regions, Buddhists lineages, and the political strategy of *umeylam* (the Middle-Way Approach, which seeks a meaningful autonomy within the People's Republic of China) and *rangzen* (Independence). See Dhompa, forthcoming, on the politics of unity among Tibetan exiles, and for an alternative vision of unity that can encompass different histories and experiences of being a Tibetan.

29. For more on *kyidug*, see Miller 1956.

30. In January 2020, there were fourteen *kyidug* in the Dharamsala area.

31. People usually speak the exile-Tibetan dialect, but occasionally in each other's company, they switch to more local words and phrases from Kyirong, like Ani Jamyang and Mo Dickyi sometimes did.

32. See Balasubramaniam and Gupta 2019 on the unique case of Tibetans living in the Tibetan colony of Majnu Ka Tilla in New Delhi; these Tibetans are making collective claims to the land they have inhabited over the past sixty years.

33. Lokyitsang 2022.

34. Choedup 2018.

35. Choedup 2018.

36. As for example, in Darjeeling, see Gerke 2012. For other ethnographies on Darjeeling Tibetans, who live in a different social, cultural, and political landscape from Tibetans in Dharamsala, see also Basu 2018; Subba 1990.

37. See Dhompa 2014; Diehl 2002; Falcone and Wangchuk 2008; Venturino 1997.

38. Eliot in Schütz 1945, 370.

39. My Tibetan friends, all of whom are former TCV students recount how they were told that the TCV school was like a big family—the school was their home, the students were their brothers and sisters, and the teachers and the school administration were like their relatives—but that one day, they would return to their real home in Tibet. On how TCV schools became key sites for the cultivation of new forms of kinship and belonging, see Lokyitsang 2022.

40. Sonam and Sarin 2009, 2:37–2:52.

41. In the past fourteen years, the conflict between the Chinese Communist Party (CCP) and the Tibetan leadership in exile has become more and more acute. The last rounds of sino-Tibetan dialogue (going on since 1979) between representatives of the CTA and CCP took place at the end of January 2010.

42. Tsundue 2010, 25.

43. In 1979, following Mao Zedong's death in 1976 and the end of the Cultural Revolution, Tibetan regions were opened up for exiled Tibetans. Many Tibetans returned to visit their family members in Tibet. Although some chose to stay, the majority returned to exile, sometimes bringing with them family members, such as aging parents. Two of the elderly I became acquainted with had returned to central Tibet in the early 1980s, and one of them brought a family member with him into exile.

44. Dhompa 2014, 115–116.

45. Lama 2022, 105. These echoes of displacement and longing can also be heard in the works of other Tibetan poets and artists. See, for example, Jigme 2020; Kaysang 2016; TenPhun 2017; Topgyal 2014.

46. See also Wangmo 2019, where filmmaker Tsering Wangmo, through conversations with her mother and by providing glimpses into her daily life, tenderly evokes how her mother, like other Tibetan women from nomadic backgrounds, courageously rebuilt a life for herself and her family in exile.

47. Lama 2022, 266.

48. Gill 2023b.

49. The literal meaning of the word is "compassion." Tibetans use the word to express pity, sympathy, or compassion.

50. Dhompa 2014, 108.

51. McGranahan 2010, 139.

52. McGranahan 2010, 139.

53. Irving 2017, 9.

54. Williams, in Mattingly 2014, 12; Williams 1981.

55. Williams, in Mattingly 2014, 12.

56. Irving 2017, 3.

57. Irving 2017, 218.

58. Irving understands this as a creative act of poesis (2017, 218).

59. Irving 2017, 31.

60. Irving 2017, 1–8.

61. Danely 2014, 188.

62. *Anna* is a former currency unit in India that was introduced by the British.

63. Craig 2020b.

64. Sonam 2023. For an intimate portrait of the Dalai Lama, written by his longtime friend, see Iyer 2008.

65. The joint religious-political system of the Tibetan state (which the 14th Dalai Lama devolved in 2011) came into place in 1642, during the reign of the 5th Dalai Lama. George Dreyfus (1994, 2002) dismisses the emphasis on Tibetan nationalism as a modern creation only and argues that a form of proto-nationalism has existed, at least in central Tibet, since the thirteenth and fourteenth centuries. This involved the perception of belonging to a distinct country and was based on the idea that Tibet was civilized by Avalokiteśvara, who manifested as the Dharma kings who introduced Buddhism to Tibet.

66. McGranahan 2010.

67. Magnetta 2018, 93.

68. Choklay 2013.

69. Magnetta 2018, 93.

70. Choklay 2013, 1:11:33–1:11:35.

71. Choklay 2013, 1:11:36–1:11:37.

72. Choklay 2013, 1:11:47.

73. Choklay 2013, 1:11:53–1:11:54.

74. Choklat 2013, 1:12:02–1:13:04.

75. Dalai Lama 2016, 211.

76. Woeser, n.d.

77. Translated from Tibetan by Bhuchung D. Sonam: https://www.tibetanyouthcongress
.org/85-sangay-dolma/

78. Many of the self-immolators who have left behind messages have called for the return of
the Dalai Lama to Tibet (Barnett 2012; Buffetrille 2012; Shakya 2012).

79. See also Klieger 1992; Venturino 1997.

80. Choklay 2013, 1:17:47–1:18:97.

Chapter 5

1. *Thugdam* refers to the meditative state in which great Buddhist masters die consciously. It
can last from a few hours to several days. See, for example, Lama Kunsang, Lama Pemo, and
Aubele 2012, 42, on the *thugdam* of Dusum Khyenpa, known as the first Karmapa. For an ethnography of *phoba*, see Kapstein 1998.

2. Aporia is a central concept in the French philosopher Janques Derrida's "deconstruc-
tion," see Derrida 1993.

3. Bubandt 2014, 35.

4. Bubandt 2014, 58.

5. Bubandt 2014, 35.

6. Bubandt 2014, 38.

7. She was the daughter of his younger brother who lived in Lhasa. All three of Genla's siblings (with whom he shares the same mother and father) lived in Tibet. He only knew the whereabouts of his younger brother and nothing of his two sisters.

8. Childs 2004, 2014.

9. Childs 2014, 234.

10. Desjarlais 2016.

11. Gouin 2010, 13.

12. Desjarlais 2016, 9. On Tibetan Buddhist death rituals, see also Ramble 1982.

13. Chandigarh is the capital of the state of Punjab and Haryana. Buses run daily between
Dharamsala and Chandigarh and further to New Delhi. Tibetans usually get to Chandigarh on the
night bus that runs to New Delhi. By bus, the journey to Chandigarh takes at least seven hours.

14. On divination in exile: Gerke 2012; Smith 2021.

15. Desjarlais 2016, 30.

16. Despite *Bardo Thodol*'s popularity in translation, it is one of many funerary practices
and not something every Tibetan will follow.

17. Gungtang Rinpoche 1975.

18. Namgyal 1986.

19. Gungtang Rinpoche 1975.

20. Gungtang Rinpoche 1975.

21. They usually recite the following mantras: *oṃ maṇi padme hūṃ* (Mantra of
Avalokiteśvara), *Ōṃ tāre tutattāre ture svāhā* (Mantra of Bodhisattva Jetsun Dolma/Green
Tara), *Ōṃ muni muni mahā muni ye svāhā* (Mantra of Buddha Śakyamuni), and also a prayer
for the long life of the Dalai Lama.

22. It is believed that one *Nyungne* practice (over two days) has the potential to purify forty
thousand eons of negative karma (Lama Zopa Rinpoche, n.d.).

23. Chodron 2009.

24. Some of the texts Genla read were: (1) a selection of self-visualizations/self-generations
of guru yoga and the personal deities prayers (*bla ma'i rnal 'byor dang yi dam khag gi bdag*

bskyed sogs zhal 'don gces btus bzhugs so); (2) the exalted sutra on the perfection of wisdom ("The Diamond Cutter"—*'phags pa shes rab kyi pha rol tu phyin pa rdo rje gcod pa zhes bya ba bzhugs so*); (3) praise of dependent arising by Tsongkhapa (*rten 'brel bstod pa bzhugs so*); (4) Samantabhadra-caryā-prannidhāna-rāja (*'phags pa bzang po spyod pa'i smon lam gyi rgyal po bzhugs so*); (5) a collection of specific chanting prayers given by the Dalai Lama during a teaching to Russian Buddhists (*spyi nor gong sa skyabs mgon chen po mchog nas au ru su'i nang par dmigs bsal gsung chos skabs kyi zhal 'don nyer mkho phyogs bsdus 'zhugs so*).

Some of the texts Anila read were: (1) the great tantric stages by Tsongkhapa (*snags rim chen mo'i smon lam bzhugs so*); (2) supplication to white Mahākāla and praise to the six-armed Mahākāla (*mgon dkar gyi 'phrin bskul dang myur mdzad mgon po'i bstod pa bcas bzhugs so*); (3) supplication prayer to lamrim lineage masters called "opening the gateway to the supreme paths" (*lam rim gsol 'debs lam mchog sgo 'byed ces bya ba bzhugs so*); (4) the dhāraṇī mantra of Uṣṇīṣavijayā (*gtsug tor rnam par rgyal ma'i gzungs sngags bzhugs so*); (5) compilation of prayers for making offerings (*mchod 'bul zhal 'don phyogs sgrig bzhugs so*). In addition, she read from another collection of prayers. Some of these were: the praise to Tara with twenty-one verses of homage; prayer for the long life of His Holiness the Dalai Lama; the verses that saved Sakya from sickness—a prayer for pacifying the fear of disease, Guhyasamāja tantra or Cakrasamvara tantra (the complete elucidation of the hidden meanings).

25. *Sobyong* takes place approximately every fourteen days at the Tsuglagkhang.

26. Genla used to receive INR 1,000 a month, but in 2018, that was increased to INR 3,000. The payment was, however, not stable. In 2022, he only received money twice, INR 4,000 each time.

27. Choedup 2018, 87.

28. If his niece happens to be in McLeod Ganj at the time of his death, she will take on the responsibilities. The uncertainty Genla expressed had to do with the constant travels of his niece, who shifts between living in different places throughout the year.

29. The horoscopic divination is known as *tserab letsi* ("natal horoscope").

30. Prayers and offerings are also made on the day of the first anniversary of the death. Mo Samdrup Drolma used to invite monks for prayers and make *tsog* offerings to her fellow Kyirong Tibetans every year after the death of her husband. This annual practice stopped in 2018, when she became too frail.

31. One bag for each household. I received one (bag) *tsog* offering on the final day and one during the *tsog* offerings made several weeks earlier.

32. See Choedup 2018.

33. Pola's dismissal of curses by *lha* or *lhu* does not mean that he doubted the existence of Buddhist deities, nagas, and ghosts.

34. Others also emphasize the importance of completing a pilgrimage to Bodhgaya in old age. An elderly relative of a friend, who in January 2020 completed what will be his final pilgrimage to Bodhgaya, said that he now had no regrets in life. All of my elderly friends have completed at least one pilgrimage to Bodhgaya.

35. The Tibetan word for "blessing" is *chinlab*. *Chin* can be translated as "magnificent potential," and *lab* as "to transform." Together: "transforming into magnificent potential."

36. Desjarlais 2016, 13.

37. Gell 2001.

38. Willerslev, Christensen, and Meinert 2013, 4.

39. See Desjarlais 2016; Flaherty 2003, 2011; Gerke 2012; Williams and Meinert 2020.

40. In Patrul Rinpoche 1999, 41.

41. Pandian 2014, 198.

42. Pandian 2014, 197.

Conclusion

1. Tibetans do not eat cats. This expression was traditionally used, among others, for yaks, and its female counterpart, *dri*, that Tibetans eat in Tibet.

2. Ortega 2016, 49–63.

3. Ortega 2016, 50.

4. Lahiri 2022, 17.

5. Greenfield-Sanders 2019, 1:51:31–1:52:28.

6. Craig 2023, 13; Pallasmaa 2005, 46.

7. My use of Dante Alighieri is inspired by artist Ali Banisadr's (2021) exhibition "Beautiful Lies," displayed at the Stefano Bardini Museum and the Palazzo Vecchio in Florence in August 2021, in honor of the 700th anniversary of the death of Dante Alighieri (http://www .alibanisadr.com/publications/ali-banisadr-beautiful-lies). For more about the exhibition, see Risaliti 2022.

BIBLIOGRAPHY

Abu-Lughod, Lila. 1986. *Veiled Sentiments: Honor and Poetry in a Bedouin Society*. Berkeley: University of California Press.

———. 1991. "Writing Against Culture." In *Recapturing Anthropology: Working in the Present*, edited by Richard G. Fox, pp. 137–162. Santa Fe, NM: School of American Research Press.

Adams, Vincanne. 1996. *Tigers of the Snow and Other Virtual Sherpas: An Ethnography of Himalayan Encounters*. Princeton, NJ: Princeton University Press.

———. 1998. "Suffering the Winds of Lhasa: Politicized Bodies, Human Rights, Cultural Difference, and Humanism in Tibet." *Medical Anthropology Quarterly* 12 (1), pp. 74–102.

Ahmed, Sara. 2000. *Strange Encounters: Embodied Others in Post-Coloniality*. London: Routledge.

Amrith, Megha, Victoria K. Sakti, and Dora Sampaio. 2023. *Aspiring in Later Life: Movements Across Time, Space, and Generations*. New Brunswick, NJ: Rutgers University Press.

Anand, Dibyesh. 2000. "(Re)imagining Nationalism: Identity and Representation in the Tibetan Diaspora of South Asia." *Contemporary South Asia* 9 (3), pp. 271–287.

———. 2007. *Geopolitical Exotica: Tibet in Western Imagination*. Minneapolis: University of Minnesota Press.

Annaud, Jean-Jacques, dir. 1997. *Seven Years in Tibet*. Film, 136 min. Los Angeles: TriStar Pictures and Mandalay Entertainment.

Anzaldúa, Gloria E. 1987. *Borderlands/La Frontera: The New Mestiza*. San Francisco: Aunt Lute.

Appadurai, Arjun, ed. 1988. *The Social Life of Things: Commodities in Cultural Perspective*. Cambridge: Cambridge University Press.

Asad, Talal, ed. 1995 [1973]. *Anthropology and the Colonial Encounter*. Lanham, MD: Rowman and Littlefield.

Atwill, David G. 2018. *Islamic Shangri-La: Inter-Asian Relations and Lhasa's Muslim Communities, 1600 to 1960*. Berkeley: University of California Press.

Avedon, John F. 2015 [1979]. *In Exile from the Land of Snows*. New York: Vintage Books.

Baars, Jan. 2017. "Aging: Learning to Live a Finite Life." *Gerontologist* 57 (5), pp. 969–976.

Bachelard, Gaston. 2014 [1958]. *The Poetics of Space*. New York: Penguin Classics.

Balasubramaniam, Madhura, and Sonika Gupta. 2019. "From Refuge to Rights: Majnu Ka Tilla Tibetan Colony in New Delhi." *Kritisk Ethnografi: Swedish Journal of Anthropology* 2 (1–2), pp. 95–109.

Banisadr, Ali. 2021. "Beautiful Lies." Paintings, solo show. 30 April 2021–29 August 2021. The Stefano Bardini Museum and the Palazzo Vecchio, Florence.

Barnett, Robert. 2012. "Political Self-Immolation in Tibet: Causes and Influences." *Revue d'Etudes Tibétaines* 25, pp. 41–64.

———. 2014. "Introduction: A Note on Context and Significance." In *My Tibetan Childhood: When Ice Shattered Stone*, by Naktsang Nulo, translated by Angus Cargill and Sonam Lhamo, pp. xv–li. Durham, NC: Duke University Press.

Basu, Sudeep. 2018. *In Diasporic Lands: Tibetan Refugees and Their Transformation Since the Exodus*. Hyderabad, India: Orient BlackSwan.

Beauvoir, Simone de. 1996 [1970]. *The Coming of Age*. New York: W. W. Norton.

Behar, Ruth. 2022 [1996]. *The Vulnerable Observer: Anthropology That Breaks Your Heart*. Boston: Beacon Press.

Benson, Peter, and Kevin L. O'Neill. 2007. "Facing Risk: Levinas, Ethnography, and Ethics." *Anthropology of Consciousness* 18 (2), pp. 29–55.

Bergen-Aurand, Brian K. 2002. "Solitude and the Infinite in Soldati and Levinas." *Romance Studies* 20 (2), pp. 165–178.

Berkeley, George. 1709. *An Essay Towards a New Theory of Vision*. Dublin: printed by Aaron Rhames, for Jeremy Pepyat. Text Creation Partnership: http://name.umdl.umich.edu/004848514.0001.000.

Bernert, Christian, trans. 2019 [2013]. "The Sūtra on Impermanence." In volume 1.22, edited by Vivian Paganuzzi, *Toh 309, Degé Kangyur 72 (mdo sde, sa)*, folios 155.a–155.b. 84000: Translating the Words of the Buddha. https://read.84000.co/translation/toh309.html#UT22084-072-009-section-1.

Bhabha, Homi K. 1983. "The Other Question: The Stereotype and Colonial Discourse." *Screen* 24 (6), pp. 18–36.

———. 1994. *The Location of Culture*. London: Routledge.

Bhoil, Shelly, and Enrique Galvan-Alvarez, eds. 2018. *Tibetan Subjectivities on the Global Stage: Negotiating Dispossession*. Lanham, MD: Lexington Books.

Biehl, João. 2005. *Vita: Life in a Zone of Social Abandonment*. Berkeley: University of California Press.

Blake, Rosemary J. 2011. "Ethnographies of Touch and Touching Ethnographies: Some Prospects for Touch in Anthropological Enquiries." *Anthropology Matters* 13 (1), pp. 1–12. https://anthropologymatters.com/index.php/anth_matters/article/view/224/409.

Bourgois, Philippe, and Jeff Schonberg. 2009. *Righteous Dopefiend*. Berkeley: University of California Press.

Brauen, Martin, Renate Koller, and Markus Vock. 2004. *Dreamworld Tibet: Western Illusions*. Trumbull, CT: Weatherhill.

Brox, Trine. 2012. "Constructing a Tibetan Demons in Exile." *Citizenship Studies* 16 (3–4), pp. 451–467.

Bubandt, Nils. 2014. *The Empty Seashell: Witchcraft and Doubt on an Indonesian Island*. Ithaca, NY: Cornell University Press.

Buch, Elana. 2013. "Senses of Care: Embodying Inequality and Sustaining Personhood in the Home Care of Older Adults in Chicago." *American Ethnologist* 40 (4), pp. 637–650.

———. 2014. "Troubling Gifts of Care: Vulnerable Persons and Threatening Exchanges in Chicago's Home Care Industry." *Medical Anthropology Quarterly* 28 (4), pp. 599–615.

Buffetrille, Katia. 2012. "Self-Immolation in Tibet: Some Reflections on an Unfolding History." *Revue d'Etudes Tibétaines* 25, pp. 1–17.

Bureau of His Holiness the Dalai Lama. 1969. *Tibetans in Exile: A Report on Ten Years of Rehabilitation in India*. Department of Information and International Relations, Central Tibetan Administration.

Butler, Judith. 2012. "Can One Lead a Good Life in a Bad Life?" Adorno Prize Lecture, Frankfurt, Germany, 11 September 2012.

——— 2015. *Notes Toward a Performative Theory of Assembly*. Cambridge, MA: Harvard University Press.

Cacioppo, John T., and William Patrick. 2009. *Loneliness: Human Nature and the Need for Social Connection*. New York: W. W. Norton.

Campt, Tina M. 2023 [2021]. *A Black Gaze. Artists Changing How We See*. Cambridge, MA: MIT Press.

Choudary, Srishti. 2019. "Pastoralists of Himachal Pradesh an Unusual Casualty of Global Warming." *Mint*, 26 Jun 2019. https://www.livemint.com/news/india/carpet-weavers-of-himachal-pradesh-an-unusual-casualty-of-global-warming-1561488151014.html.

Chen, Xuewei, Divya Talwar, and Qian Ji. 2015. "Social Network and Social Support Among Elderly Asian Immigrants in the United States." *Global Journal of Anthropology Research* 2 (2), pp. 15–21.

Chettri, Mona. 2017. *Ethnicity and Democracy in the Eastern Himalayan Borderland*. Amsterdam: Amsterdam University Press.

Childs, Geoff. 2001. "Old-Age Security, Religious Celibacy, and Aggregate Fertility in a Tibetan Population." *Journal of Population Research* 18 (1), pp. 52–67.

———. 2004. *Tibetan Diary: From Birth to Death and Beyond in a Himalayan Valley of Nepal*. Berkeley: University of California Press.

———. 2008. *Tibetan Transitions: Historical and Contemporary Perspective on Fertility, Family, Planning, and Demographic Change*. Leiden: Brill.

———. 2014. "Hunger, Hard Work, and Uncertainty: Tashi Dondrup Reminisces on Life and Death in a Tibetan Village." In *Buddhists: Understanding Buddhism Through the Lives of Practitioners*, edited by Todd Lewis, pp. 228–235. Chichester: John Wiley & Sons Ltd.

Childs, Geoff, Melvyn C. Goldstein, and Tsering Wangdui. 2011. "Externally-Resident Daughters, Social Capital, and Support for the Elderly in Rural Tibet." *Journal of Cross-Cultural Gerontology* 26, pp. 1–22.

Childs, Geoff, Melvyn C. Goldstein, Puchung Wangdui, and Namgyal Choedup. 2021. "What Constitutes 'Successful Aging' in a Tibetan Context?" In *Aging Across Cultures: Growing Old in the Non-Western World*, edited by Helaine Selin, pp. 229–244. Cham: Springer Cham.

Childs, Geoff, and Namgyal Choedup. 2019. *From a Trickle to a Torrent. Education, Migration, and Social Change in a Himalayan Valley of Nepal*. Berkeley: University of California Press.

———. 2023. "Resistance to Marriage, Family Responsibilities, and Mobility: A Turbulent Life Story from Kyidrong." In "Writing with Care: Ethnographies from the Margins of Tibet and the Himalayas," edited by Harmandeep K. Gill and Theresia Hofer. Special issue, *Himalaya* 43 (1), pp. 92–107.

Chittick, William C. 1989. *The Sufi Path of Knowledge: Ibn al-ʿArabi's Metaphysics of the Imagination*. Albany, NY: State University of New York Press.

Chodron, Thubten. 2009. "Preliminary Practice (*Ngöndro*) Overview." Venerable Thubten Chodron. 1 September. https://thubtenchodron.org/2009/09/clearing-and-enriching-mind/.

Choedak, Jigme. 2023. "(Un)tying Knots." Paintings, solo show. 13 December 2023–2 January 2024. *Wind Horse Gallery*, Kathmandu.

Choedup, Namgyal. 2018. "'Old people's homes,' Filial Piety, and Transnational Families: Change and Continuity in Elderly Care in the Tibetan Settlements in India." In *Care Across Distance: Ethnographic Explorations of Aging and Migration*, edited by Azra Hromadzic and Monika Palmberger, pp. 75–94. New York: Berghahn Books.

Choedup, Ugyan. 2017. "Historical Trajectory of Tibetan Identity: Some Preliminary Notes on the Role of Exile Educational Institutions." *Tibet Journal* 42 (2), pp. 93–110.

———. 2023. "Competing Visions: Schooling the Nation and the 'Revolt' at the Ockenden Tibetan School." *International Journal of Asian Studies* 20, pp. 497–512.

Choklay, Tenzin T., dir. 2013. *Bringing Tibet Home*. Documentary, 82 min. Produced by T. Tenzin, T. Choklay, and Tenzin Rigdol. New York: Five by Nine Films.

Christopher, Stephen. 2020. "Divergent Refugee and Tribal Cosmopolitanism in Dharamsala." *Copenhagen Journal of Asian Studies* 38 (1), pp. 33–56.

Cohen, Lawrence. 1994. "Old Age: Cultural and Critical Perspectives." *Annual Review of Anthropology* 23, pp. 153–178.

———. 1998. *No Aging in India: Alzheimer's, the Bad Family, and Other Modern Things.* Berkeley: University of California Press.

———. 2003. "Senility and Irony's Age." *Social Analysis* 7 (2), pp. 122–134.

Cole, Jennifer, and Deborah L. Durham, eds. 2007. *Generations and Globalization: Youth, Age, and Family in the New World Economy.* Bloomington: Indiana University Press.

Corwin, Anna I. 2012. "Let Him Hold You: Spiritual and Social Support in a Catholic Convent Infirmary." *Anthropology of Aging Quarterly* 33 (4), pp. 120–129.

Cotton, Shelia R., George Ford, Sherry Ford, and Timothy M. Hale. 2014. "Internet Use and Depression Among Retired Older Adults in the United States: A Longitudinal Analysis." *Journals of Gerontology. Series B, Psychological Sciences and Social Sciences* 69, pp. 763–771.

Craig, Sienna R. 2012. *Healing Elements: Efficacy and the Social Ecologies of Tibetan Medicine.* Berkeley: University of California Press.

———. 2020a. *The Ends of Kinship: Connecting Himalayan Lives Between Nepal and New York.* Seattle: University of Washington Press.

———. 2020b. "The Forest of (Be)Longing." In *Flash Ethnography*, edited by Carole McGranahan and Nomi Stone. *American Ethnologist* (website). 26 October. https://americanethnologist.org/online-content/collections/flash-ethnography/the-forest-of-belonging/.

———. 2023. "Foreword: The Politics and Poetics of Himalayan Lives." In "Writing with Care: Ethnographies from the Margins of Tibet and the Himalayas," edited by Harmandeep K. Gill and Theresia Hofer. Special issue, *Himalaya* 43 (1), pp. 12–19.

Crapanzano, Vincent. 1980. *Tuhami: Portrait of a Moroccan.* Chicago: University of Chicago Press.

———. 2004. *Imaginative Horizons. An Essay in Literary-Philosophical Anthropology.* Chicago: University of Chicago Press.

Crosby, Christina. 2016. *A Body, Undone. Living on After Great Pain.* New York: New York University Press.

D'Amico-Samuels, Deborah. 1991. "Undoing Fieldwork: Personal, Political, and Theoretical Implications." In *Decolonizing Anthropology*, edited by Faye V. Harrison, pp. 68–87. Washington, DC: American Anthropological Association.

Dalai Lama. 2016 [1962]. *My Land and My People: Memories of the Dalai Lama of Tibet.* New Delhi: Timeless Books.

Danely, Jason. 2014. *Aging and Loss: Mourning and Maturity in Contemporary Japan.* New Brunswick, NJ: Rutgers University Press.

———. 2017. "Carer Narratives of Fatigue and Endurance in Japan and England." *Subjectivity* 10, pp. 411–426.

———. 2022. *Fragile Resonance: Caring for Older Family Members in Japan and England.* Ithaca, NY: Cornell University Press.

Darwish, Mahmoud. 2005. "To Our Land." *Poetry*, December 2005. https://www.poetryfoundation.org/poetrymagazine/browse?contentId=46724.

———. 2009. "Lose One of Your Stars." In *A River Dies of Thirst: Journals*, translated by Catherine Cobham, pp. 80. Brooklyn, NY: Archipelago Books.

———. 2010. *Absent Presence.* London: Hesperus Press Limited.

Das, Veena. 2006. *Life and Words: Violence and the Descent into the Ordinary.* Berkeley: University of California Press.

———. 2014. Afterword to *Ayya's Accounts: A Ledger of Hope in Modern India*, by Anand Pandian and M. P. Mariappan, pp. 199–205. Bloomington: Indiana University Press.

———. 2020. *Textures of the Ordinary: Doing Anthropology After Wittgenstein.* New York: Fordham Press.

Dasel, Tenzin, dir. 2016. *Royal Café*, directed with Remi Caritey. Independent film, 40 min.

Davé, Naisargi. 2021. "Afterword: For a Synaesthetics of Seeing." *Cambridge Journal of Anthropology* 39 (1), pp. 143–149.

Derrida, Jacques. 1993. *Aporias*. Stanford, CA: Stanford University Press.

Desjarlais, Robert. 1997. *Shelter Blues: Sanity and Selfhood Among the Homeless*. Philadelphia: University of Pennsylvania Press.

———. 2003. *Sensory Biographies: Lives and Deaths Among Nepal's Yolmo Buddhists*. Berkeley: University of California Press.

———. 2016. *Subject to Death: Life and Loss in a Buddhist World*. Chicago: University of Chicago Press.

Dhompa, Tsering W. 2014 [2013]. *A Home in Tibet*. New Delhi: Penguin Books.

———. 2023. "Cotton Singers." In "Writing with Care: Ethnographies from the Margins of Tibet and the Himalayas," edited by Harmandeep K. Gill and Theresia Hofer. Special issue, *Himalaya* 43 (1), pp. 148–149.

———. Forthcoming. *Politics of Sorrow: A Story of Unity and Allegiance Across Tibetan Exile*. New York: Columbia University Press.

Dickie, Tenzin. 2023. *The Penguin Book of Modern Tibetan Essays*. New Delhi: Penguin Random House India.

Dickinson, Anna, and Robin L. Hill. 2007. "Keeping in Touch: Talking to Older People About Computers and Communication." *Educational Gerontology* 33 (8), pp. 613–630.

Didi-Huberman, Georges. 2005. *Confronting Images: Questioning the Ends of a Certain History of Art*. Translated by John Goodman. Philadelphia: Pennsylvania State University Press.

Diehl, Keila. 2002. *Echoes from Dharamsala: Music in the Life of a Tibetan Refugee Community*. Berkeley: University of California Press.

Dodin, Thierry, and Heinz Räther, eds. 2001. *Imagining Tibet: Perceptions, Projections, and Fantasies*. Somerville, MA: Wisdom.

Dolma, Kunsang, and Evan Denno. 2013. *A Hundred Thousand White Stones: An Ordinary Tibetan's Extraordinary Journey*. Somerville, MA: Wisdom.

Dorjee, Pema. 2005. *The Spiritual Medicine of Tibet: Heal Your Spirit, Heal Yourself*. London: Watkins.

Dossa, Parin, and Cati Coe, eds. 2017. *Transnational Aging and Reconfigurations of Kin Work*. New Brunswick, NJ: Rutgers University Press.

Dreyfus, George. 1994. "Proto-Nationalism in Tibet." In *Tibetan Studies, Proceedings of the 6th Seminar of the International Association for Tibetan Studies. Fagernes 1992*, edited by Per Kværne, pp. 205–218. Oslo: Institute for Comparative Research in Human Culture.

———. 1995. "Are We Prisoners of Shangri-la? Orientalism, Nationalism, and the Study of Tibet." *Journal of the International Association for Tibetan Studies* 1, pp. 1–21.

———. 2002. "Tibetan Religious Nationalism: Western Fantasy or Empowering Vision?" In *Tibet, Self, and the Tibetan Diaspora*, edited by Christian P. Klieger, pp. 37–56. Leiden: Brill.

Duckworth, Douglas S. 2019. *Tibetan Buddhist Philosophy of the Mind and Nature* [South Asia Edition]. New Delhi: Oxford University Press.

Ehrhard, Franz-Karl. 2004. "Die Statue und der Tempel des Arya Va-ti Bzang-po: Ein Beitrag Zu Geschichte und Geographie des Tibetischen Buddhismus." In *Contributions to Tibetan Studies*, vol. 2, edited by David P. Jackson. Wiesbaden: Dr. Ludwig Reichert Verlag.

Ekvall, Robert B. 1980. "The High-Pasturage Ones of Tibet Also Grow Old." *Proceedings of the American Philosophical Society* 124 (6), pp. 429–437.

Eriksen, Thomas H. 2005. *Engaging Anthropology: The Case for a Public Presence*. New York: Routledge.

Ewing, Katherine P. 1990. "The Illusion of Wholeness: Culture, Self, and the Experience of Inconsistency." *Ethos* 18, pp. 251–278.

———. 1991 "Can Psychoanalytic Theories Explain the Pakistani Woman? Intrapsychic Autonomy and Interpersonal Engagement in the Extended Family." *Ethos* 19, pp. 131–160.

Fabian, Johannes. 2014 [1972]. *Time and the Other: How Anthropology Makes Its Object*. New York: Columbia University Press.

"Facts and Figures About the Kangyur and Tengyur." 2010. 84000: Translating the Words of the Buddha. 2 January. https://84000.co/facts-and-figures-about-kangyur-and-tengyur.

Falcone, Jessica, and Tsering Wangchuk. 2008. "'We're Not Home': Tibetan Refugees in India in the Twenty-First Century." *India Review* 7 (3), pp. 164–199.

Fanon, Frantz. 2021 [1967]. *Black Skin, White Masks*. New York: Penguin Random House.

Fjeld, Heidi E. 2005. *Commoners and Nobles: Hereditary Divisions in Tibet*. Copenhagen: NIAS Press.

———. 2008. "Pollution and Social Networks in Contemporary Rural Tibet." In *Proceedings of the Tenth Seminar of the IATS, 2003. Vol. 11: Tibetan Modernities: Notes from the Field on Cultural and Social Change*, edited by Robert Barnett and Ronald D. Schwartz, pp. 113–137. Leiden: Brill.

Flaherty, Michael G. 2003. "Time Work: Customizing Temporal Experience." *Social Psychology Quarterly* 66 (1), pp. 17–33.

———. 2011. *The Textures of Time: Agency and Temporal Experience*. Philadelphia: Temple University Press.

Frechette, Ann. 2002. *Tibetans in Nepal: The Dynamics of International Assistance Among a Community in Exile*. New York: Berghahn Books.

Gagné, Karine. 2018. *Caring for Glaciers; Land, Animals, and Humanity in the Himalayas*. Seattle: University of Washington Press.

Gammeltoft, Tine. 2006. "Beyond Being: Emergent Narratives of Suffering in Vietnam." *Journal of the Royal Anthropological Institute* 12, pp. 589–605.

Gandhi, Leela. 2006. *Affective Communities: Anticolonial Thought, Fin-de-Siècle Radicalism, and the Politics of Friendship*. Durham, NC: Duke University Press.

Garcia, Angela. 2010. *The Pastoral Clinic: Addiction and Dispossession Along the Rio Grande*. Berkeley: University of California Press.

Gardner, Alexander. 2019. *The Life of Jamgon Kongtrul the Great*. Ithaca, NY: Snow Lion.

Gayley, Holly. 2017. *Love Letters from Golok: A Tantric Couple in Modern Tibet*. New York: Columbia University Press.

Geismar, Haidy, Ton Otto, and Cameron D. Warner. 2022. *Impermanence: Exploring Continuous Change Across Cultures*. London: UCL Press.

Gell, Alfred. 2001 [1992]. *The Anthropology of Time: Cultural Constructions of Temporal Maps and Images*. London: Routledge.

Gellner, David N. 2007. *Resistance and the State: Nepalese Experiences*. New York: Berghahn Books.

———, ed. 2013. *Borderland Lives in Northern South Asia*. Durham, NC: Duke University Press.

Gerke, Barbara. 2012. *Long Lives and Untimely Deaths: Life-Span Concepts and Longevity Practices Among Tibetans in the Darjeeling Hills, India*. Leiden: Brill.

Gill, Harmandeep K. 2022: "Imagining Self and Other: Carers, TV and Touch." In *Imagistic Care: Growing Old in a Precarious World*, edited by Cheryl Mattingly and Lone Grøn, pp. 163–184. New York: Fordham Press.

———. 2023a. "'Setting Off from the Mountain Pass': Facing Death and Preparing for the Journey Ahead in Tibetan Exile." In *Aspiring in Later Life: Making Selves, Places, Relations Across Locales*, edited by M. Amrith, V. K. Sakti, and D. Sampaio, pp. 159–175. New Brunswick, NJ: Rutgers University Press.

———. 2023b. "Old Tibetan Hands." In "Writing with Care: Ethnographies from the Margins of Tibet and the Himalayas," edited by Harmandeep. K. Gill and Theresia Hofer. Special issue, *Himalaya* 43 (1), pp. 150–181.

Gill, Harmandeep K., and Theresia Hofer, eds. 2023. "Writing with Care: Ethnographies from the Margins of Tibet and the Himalayas." Special issue, *Himalaya* 43 (1).

Glissant, Édouard. 1997. *Poetics of Relation*. Ann Arbor: University of Michigan Press.

Goldstein, Melvyn C. 1989. *A History of Modern Tibet*. Vol. 1, *1913–1951, The Demise of the Lamaist State*. Berkeley: University of California Press.

———. 1997. *The Snow Lion and the Dragon: China, Tibet, and the Dalai Lama*. Berkeley: University of California Press.

———. 1998. *Introduction to Buddhism in Contemporary Tibet: Religious Revival and Cultural Identity*, edited by Melvyn C. Goldstein and Matthew T. Kapstein, pp. 1–14. Delhi: Motilal Banarsidass Publishers.

Goldstein, Melvyn C., and Cynthia M. Beall. 1997. "Growing Old in Tibet: Tradition, Family, and Change." *Aging Asian Concepts and Experiences Past and Present* 643, pp. 155–176.

Goodman, Michael H. 1986. *The Last Dalai Lama: A Biography*. Boston: Shambala.

Gouin, Margaret. 2010. *Tibetan Rituals of Death: Buddhist Funerary Practices*. London: Routledge.

Greenfield-Sanders, Timothy, dir. 2019. *Toni Morrison: The Pieces I Am*. Documentary, 119 min. Produced by Johanna Giebelhaus, Timothy Greenfield-Sanders, Chad Thompson, and Tommy Walker. New York: Magnolia Pictures.

Grunfeld, Tom A. 1987. *The Making of Modern Tibet*. London: Zed Books.

Grøn, Lone, and Cheryl Mattingly. 2017. "In Search of Good Old Life: Ontological Breakdown and Responsive Hope at the Margins of Life." *Death Studies* 42 (5), pp. 306–313.

Guenther, Lisa. 2011. "The Ethics of Politics of Otherness: Negotiating Alterity and Racial Difference." *PhiloSOPHIA* 1 (2), pp. 195–214.

———. 2012. "Should You Ever Find Yourself in Solitary." Paper presented at the New York Institute for the Humanities, New York, NY, 17 November.

———. 2013. *Solitary Confinement: Social Death and Its Afterlives*. Minneapolis: University of Minnesota Press.

Gungtang Rinpoche. 1975. *Nyams-myong rgan-po'i 'bel-gtam* [Advice from an Experienced Old Man] Oral translation by Sharpa Rinpoche. Notes taken by Alexander Berzin in 1975, Dharamala, India. Berzin Archives. https://studybuddhism.com/en/advanced-studies/lam-rim/impermanence-death/paraphrase-of-advice-from-an-experienced-old-man.

Gutschow, Kim. 2004. *Being a Buddhist Nun: The Struggle for Enlightenment in the Himalayas*. Cambridge, MA: Harvard University Press.

Gyal, Dondrup, and Tsering Dondrup. 1983. "rGyu 'bras med pa'i mna' ma" [A shameless bride]. *sBrang char* 2, pp. 41–55.

Gyal, Huatse. 2021. "Our Indigenous Land Is Not a Wasteland." AES [American Ethnological Society]. 6 February. https://americanethnologist.org/online-content/essays/our-indigenous-land-is-not-a-wasteland/.

Gyalpo, Changchan Gung S. 1963. *Rgan byis gsum gyi 'bel gtam snang ba rab gsal zhes bya ba bzhugso* ['A moral advice of an old woman' to two young women, regarding mortal decay], edited and published by Gergan D. Tharchin. Kalimpong: Tibet Mirror Press.

Gyatso, Janet. 2016. *Being Human in a Buddhist World*. New York: Columbia University Press.

Hall, Stuart. 1981. "The Whites of Their Eyes: Racist Ideologies and the Media." In *Silver Linings: Some Strategies for the Eighties*, edited by Geroge Bridges and Rosalind Brunt, pp. 89–93. London: Lawrence and Wishart.

———. 1997. "The Spectacle of the 'Other.'" In *Representation: Cultural Representations and Signifying Practices*, edited by Stuart Hall, pp. 225–285. Thousand Oaks, CA: Sage Publications Ltd.

———. 2021. *Selected Writings on Race and Difference*, edited by Paul Gilroy and Ruth W. Gilmore. Durham, NC: Duke University Press.

Haraway, Donna. 1988. "Situated Knowledges: The Science Question in Feminism and the Privilege of Partial Perspective." *Feminist Studies* 14 (3), pp. 575–599.

Harris, Clare E. 2012. *The Museum on the Roof of the World: Art, Politics, and the Representation of Tibet*. Chicago: University of Chicago Press.

Harrison, Faye V., ed. 1991. *Decolonizing Anthropology: Moving Further Toward an Anthropology for Liberation*. Washington, DC: American Anthropological Association.

Havnevik, Hanna. 1989. *Tibetan Buddhist Nuns: History, Cultural Norms and Social Reality*. Oslo: Norwegian University Press.

Hess, Julia M. 2009. *Immigrant Ambassadors: Citizenship and Belonging in the Tibetan Diaspora*. Stanford, CA: Stanford University Press.

Hilton, James. 1933. *Lost Horizon*. London: Macmillan.

Hofer, Theresia, ed. 2014. *Bodies in Balance: The Art of Tibetan Medicine*. Seattle: University of Washington Press.

———. 2018. *Medicine and Memory in Tibet: Amchi Physicians in an Age of Reform*. Seattle: University of Washington Press.

Holmberg, David. 2007. "Outcastes in an 'Egalitarian' Society: Tamang/Blacksmith Relations from a Tamang Perspective." *Occasional Papers in Sociology and Anthropology* 10, pp. 124–140.

hooks, bell. 1990. *Yearning: Race, Gender, and Cultural Politics*. Boston, MA: South End Press.

———. 2019 [2009]. *Belonging: A Culture of Place*. New York: Routledge.

Houston, Serin, and Richard Wright. 2003. "Making and Remaking Tibetan Diasporic Identities." *Social and Cultural Geography* 4 (2), pp. 217–232.

Hromadzic, Azra, and Monika Palmberger, eds. 2018. *Care Across Distance: Ethnographic Explorations of Aging and Migration*. New York: Berghahn Books.

Hurston, Zora N. 1935. *Mules and Men*. Philadelphia: J. B. Lippincott.

———. 2018. *Barracon: The Story of the Last "Black Cargo."* New York: Amistad Press.

Information Office of His Holiness the Dalai Lama. 1981. *Tibetans in Exile: 1959–1980*. New Delhi: Model Press.

International Campaign for Tibet. 2023. "China's New 'White Paper' on Tibet: Ominous Silence Amid Barrage of Party Language." 15 November 2023. https://savetibet.org/wp-content/uploads/2023/11/Chinas-new-'White-Paper-on-Tibet-Ominous-silence-amid-barrage-of-party-language.pdf.

Irving, Andrew. 2017. *The Art of Life and Death: Radical Aesthetics and Ethnographic Practice*. Chicago: Hau Books.

Iyer, Pico. 2009 [2008]. *The Open Road: The Global Journey of the Fourteenth Dalai Lama*. London: Bloomsbury.

Jabb, Lama. 2015. *Oral and Literary Continuities in Modern Tibetan Literature: The Inescapable Nation*. Lanham, MD: Lexington Books.

Jackson, Michael. 2005. *Existential Anthropology: Events, Exigencies and Effects*. New York: Berghahn Books.

———. 2013. *Lifeworlds: Essays in Existential Anthropology*. Chicago: University of Chicago Press.

———. 2017. *How Lifeworlds Work: Emotionality, Sociality, and the Ambiguity of Being*. Chicago: University of Chicago Press.

Jigme, Tenzin. 2020. *Allegories of the Self* and *In Loving Memory*. Paintings exhibited as part of *Prayer Flags: Art from the Himalayas*, 29 February–12 April 2020. Wind Horse Gallery, Kathmandu.

Jinba, Tenzin. 2023. *The Beggar Lama: The Life of the Gyalrong Kuzhap*. New York: Columbia University Press.

Kajal, Kapil. 2021. "In Himachal Pradesh, Climate Change and Unplanned Development Are Causing Disasters." Scroll.in. 10 September. https://scroll.in/article/1004622/in-himachal-pradesh-climate-change-and-unplanned-development-are-causing-disasters.

Kapstein, Matthew T. 1998. "A Pilgrimage of Rebirth Reborn: The 1992 Celebration of the Dri-gung Powa Chenmo." In *Buddhism in Contemporary Tibet: Religious Revival and Cultural Identity*, edited by Melvyn C. Goldstein and Matthew T. Kapstein, pp. 95–119. Berkeley: University of California Press.

———. 2009 [2006]. *The Tibetans*. India Edition. New Delhi: Wiley Blackwell.

Karmay, Samten G. 1998. *The Arrow and the Spindle: Studies in History, Myths, Rituals and Be-liefs in Tibet*. Kathmandu: Mandala.

Katz, Stephen. 2006. "From Chronology to Functionality: Critical Reflection on the Gerontol-ogy of the Body." In *Aging, Globalization and Inequality: The New Critical Gerontology*, ed-ited by Jan Baars, Dale Dannefer, Chris Phillipson, and Alan Walker, pp. 123–138. Amityville, NY: Baywood.

Katz, Stephen, and Barbara L. Marshall. 2004. "Is the Functional 'Normal'? Aging, Sexuality and the Bio-Marking of Successful Living." *History of the Human Sciences* 17 (1), pp. 53–75.

Kaysang. 2016. *Broken Portraits*. Dharamsala: TibetWrites.

Kellner, Birgit. 2010. "Self-Awareness (*svasaṃvedana*) in Dignāga's *Pramāṇasamuccaya* and -*vṛtti*: A Close Reading." *Journal of Indian Philosophy* 38 (3), pp. 203–231.

Kerouac, Jack. 1958. *The Dharma Bums*. New York: Viking.

Khrinley, Dungkar L. 2002. *Dungkar Tibetological Great Dictionary*. Beijing: China Tibetology Publishing House.

Kleinman, Arthur. 2012. "The Art of Medicine: Caregiving as Moral Experience." *Lancet* 380, pp. 1550–1551.

———. 2020. *The Soul of Care: The Moral Education of a Husband and a Doctor*. London: Pen-guin Books.

Kleinman, Arthur, and Sjakk van der Geest. 2009. "'Care' in Health Care: Remaking the Moral World of Medicine." *Medische Antropologie* 21 (1), pp. 159–168.

Klieger, Christian P. 1992. *Tibetan Nationalism: The Role of Patronage in the Accomplishment of a National Identity*. Meerut, India: Archana.

Kong, Byung-Hye. 2008. "Levinas' Ethics of Caring: Implications and Limits in Nursing." *Asian Nursing Research* 2 (4), pp. 208–213.

Lahiri, Jhumpa. 2022. *Translating Myself and Others*. Princeton, NJ: Princeton University Press.

Lama, Jigme Y. 2023. "'To Be or Not to Be': Tibetans and the Question of Citizenship." In *Citi-zenship in Contemporary Times: The Indian Context*, edited by Gorky Chakraborty, pp. 217–229. New York: Taylor and Francis.

Lama Kunsang, Lama Pemo, and Marie Aubele. 2012. *History of the Karmapas: The Odyssey of the Tibetan Masters with the Black Crown*. Ithaca, NY: Snow Lion.

Lama, Tsering Y. 2022. *We Measure the Earth with Our Bodies*. New York: Bloomsbury.

Lama Zopa Rinpoche. n.d. "Abiding in the Retreat: A Nyung Nä Commentary." Edited by Ven. Alisa Cameron. https://www.lamayeshe.com/article/chapter/1-benefits-nyung-nä-practice/.

Lamb, Sarah. 1997. "The Making and Unmaking of Persons: Notes on Aging and Gender in North India." *Ethos* 25 (3), pp. 279–302.

———. 2000. *White Saris and Sweet Mangoes: Aging, Gender and Body in North India*. Berkeley: University of California Press.

———. 2009. *Aging and the Indian Diaspora: Cosmopolitan Families in India and Abroad*. Bloomington: Indiana University Press.

———. 2014. "Permanent Personhood or Meaningful Decline? Toward a Critical Anthropology of Successful Aging." *Journal of Aging Studies* 29, pp. 41–52.

Leder, Drew. 1991. *The Absent Body*. Chicago: University of Chicago Press.

Levinas, Emmanuel. 1996 [1962]. "Transcendence and Height." In *Emmanuel Levinas: Basic Philosophical Writings*, edited by Adriaan Peperzak, Simon Critchley, and Robert Ber-nasconi, pp. 11–31. Bloomington: Indiana University Press.

Lewis, Todd, ed. 2014. *Buddhists: Understanding Buddhism Through the Lives of Practitioners.* Malden, MA: Wiley-Blackwell.

Liang, Jaylene, and Baozhen Luo. 2012. "Toward a Discourse Shift in Social Gerontology: From Successful Aging to Harmonious Aging." *Journal of Aging Studies* 26, pp. 327–334.

Loden, dir. 2023. *Origin (rten 'brel)*. Independent film, 13 min, 50 sec.

Lokyitsang, Dawa. 2022. "Sovereignty in Settler Colonial Times: Kinship and Education in the Tibetan Exile Community." AES [American Ethnological Society]. 3 March. https://ameri canethnologist.org/online-content/essays/sovereignty-in-settler-colonial-times-kinship -and-education-in-the-tibetan-exile-community/.

Lopez Jr., Donald S. 1998. *Prisoners of Shangri-La: Tibetan Buddhism and the West.* Chicago: University of Chicago Press.

Løgstrup, Knud E. 1997. *The Ethical Demand.* Notre Dame, IN: University of Notre Dame Press.

Magnetta, Sarah. 2018. "Common Ground: Place and Identity in Contemporary Tibetan Art." *South Asian Studies* 34 (2), pp. 186–196.

Makley, Charlene E. 2007. *The Violence of Liberation: Gender and Tibetan Buddhist Revival in Post-Mao China.* Berkeley: University of California Press.

March, Kathryn S. 2002. *If Each Comes Halfway: Meeting Tamang Women in Nepal.* Ithaca, NY: Cornell University Press.

Martin, Emma. 2017. "Collecting Tibet: Dreams and Realities." *Journal of Museum Ethnography* 30, pp. 59–78.

Mattingly, Cheryl. 2014. *Moral Laboratories: Family Peril and the Struggle for a Good Life.* Berkeley: University of California Press.

———. 2019. "Defrosting Concepts, Destabilizing Doxa: Critical Phenomenology and the Perplexing Particular." *Anthropological Theory* 19 (4), pp. 415–439.

Mattingly, Cheryl, and Lone Grøn, eds. 2022. *Imagistic Care: Growing Old in a Precarious World.* New York: Fordham University Press.

Maurette, Pablo. 2018. *The Forgotten Sense: Meditations on Touch.* Chicago: University of Chicago Press.

McConnell, Fiona. 2013. "Citizens and Refugees: Constructing and Negotiating Tibetan Identities in Exile." *Annals of the Association of American Geographers* 103 (4), pp. 967–983.

McGranahan, Carole. 2006. "Tibet's Cold War: The CIA and the Chushi Gangdrug Resistance 1956–1974." *Journal of Cold War Studies* 8 (3), pp. 102–130.

———. 2010. *Arrested Histories: Tibet, The CIA, and Memories of a Forgotten War.* Durham, NC: Duke University Press.

———. 2018a. "Ethnography Beyond Method: The Importance of an Ethnographic Sensibility." *Sites: A Journal of Social Anthropology and Cultural Studies* 44 (2), pp. 1–10.

———. 2018b. "Refusal as Political Practice: Citizenship, Sovereignty, and Tibetan Refugee Status." *American Ethnologist* 45 (3), pp. 367–379.

———. 2020. "Ethnographic Writing with Kirin Narayan: An Interview." In *Writing Anthropology: Essays on Craft and Commitment*, edited by Carole McGranahan, pp. 87–92. Durham, NC: Duke University Press.

———. 2022. "Theory as Ethics." *American Ethnologist* 49 (3), pp. 289–301.

McHugh, Ernestine L. 1989. "Concepts of the Person Among the Gurungs of Nepal." *American Ethnologist* 16, pp. 75–86.

Mead, Margaret. 1928. *Coming of Age in Samoa: A Psychological Study of Primitive Youth for Western Civilisation.* New York: William Morrow.

Meinert, Lotte. 2022. "Keeping Quiet: Liminal Responsiveness and Shadows of Sharing in Ik Borderlands." Paper presented at Liminal Ethics: Phenomenologies of Moral Community (conference), 11–12 October, Moesgård Museum, Aarhus University, Denmark.

Meinert, Lotte, and Susan R. Whyte. 2023. *This Land Is Not For Sale: Trust and Transitions in Northern Uganda*. New York: Berghahn Books.

Merleau-Ponty, Maurice. 1964a. "Eye and Mind." In *The Primacy of Perception*, edited by James E. Edie, translated by Carleton Dallery, pp. 159–190. Evanston, IL: Northwestern University Press.

———. 1964b. "Cézanne's Doubt." In *Sense and Non-Sense: Studies in Phenomenology and Existential Philosophy*, translated by Hubert L. Dreyfus and Patricia A. Dreyfus, pp. 9–25. Evanston, IL: Northwestern University Press.

———. 2013 [1945]. *Phenomenology of Perception*. Translated by Donald Landes. London: Routledge.

Miller, Beatrice D. 1956. "Ganye and Kidu: Two Formalized Systems of Mutual Aid Among the Tibetans." *Southwestern Journal of Anthropology* 12, pp. 157–170.

Miller, Kei. 2021. *Things I Have Withheld*. Edinburgh: Canongate Books.

Mitzner, Tracy L., Jyoti Savla, Walter R. Boot, Joseph Sharit, Neil Charness, Sara J. Czaja, and Wendy A. Rogers. 2019. "Technology Adoption by Older Adults: Findings from the PRISM Trial." *Gerontologist* 59 (1), pp. 34–44.

Moody, Harry. 2009. "From Successful Aging to Conscious Aging." In *The Cultural Context of Aging: Worldwide Perspectives*, 3rd ed., edited by Jay Sokolovsky, pp. 67–76. Westport, CT: Praeger.

Morgan, Michael L. 2013 [2011]. *The Cambridge Introduction to Emmanuel Levinas*. Cambridge: Cambridge University Press.

Murphy, Robert F. 2001. *The Body Silent—The Different World of the Disabled*. New York: W. W. Norton.

Namgyal, Lobsang. 1986. "Nyams char rgan po'i dri lan" [The Questions and Answers of the Weak and Old Man]. In *Dzo mo glang ma*, vol. 2, pp. 62–63. Shigatse, Tibet.

Narayan, Kirin. 1989. *Storytellers, Saints, and Scoundrels: Folk Narrative in Hindu Religious Teaching*. Philadelphia: University of Pennsylvania Press.

———. 2007. *My Family and Other Saints*. Chicago: University of Chicago Press.

———. 2012. *Alive in the Writing: Crafting Ethnography in the Company of Chekhov*. Chicago: University of Chicago Press.

Navaro, Yael. 2009. "Affective Spaces, Melancholic Objects: Ruination and the Production of Anthropological Knowledge." *Journal of the Royal Anthropological Institute* 15, pp. 1–18.

Ngorchen Konchog Lhundrub. 1991 [1535]. *The Beautiful Ornament of the Three Visions*. Translated by Lobsang Dakpa and Jay Goldberg. Ithaca, NY: Snow Lion.

Norbu, Dawa. 1987 [1974]. *Red Star over Tibet*. New Delhi: Sterling.

———. 1992. "'Otherness' and the Modern Tibetan Identity." *Himāl Southasian* 5 (3), pp. 10—11.

Norbu, Jamyang. 1986 [1979]. *Warriors of Tibet: The Story of Aten and the Khampas' Fight for the Freedom of Their Country*. London: Wisdom.

———. 2007. *Shadow Tibet: Selected Writings 1989 to 2004*. New Delhi: Srishti.

———. 2016. "Untangling a Mess of Petrified Noodles." *Shadow Tibet* (blog). 26 June. https://www.jamyangnorbu.com/blog/2016/06/29/untangling-a-mess-of-petrified-noodles/.

Nowak, Margaret. 1984. *Tibetan Refugees: Youth and the New Generation of Meaning*. New Brunswick, NJ: Rutgers University Press.

Nulo, Naktsang. 2014. *My Tibetan Childhood: When Ice Shattered Stone*, translated by Angus Cargill and Sonam Lhamo. Durham, NC: Duke University Press.

Odgaard, Marie R. B. 2022. "A Staircase Between the Sun and the Moon: The Arts of Living Queerly in Amman." PhD diss., Department of Anthropology, Aarhus University.

Ortega, Mariana. 2016. *In-Between: Latina Feminist Phenomenology, Multiplicity, and the Self*. Albany, NY: State University of New York Press.

Ortner, Sherry B. 1995. "The Case of the Disappearing Shamans, or No Individualism, No Relationism." *Ethos* 23, pp. 355–390.

Ozawa-de Silva, Chikako, and Brendan R. Ozawa-de-Silva. 2011. "Mind/Body Theory and Practice in Tibetan Medicine and Buddhism." *Body and Society* 17 (1), pp. 95–119.

Pahuus, Mogens. 2018. *Dialog med Løgstrup: Løgstrups fænomenologi.* Aalborg, Denmark: Aalborg Universitetsforlag.

Pallasmaa, Juhani. 2005 [1996]. *The Eyes of the Skin. Architecture and the Senses.* Chichester: John Wiley & Sons Ltd.

Pandian, Anand, and M. P. Mariappan. 2014. *Ayya's Accounts: A Ledger of Hope in Modern India.* Bloomington: Indiana University Press.

———. 2015. *Reel World: An Anthropology of Creation.* Durham, NC: Duke University Press.

Parrott, Fiona R. 2010. "Bringing Home the Dead: Photographs, Family Imaginaries and Moral Remains." In *An Anthropology of Absence: Materializations of Transcendence and Loss,* edited by Mikkel Bille, Frida Hastrup, and Tim F. Sørensen, pp. 131–146. New York: Springer.

Patrul Rinpoche. 1999 [1994]. *The Words of My Perfect Teacher: A Complete Translation of a Classic Introduction to Tibetan Buddhism.* Translated by Padmakara Translation Group. New Delhi: Vistaar.

Peloquin, Susan. 1989. "Helping Through Touch: The Embodiment of Caring." *Journal of Religion and Health* 28 (4), pp. 299–320.

Powers, John. 1995. *Introduction to Tibetan Buddhism.* Ithaca, NY: Snow Lion.

Ramble, Charles. 1982. "Status and Death: Mortuary Rites and Attitudes to the Body in a Tibetan Village." *Kailash* 9 (4), pp. 333–359.

Ramble, Charles, Peter Schwieger, and Alice Travers, eds. 2013. *Tibetans Who Escaped the Historian's Net: Studies in the Social History of Tibetan-Speaking Societies.* Kathmandu: Vajra Books.

Rajan, Hamsa. 2018. "When Wife-Beating Is Not Necessarily Abuse: A Feminist and Cross-Cultural Analysis of the Concept of Abuse as Expressed by Tibetan Survivors of Domestic Violence." *Violence Against Women* 24 (1), pp. 3–27.

Richardson, Hugh E. 1984 [1962]. *Tibet and Its History.* Boston: Shambala.

Risaliti, Sergio. ed. 2022. [exhibition catalog]. *ALI BANISADR. Beautiful Lies.* Milan: Forma Edizioni.

Robin, Francoise. 2015. "Caring for Women's Words and Women's Bodies: A Field Note on Palmo and Her 'Demoness Welfare Association for Women.'" *Revue d'Etudes Tibetaines* 34, pp. 153–169.

Rowe, John W., and Robert L. Kahn. 1987. "Human Aging: Usual and Successful." *Science* 237 (4811), pp. 143–149.

Said, Edward. 1978. *Orientalism.* New York: Pantheon Books.

———. 1993. *Culture and Imperialism.* London: Chatto and Windus.

Samuel, Geoffrey. 1993. *Civilized Shamans: Buddhism in Tibetan Societies.* Washington, DC: Smithsonian Institution Press.

———. 2014. "Body and Mind in Tibetan Medicine and Tantric Buddhism." In *Bodies in Balance: The Art of Tibetan Medicine,* edited by Theresia Hofer, pp. 32–45. Seattle: University of Washington Press.

Sarkar, Priyambada. 2021. *Language, Limits, and Beyond: Early Wittgenstein and Rabindranath Tagore.* New Delhi: Oxford University Press.

Scarry, Elaine. 1985. *The Body in Pain: The Making and Unmaking of the World.* Oxford: Oxford University Press.

Scheper-Hughes, Nancy. 2001 [1979]. *Saints, Scholars, and Schizophrenics: Mental Illness in Rural Ireland.* Berkeley: University of California Press.

———. 1993 [1992]. *Death Without Weeping: The Violence of Everyday Life in Brazil*. Berkeley: University of California Press.

Schlütter, Mette, and Tenna Jensen. 2023. "Striving to Belong: Everyday Enactments of Belonging Among Older Adults in Greenland." *Anthropology and Aging* 44 (1), pp. 19–36.

Schütz, Alfred. 1945. "The Homecomer." *American Journal of Sociology* 50 (5), pp. 369–376.

Schwartz, Ronald D. 1994. *Circle of Protest: Political Ritual in the Tibetan Uprising*. New York: Columbia University Press.

Shakya, Tsering. 1991. "Tibet and the Occident: The Myth of Shangri-la." *Lungta* 5, pp. 21–23.

———. 1993. "Whither the Tsampa Eaters?" Himāl *Southasian* 6 (5), pp. 8–11.

———. 1999. *The Dragon in the Land of Snows: A History of Modern Tibet Since 1947*. New York: Penguin Compass.

———. 2012. "Self-Immolation, the Changing Language of Protest in Tibet." *Revue d'Etudes Tibétaines* 25, pp. 19–39.

Shneiderman, Sara B. 2006. "Living Practical Dharma: A Tribute to Chomo Khandru and the Bonpo Women of Lubra Village, Mustang, Nepal." In *Women's Renunciation in South Asia: Nuns, Yoginis, Saints, and Singers*, edited by Meena Khandelwal, Sandra L. Hausner, and Ann G. Gold, pp. 69–94. London: Palgrave Macmillan.

Singh, Julietta. 2018. *No Archive Will Restore You*. Santa Barbara, CA: Punctum Books.

Smith, Alexander K. 2021. *Divination in Exile: Interdisciplinary Approaches to Ritual Prognostication in the Tibetan Bon Tradition*. Leiden: Brill.

Snellgrove, David L., and Hugh E. Richardson. 2003. *A Cultural History of Tibet*. Bangkok: Orchid Press.

Sonam, Bhuchung D. 2012. *Yak Horns: Notes on Contemporary Tibetan Writing, Music, Film, and Politics*. Dharamsala: TibetWrites.

———. 2015. *Songs of the Arrow*. Dharamsala: Blackneck Books.

———. 2022. Introduction to *Under the Blue Skies. A Tibetan Reader*, edited by Bhuchung D. Sonam, pp. 11–14. Dharamsala: Blackneck Books.

———. 2023. "Who Will Be the Dalai Lama's Successor? China Won't Have a Say." *Washington Post*, 3 October. https://www.washingtonpost.com/opinions/2023/10/03/china-tibet-dalai-lama-succession/.

Sonam, Tenzing, and Ritu Sarin, dir. 2009. *The Sun Behind the Clouds: Tibet's Struggle for Freedom*. Documentary, 79 min. Produced by Ritu Sarin, Tenzin T. Choklay, Babeth M. Van-Loo, and John Sergeant. New York: Zeitgeist Films.

Sperling, Elliot. 1979. "Old Age in the Tibetan Context." *Saeculum* 30 (4), pp. 434–442.

Stevenson, Lisa. 2014. *Life Beside Itself: Imagining Care in the Canadian Arctic*. Berkeley: University of California Press.

Stoller, Paul. 1989. *The Taste of Ethnographic Things: The Senses in Anthropology*. Philadelphia: University of Pennsylvania Press.

———. 1997. *Sensuous Scholarship*. Philadelphia: University of Pennsylvania Press.

———. 2008. *The Power of the Between: An Anthropological Odyssey*. Chicago: University of Chicago Press.

Subba, Tanka B. 1990. *Flight and Adaptation: Tibetan Refugees in the Darjeeling–Sikkim Himalaya*. Dharamsala: Library of Tibetan Works and Archives.

Suhr, Christian. 2019. *Descending with Angels: Islamic Exorcism and Psychiatry: A Film Monograph*. Manchester: Manchester University Press.

Swank, Heidi. 2014. *Rewriting Shangri-la: Tibetan Youth, Migrations and Literacies in McLeod Ganj, India*. Leiden: Brill.

Tagore, Rabindranath. 1933 [1917]. *My Reminiscences*. Translated by Surendranath Tagore. London: Macmillan.

———. 2010 [2006]. *My Life in My Words*. Selected and edited with an introduction by Uma Das Gupta. New Delhi: Penguin Books.

Taylor, Chloe. 2005. "Levinasian Ethics and Feminist Ethics of Care." *Contemporary Issues in Philosophical Ethics* 9 (2), pp. 217–239.

Taylor, Janelle S. 2008. "On Recognition, Caring and Dementia." *Medical Anthropology Quarterly* 22 (4), pp. 313–335.

Tenphun. 2017. *Sweet Butter Tea: A Book of Poems*. Dharamsala: Blackneck Books.

Thera, Nyanaponika. 2013. Preface to "The Three Basic Facts of Existence: I. Impermanence (Anicca)." Access to Insight (BCBS Edition). 30 November. https://www.accesstoinsight.org/lib/authors/various/wheel186.html#preface.

Thornton, Rebecca M. 2015. "Speaking an Elderly Body into a Visible Space: Defining Moments." *Qualitative Theory* 21 (1), pp. 66–76.

Topgyal, Tsering. 2014. "Tibet's Exiles." Featuring the photographs of Tsering Topgyal. *Spotlight, Associated Press (AP) Images* (blog). Associated Press, 5 May. https://apimagesblog.com/blog/2014/11/05/tibets-exiles/.

Tsagong, Tenzin. 2023. "An Exiled Publisher Creates a 'Brotherhood Across Tibetans.'" *New York Times*, 12 July. https://www.nytimes.com/2023/07/12/books/booksupdate/tibetan-literature-tibetwrites.html.

Tseden, Pema, dir. 2011. *Old Dog*. Film, 93 min. Written by Pema Tseden. Produced by Zhang Xianmin. Beijing: Himalaya Audio and Visual Culture Communication.

———, dir. 2015. *Tharlo*. Film, 138 min. Written by Pema Tseden. Produced by Wu Leilei, Wang Xuebo, and Zhang Xianmin. Beijing: Heaven Pictures; Culture and Media; YiHe Star Film Production; Ocean and Time Culture Communication.

———, dir. 2019. *Balloon*. Film, 102 min. Written by Pema Tseden. Beijing: Shengtang Times Culture Communication; Factory Gate (Tianjin) Film; Qinghai Manishi Film; China Film Stellar Theatre Chain.

Tsering, Lhasang. 2012. *Wondering*. Dharamsala: TibetWrites.

Tsering, Tashi. 1997. "Themes and Perspectives on Tibetan History with Emphasis on nGo-log and Preliminary Remarks on Some New Sources." Paper presented at the History of Tibet: New Resources and Perspectives Conference, 23–24 May, Oxford University, Oxford, England.

Tseten, Sonam, dir. 2020. *Settlement*. Film, 4 min. Dharamsala: Drung Films Collective.

Tsing, Anna. 2013. "Sorting Out Commodities: How Capitalist Value Is Made Through Gifts." *HAU: Journal of Ethnographic Theory* 3, pp. 21–43.

Tsundue, Tenzin. 2010 [2002]. *Kora: Stories and Poems*. Dharamsala: TibetWrites.

Valentin, Karen, and Uma Pradhan, eds. 2023. *Anthropological Perspectives on Education in Nepal: Educational Transformations and Avenues of Learning*. New Delhi: Oxford University Press.

Venturino, Steven J. 1997. "Reading Negotiations in the Tibetan Diaspora." In *Constructing Tibetan Culture: Contemporary Perspectives*, edited by Frank J. Korom, pp. 98–121. Quebec: World Heritage Press.

Von Herder, Johann G. 2009 [1778]. *Plastik*. Whitefish, MT: Kessinger.

Wangmo, Tenzin. 2010. "Changing Expectations of Care Among Older Tibetans Living in India and Switzerland." *Aging and Society* 30, pp. 879–896.

Wangmo, Tenzin, and Pamela B. Teaster. 2009. "The Bridge from Then and Now: Tibetan Elders Living in Diaspora." *Journal of Applied Gerontology* 29 (4), pp. 434–454.

Wangmo, Tsering, dir. 2019. *Conversations With My Mother*. Independent documentary, 6 min, 3 sec.

Warner, Cameron D. 2011. "Re/crowning the Jowo Śākyamuni: Texts, Photographs, and Memories." *History of Religions* 51 (1), pp. 1–30.

Weil, Andrew. 2005. *Healthy Aging: A Lifelong Guide to Your Well-Being.* New York: Anchor Books.

Wikan, Unni. 2012. *Resonance: Beyond the Words.* Chicago: University of Chicago Press.

Willerslev, Rane, Dorthe R. Christensen, and Lotte Meinert. 2013. Introduction to *Taming Time, Timing Death: Social Technologies and Ritual,* edited by Rane Willerslev and Dorthe R. Christensen, pp. 1–16. Farnham: Ashgate.

Williams, Bernard. 1981. *Moral Luck: Philosophical Papers.* Cambridge: Cambridge University Press.

Williams, Lars, and Lotte Meinert. 2020. "Repetition Work: Healing Spirits and Trauma in the Churches of Northern Uganda." In *Time Work: Studies of Temporal Agency,* edited by Michael G. Flaherty, Lotte Meinert, and Anne L. Dalsgård, pp. 31–49. New York: Berghahn Books.

Woeser, Tsering. 2020. *Forbidden Memory: Tibet During the Cultural Revolution.* Edited by Robert Barnett. Translated by Susan T. Chen. Sterling, VA: Potomac Books.

———. n.d. "An Interview with Tsering Woeser." By Kamila Hladíková. *Asymptote.* https://www.asymptotejournal.com/interview/an-interview-with-tsering-woeser/.

Yeh, Emily T. 2007. "Exile Meets Homeland: Politics, Performance, and Authenticity in the Tibetan Diaspora." *Environment and Planning D: Society and Space* 25 (4), pp. 648–667.

INDEX

Note: Page numbers in italic type refer to photographs. Institutions are in McLeod Ganj/ Dharamsala unless otherwise indicated. Names of elderly Tibetans-in-exile are both actual and pseudonymous. See the author's note on names on pp. xvii–xviii.

Derrida, Jacques, 247n2
Desjarlais, Robert, 14, 184, 186, 190, 237n55
Dharamkot village, 47
Dharamsala/McLeod Ganj: aging in, 50–55;
    animals in and around, 45, 47, 51–53;
    author's experience of, 23, 25, 47, 52;
    businesses in, 45; as capital of Tibetans-in-
    exile, 1, 25, 35, 43–50, 171; descriptions of,
    xxvii; development in, 240n46; diversity
    of, 49–50; environmental changes in, 49,
    52; history of, 35, 44–45; images of, 8, 24,
    40, 46, 54; lower and upper, 35, 44; name
    of, 23, 44; physical environs of, 50–51;
    tourism in, 45, 47, 52; weather in, 51–53,
    60, 89, 96, 172, 176
Dhargye, Tenzin, 88
Dharmakīrti, 18, 19
Dhauladhar range, xxvii, 44, 47, 51, 52, 172
Dhompa, Tsering Wangmo, xii, 152, 154, 156,
    162, 256n28
Dhondrup, Akhu, 80, 82–84, 86–88, 142,
    147–48, 203
Dickyi Larsoe Settlement, 37
Diehl, Keila, 240n48
Doeguling Settlement, 38, 42–43, 149–50, 201
Dolkar, Yangchen, 138
Dolma, Sangay, 171
Dolma, Tsering, 38
Dondrup, Tashi, 184
Drepung Monastery, Tibet and Doeguling
    Settlement, 38, 82, 164, 199
Dreyfus, George, 246n65
Drolma, Samdrup: aging experiences of, 63,
    214, 220–21; character/personality/habits of,
    220–21, 223; and death, xxiii–xxiv, 3, 192,
    214–15; everyday activities of, xxiii, 219–20;
    and exile, 81–82; and her body, 220; home's
    significance for, 154, 161; late husband of,
    66, 80–82, 142, 154, 223; memories of,
    79–80, 154; photographs related to, xxiv,
    145, 153, 193; profile of, xv; raising of Dickyi
    Sangmo's son by, 83–84; relative of, 35–36;
    sisters of, 26–27, 63, 65, 66, 79, 91, 189, 203,
    205–6, 211, 213, 215, 221; Tibetan Buddhist
    practices of, 195, 208; voice of, 221
Drukpa Kagyu order, 205
dü chungpa (small householders), 79

Ekvall, Robert B., 5
Eliot, Thomas S., 150

embodied knowing, 3, 18–22. See also care/
    caregiving: as component of ethnographic
    method; ethics of care: in ethnographic
    fieldwork; singularity of lives and
    experiences
emptiness, 7, 10, 11. See also no-self
"empty heart" metaphor, 91, 167
Establishment 22, 159
ethics: of care, 98–99, 115–19, 124–27; in
    ethnographic fieldwork, 2, 4, 14–18, 30;
    feminist theories of, 124–25, 244n60; of
    filial piety, 5; and hinges between self and
    other, 76, 78, 116; Levinas's theory of,
    98–99, 114, 116–18, 124–27; Løgstrup's
    theory of, 116–18; self-other relationship
    and, 76, 78, 114, 116–18; Tibetan Buddhist,
    11–12; and viewers' responses to television
    characters, 113–15
ethnography: biases in, 10; ethical concerns
    in, 2, 4, 14–18, 30; interpretation and
    meaning in, 2–4, 15, 20, 22; phenomeno-
    logical approach to, 4, 18–19, 22; reciprocity
    in fieldwork, 2, 30; singularity as a
    principle in theory and practice of, 4,
    14–19, 22
exercise, xxix, 172, 174, 196, 198, 223
exile: death in, 31, 150, 154; Dharamsala/
    McLeod Ganj as capital in, 1, 25, 35,
    43–50; early efforts in, 36–41; escapes into,
    31, 80–82, 100, 155, 158–59, 204; home in,
    135–38, 142, 149–50, 150–51, 167; overview
    of settlements in, 41; present status of
    communities in, 41–43; psychological
    experience of, 33–34, 152, 154; Tibetan
    deaths in, 36–37. See also Tibetans-in-exile

face, and the ethical encounter, 116–18, 126, 127
family: and caregiving in old age, 5–6, 43,
    105–10; designation of children as monks
    or nuns, 107; filial piety, 5, 43, 107–8. See
    also aging/old age: absence/presence of
    significant others in
feminism, 98, 124–25, 244n60
filial piety, 5, 43, 107–8
Fraser, Nancy, 115
freedom. See aging/old age: dependence/lack
    of freedom experienced in

Gaddis, 44, 47, 49, 240n48
Gallu Temple, 47

ACKNOWLEDGMENTS

In 2011, I visited McLeod Ganj for the first time. On my return from India, I bought the book *Nine Lives: In Search of the Sacred in Modern India* by William Dalrymple at Delhi Airport, in which I read a story that deeply affected me. The story was about an elderly Tibetan monk, Tashi Passang, who at the time lived in McLeod Ganj. After the Chinese colonization of Tibet, he renounced his monastic vows to fight against the People's Liberation Army. As a result, his mother was grotesquely tortured by Chinese soldiers. Shortly after reading Tashi Passang's story, I decided to become engaged with the Tibetan freedom struggle. Little did I know that, in a few years, my life would become seriously intertwined with Tashi Passang's generation of exiled Tibetans, not many of whom remain in exile now. I am forever grateful to Tashi Passang, whose courage, dedication, and hopefulness inspired me to work with Tibetans-in-exile.

Writing a book and doing fieldwork are not solitary endeavors. This book, and the fieldwork it builds on, would not have been possible without inspiration from, support from, and collaboration with many precious individuals—friends, colleagues, strangers—and institutions that gave me the opportunity and courage to develop my voice.

I bow in immense gratitude to my precious teachers, my elderly friends in McLeod Ganj and in Kathmandu, who opened up their homes to me and allowed me to become a part of their lives. It is strange how we serendipitously found each other in this lifetime, despite being born in radically different times and places, separated by more than fifty years. Some of my friends passed away in the process of writing this book, but I continue to feel their presence, visualize their faces, and hear their voices in my mind. It is as if they are still here, making it difficult for me to come to terms with their physical absence. The time I spent with them will stand as one of the most humbling and memorable periods of my life.

I am indebted to the Tibetan Children's Village school administration for granting me permission to do fieldwork at their old-age home. More than anyone, Tsering Youdon la made it possible: thank you so much for your friendship and loving support over the years. I am also incredibly grateful to the director of Tibet Charity in McLeod Ganj, Tsering Thundup la, for taking me in as a volunteer in 2018. I am much obliged to Acha Tenzing la and Acha Jigme la, who took me in as if I were a part of the Tibet Charity family. I am grateful to the Central Tibetan Administration for allowing me to do interviews at the Jampaling Old People's Home. I offer a sincere thank-you to Ama Drolma Samten la for her kindness and for helping me during my fieldwork in Boudhanath in 2018.

I bow to my precious teachers, Lotte Meinert and Lone Grøn, who invited me to be a doctoral student in their research project, "Aging as a Human Condition: Radical Uncertainty and the Search for a Good (Old) Life," funded by the Velux Foundation, at Aarhus University from 2017 to 2020. This book largely builds on the fieldwork I carried out during those doctoral studies. I am immensely grateful to you both for being my biggest supporters over the years and for teaching me so much, not only through your scholarship but also by being living embodiments of compassionate teachers. It has been an immense pleasure to learn from other scholars and artists in this project: Susan Whyte, Cheryl Mattingly, Maria Louw, Helle Wentzer, Rasmus Dyring, Tove Nyholm, and Maria Speyer. It has also been humbling to learn from other scholars who engaged with the project in various capacities: Anne-Marie Pahuus, Lawrence Cohen, Janelle Taylor, Thomas Wentzer, Julie Livingston, Tine Rostgaard, Joel Robbins, Jason Danely, Robert Desjarlais, and Sverre Raffnsøe. I am immensely grateful to Cheryl Mattingly, whose writings marked a turning point for me. Thanks are also due to Cameron Warner, who acted as a cosupervisor for my doctoral studies and engaged with my work then. I am grateful to my excellent doctoral assessment committee—Carole McGranahan, Mikkel Rytter, and Robert Desjarlais—for their encouragement and insightful questions that pushed my thinking. Thank you to all the wonderful colleagues and friends at Aarhus University during my doctoral studies, especially Marie Odgaard, Katrine Bach, Mona Chettri, Mette Schlütter, Abir Ismail, Anne Chahine, Christian Suhr, Karen Waltorp, Chiara Bresciani, Anne-Mette Christensen, Mia Korsbæk, Julie Bune, and Bodil Bjerring. I extend heartfelt thanks to Anne-Marie Pahuus for her generosity and support over the years.

I am forever indebted to the Carlsberg Foundation and its board of directors for funding my postdoctoral research through their *Visiting Fellowships at University of Oxford* program, which made it possible for me to do more fieldwork in McLeod Ganj and work on writing this book. The Carlsberg Foundation also granted funding for the publication of this book (grant number CF23-1814), for which I am immensely grateful. Thank you to Linacre College for providing me with a college affiliation during my fellowship and also a Junior Research Fellowship grant to travel to India for fieldwork. An immense thank-you goes to Ulrike Roesler and Lama Jabb, who supported my application to the Carlsberg Foundation by housing me at the Faculty of Asian and Middle Eastern Studies, University of Oxford. Thank you very much to David Gellner and Clare Harris, who also supported my application. I am incredibly grateful to Lama Jabb and Darig Thokmay for generously sharing their insights on Tibetan society and language. It has been a pleasure to interact with and get to know members of the Tibetan and Himalayan studies cluster at Oxford, especially Anna Sehnalova, Robert Mayer, Caroline Picard, Thupten Kelsang, Hannah Theaker, and Rachael Griffiths. Special thanks go to Theresia Hofer for her precious support and friendship over the years, and to the most kind and thoughtful Hilary and Jon Vidnes for their hospitality. I am grateful to the community at Linacre College, especially to the other Junior Research Fellows, whose company has enriched my time in Oxford. I am also tremendously grateful to the dining hall staff at Linacre College, who prepared warm and nourishing meals for the college staff members and students five days a week, relieving me of the burden of cooking and allowing me to immerse myself in my work. I am also indebted to the board of directors of the San Cataldo Foundation for providing me with four weeks of writing residency at the Amalfi coast in Italy to work on the book. I will never forget my time there and the companionship of my fellow residents. Thank you to Linacre College for awarding me a Junior Research Fellowship grant to cover my travel expenses between the Amalfi coast and the United Kingdom.

I extend my heartfelt gratitude to the eminent Gen Tashi Tsering la for digging up several texts on old age from the towering collection of literature at the Amnye Machen Institute, including the text by Menriwa Lobsang Namgyal and Changchan Gyalpo, and allowing me to use them in my writings. Thank you to Tenzin Choephel for helping me translate the poem by Menriwa Lobsang Namgyal. I am also grateful to Heidi Fjeld for her invaluable support over the years, as a mentor and friend.

Thank you very much to my wonderful editor at the University of Pennsylvania Press, Elisabeth Maselli, for her support and for seeing this book through to publication. Thanks are also due to everyone who has been involved in the production phase. I bow to the two peer reviewers who read the manuscript with so much care and openness—thank you for offering praise and encouraging words, making invaluable comments, and raising questions that have improved the manuscript. I extend boundless gratitude to my teacher and friend, Lone Grøn, who generously offered to read the revised manuscript while being buried under multiple deadlines—thank you for raising relevant questions and making insightful comments. Thank you to Lotte Meinert, Bhuchung D. Sonam, and Heidi Fjeld for reading parts of the revised manuscript and offering encouragement and critical comments. Thanks are also due to Jigme Yeshe Lama for reading one of the chapters, raising questions, and offering kind words.

Dear friends who are a soothing presence in my life, in person and from afar, you are a part of this book too! I would like to start by thanking my dearest Tibetan friends in McLeod Ganj and other places around the world who have been priceless teachers and taught me more about the Tibetan world than books alone ever could: Tsering Choephel, Lobsang Tenchoe, Dhondup Tashi, Tsering Topgyal, Tenzin Dadon, Tenzin Norgyal, Tenzin Dickyi, Tamdin Bhuchung, Tenzin Wangchuk, Phuntsok Palden, Ama Tashi Lhatso, Dawa Tsering, Sonam Choedon, Ama Yangchen, Lhamo Khotsenang, Nyima Bhuti, and, of course, all of my neighbors on Dharamkot Road. Tsering Choephel, I am especially indebted to you for your precious friendship and help over the years; as one of my most important local Tibetan experts, you have offered much insightful advice on many matters in this book. For comforting and energizing conversations in McLeod Ganj, thanks are also due to Cherry Malagamba, Kunchok Rabten, Emma Martin, Geshe Lobsang Nyandak la, and Mili Swali. In the United Kingdom, I thank dearest Serena Tizzi and Andy Obeid, for taking me in like family (Serena, you make the best tiramisu!), as well as Emily Stevenson, Yasmeen Arif, Karen Iles, Freya Hope, Antonio Jiménez, Suleiman Halasah, Bhawani Buswala, Jose Valenzuela, Isabella Cammarota, Jotun Hein, Juni, Anthony Howarth, and Juliet Chastney. In Denmark, I thank Marie Odgaard, Katrine Bach, Josefine Pedersen, and Birgit Bune, with especially heartfelt gratitude extended to dearest Marie Odgaard for reading my texts over the years and offering loving support; and I am also forever grateful to Tove Nyholm and Michael Schmidt for taking me in as their own. In Germany, India, and

France, I thank dearest Luisa Matthias, Vandana Pathak, and Chloé Lukasiewicz. In Norway, sincere thanks go to kjæreste Marie Nilsson, Hilde Knutsen, Inger Vasstveit, Cecilie Mueenuddin, Alma Orucevic, and the board members of the Norwegian Tibet Committee—Namgyal Tsomo, Metock Yangchen, Merethe Jodalen, Grzegorz Odor, and Anniela Hegnar—with whom I had the pleasure of working. To other wonderful people who have expressed their enthusiasm for the book, I am incredibly grateful for your support.

I bow to my Mammi ji, Sukhdev Kaur, and to my Daddi ji, Ranjit Singh, for teaching me the importance of doing hard and sincere work. Thank you to the rest of our small family: Laddi, Jeevan, and my most precious Harvir, Manvir, and Goldy. Thank you to my family for allowing me to go my own (untraditional Indian) way and for extending your boundaries for me.

Finally, I bow to all the (street) dogs (especially Lychee, Babar, Devi, Mindrug, Mari, Arfi, Nagri, Poppy), cats (Senge, Hope), monkeys, cows, and bulls in McLeod Ganj who light up my life. Caring for them and loving them is a gift that keeps on giving. It has been the privilege of a lifetime to be accompanied by my dog companions—Tyler and Loofy—and cat companions—Noori, Lotus, and Semo—over the years, all of whom passed away in 2024 while I was in the process of finalizing this book. My love for them follows me in everything that I do. Thank you to my previous landlady, Ama Dawa Choezom la, and my current landlord, Po Norbu Sangpo la, in Töpa Village, for kindly allowing me to welcome dogs, cats, and monkeys to my room and balcony.

I bow in gratitude to Dharamsala—its human inhabitants, animals, birds, mountains, forests, and rivers, whose presence and companionship have provided me a home in the world. It is an immense privilege to live in Dharamsala at the same time as His Holiness the great 14th Dalai Lama—I bow to you in great reverence and gratitude.

Thank you.
Thug-je-che
Harman/Dadon

www.ingramcontent.com/pod-product-compliance
Lightning Source LLC
Chambersburg PA
CBHW041220270326
41932CB00003B/3